T0129280

Isabelle's Choice

Sally Campbell Repass

authorHOUSE®

AuthorHouse™
1663 Liberty Drive
Bloomington, IN 47403
www.authorhouse.com
Phone: 1-800-839-8640

Published by AuthorHouse 1/16/2013

ISBN: 978-1-4817-0824-1 (sc)
ISBN: 978-1-4817-0821-0 (e)

Acknowlegements

...A SPECIAL THANKS TO THE FOLLOWING PEOPLE WHO HELPED EDIT MY BOOKS...

Margaret Campbell Sharitz,
Laura Beth Peake
Robert Paul Repass,
Shirley Chapman Stansbery

...MY SINCERE THANKS TO THE FOLLOWING PEOPLE WHO SUPPLIED INFORMATION...

A Special Friend, Cathy, from Prince Edward Island, supplied lots of info for Book #3, 'FROM THE RANCH...TO THE ISLAND'

My Special friend, Karen Heath, from Medicine Bow, who supplied lots of info on Book #5, 'MEDICINE BOW...A NEW BEGINNING'

...THANKS TO THE FOLLOWING WHO SUPPLIED PHOTOS FOR THE BOOK COVERS...

Ladonna Yearout-Patton for
'FROM THE RANCH...TO THE ISLAND'
www.ladonnacherellphotography.com
MODEL: Tammy Lynn Fisher, with Okko & Rocky

Alex Zhuravlov & Joe McDonough for
'BACK HOME TO MONTANA'
(Taken from their movie 'Bethlehem')
ACTOR: Tracy Fisher

Dedication

...IN MEMORY...
of my family and friends who have
recently passed away due to cancer.

Ethel Irene Snider Pruitt - age 72
Patty Parsons Mozingo - age 74
Charlina Blevins Harden - age 65
Major Jeffery Neal Pruitt - age 48
Sarah Campbell Benson - age 43

II Timothy 4: 7
I have fought a good fight, I have finished
my course, I have kept the faith:
KJV

...In Honor...

of my family and friends who are
presently battling cancer.

Robert Paul Repass
Adam Trent Fisher
Sonya Mozingo McCollian

Hebrews 4:16
Let us therefore come boldly unto the throne of grace,
that we may obtain mercy, and find
grace to help in time of need.
KJV

John 14:14
If ye ask any thing in my name, I will do it.
KJV

John 14:18
I will not leave you comfortless: I will come to you.
KJV

Contents

Chapter 1

It had been a long, sad day for Isabelle Parker Colter, daughter of Dr. Jennifer Parker and Gabe Colter of Laurel, Montana. Her best friend, Fallon Hollister, had been laid to rest today.

A few nights ago she and Fallon had been to the Senior Prom with their boyfriends. Isabelle was dating Tracy Kelley and Fallon was with Dustin Newman. They had a wonderful time at the Prom and were heading home. They were laughing and talking and suddenly that came to a halt. A drunk driver swerved over to their side of the road and hit them head on. Dustin was driving, so that meant Fallon was in the front passenger seat. Dustin was knocked unconscious and there was no sound from Fallon. Isabelle was aching all over from the sudden impact but didn't see any blood. She turned to her companion, Tracy, who lay there with his eyes closed. Blood was oozing from his head and running down his face.

"TRACY!!!" screamed Isabelle. "Are you okay?" She took her cell phone from her purse and dialed 911. The rescue squad would be there shortly, she was told. Meanwhile, she turned to Tracy and shook him gently.

There was no response. She lay her head on his chest and could hear a faint heartbeat. "THANK YOU, GOD!!!"

Then she slid to the edge of her seat and tapped Fallon on the shoulder. "FALLON!" she yelled in a shrill voice. "Are you okay?" There was no response. She then turned to Dustin and still got no response. "Am I the only one who survived?" she asked crying so hard she could hardly speak.

She saw two sets of headlights in the dark night and felt a sigh of relief. "Please let that be help," she screamed. "P-L-E-A-S-E...Dear God... Don't let anyone die!!!" she begged.

The paramedics got out of the ambulances and headed their way. They opened both of the front car doors and bent down and looked in as they shined their flashlights into each face. They didn't like what they saw. They rushed back to the ambulances and brought four stretchers. They began with Dustin and Fallon, then came for Isabelle and Tracy. It seemed like a long ride to the hospital where they were quickly unloaded and wheeled into the Emergency Room. Isabelle had no idea how bad the others were hurt. She only knew she felt like she had been run over by a big truck. She was going to be sore. She wasn't worrying about herself; she had to know about the others. A nurse walked in and Isabelle grabbed her arm, "PLEASE...tell me, are the others okay?"

"Honey, I can't tell you anything yet. The doctors are working with them."

"Will you let me know as soon as you find out?" pleaded Isabelle.

"I will let you know," replied the nurse and walked out.

Isabelle lay there crying...yes, crying for her friends whom she loved so much. They just had to be okay. She and Fallon had been best friends all through high school. They shared secrets and could talk about anything. Friends like Fallon were few and far between. They were like sisters. For the past year or so they had been talking about college. Although they had different interests, they knew they didn't want to be too far apart when they chose a college.

Her thoughts were interrupted when the doctor walked in. "Hello, I'm Dr. Houseman. Well, Miss Colter how are you feeling?"

"Like I've been run over by a big truck," she replied with a faint smile.

He examined her closely and found no broken bones or bleeding. He asked her where she hurt, to which she replied, "All over!"

"I think you will be okay. You seem to be bruised from the impact. I think you will be okay in a week or two."

"Thank you, doctor. How are my friends?"

"I haven't seen them. Other doctors are with them."

"Can I go see them?" she asked with innocent eyes gazing at him.

"Not tonight. We're going to keep you overnight to make sure you're okay."

He could tell she wasn't happy about that but she never said anything more. He left the room and went to check on the others. Dustin had been taken into surgery and Tracy was being treated for his head wound. He looked in where the other girl was and saw that a sheet had been drawn over her head. Tears came in his eyes. What a loss, he was thinking. Just in the prime of her life and now it's over. He had a daughter the same age and he shivered when he thought that it could have been her. She was at the same dance tonight. He felt a sigh of relief for himself but his heart ached for another mom and dad somewhere. He didn't know who the girl was yet but decided it was time to find out.

He approached Dr. Baker and asked, "Can you tell me who the girl is?"

"She's Fallon Hollister, daughter of our local pharmacist, John Hollister."

"Oh no..." gasped Dr. Houseman. "We are very good friends with her family. I know this is going to devastate John and Lynette. I just can't imagine what they are going through!"

"Although I have no children," said young Dr. Baker, "I can't imagine the pain they must be going though now."

About that time John and Lynette Hollister came down the hallway. Dr. Houseman walked up to them and hugged them both as he offered his sincere condolences. Tears were running down John's face and Lynette was hysterical. Dr. Houseman held her in his arms and let her cry. He couldn't hold back his own tears. He could almost feel the pain they were going through. It kept running over and over in his mind that it could have been his daughter.

Lynette finally regained her composure and spoke, "Thank you for being here for us, Bill." She wiped her eyes and took her husband by the arm.

"We really appreciate you, Bill," said John with tears in his eyes. "Nothing will ever be the same again. I don't know how we will make it without Fallon. She was the light of our lives! I just can't believe she is gone. I guess we had better go identify her body."

"Why don't you go John, and let Lynette stay with me. It would be easier on her."

"That's a good idea, Bill. Where is she?"

Dr. Houseman pointed to the room where Fallon was and John headed that way. Lynette sat down in a chair in the hallway. She felt so weak and thought her legs were going to give away. She put her head in her hands and wept for her daughter.

John returned shortly and was crying softly. He went straight to his wife and put his arms around her. "Everything will be okay, my love. Fallon has gone to a beautiful place. At least we know where she is. I am so glad we raised her in Christian faith and love. You know she became a Christian in her early life and I feel at peace about her now. Our loss is Heaven's gain. One day we will meet her again."

"I know that John, but how are we going to live without her?" she asked.

"It won't be easy my dear... We'll have to look to God for comfort. He won't put more on us than we can bear."

"I believe that John but how does that ease the hurt I am feeling now?"

"You need to grieve and cry Lynette. That is part of the healing process." John was dying inside but knew he had to be strong for his wife.

Dr. Houseman suggested that John take his wife home as there was nothing they could do at the hospital. The funeral director would be sending someone very soon to pick up Fallon's body. He knew her parents needed to be gone before they came to get Fallon.

The next morning Isabelle was released. She went to see Tracy in the Intensive Care Unit. He was barely awake when she got there. She walked up to his bed and stood there for a few seconds. His eyes opened wider and he whispered, "Isabelle."

She took his hand and leaned over and kissed him on the cheek. A faint smile crossed his face. "How are you feeling?" she asked.

"I've been better," he answered faintly.

"You're going to be okay. I know you are. I have been praying for you. I've been praying for Fallon and Dustin too. Have you heard anything about them?"

"Not a word. I doubt if they would tell me anything."

"They won't tell me either. I'm sure my parents will know when they come to pick me up. They should be here soon. I wanted to see you before I left the hospital. I will be back to see you...I promise! Take care and I love you, Tracy!"

"I love you too," he whispered.

Isabelle left the room and headed downstairs. Her parents were waiting for her. Jennifer had spent most of the night at the hospital with her before going home around three o'clock in the morning to get a few hours of sleep. She was still anxious to see that her daughter was okay. Isabelle hugged her Mom, then her Dad. She was so blessed to have such wonderful parents. She came from a long line of Love.

"Are you ready to go home?" asked her dad, Gabe.

"Yes," she replied. "I want to come back to see Tracy later today."

"That's fine," replied her Dad.

They left the hospital and headed for their car. As soon as they were seated Isabelle asked, "Please tell me about Fallon. Is she hurt badly? They wouldn't tell me at the hospital."

Jennifer turned around in her seat where she could look Isabelle in the eye. "I'm so sorry Isabelle...she didn't make it. She died instantly after the impact."

"Oh no..." she cried out, "FALLON CAN'T BE DEAD!!! She is my best friend. We have so many plans for our future. She just can't be gone!"

"I'm so sorry, Isabelle!" exclaimed her mom, Jennifer. "As sad as it is, it was God's time to take her home to

Heaven. I am just so thankful she had accepted Jesus as her Savior in the past. She was called out to meet Him so suddenly. That's why it pays to be ready because we know not what hour He will call us."

"I know that is true Mom but it's still hard for me to let go of her. I still can't believe she's gone. We will never get to be together again. All the plans we made for college are gone. I don't want to feel bitter at God for taking her... but I just don't understand."

"It's not for us to understand, Isabelle. We must not question God for we know that He never makes a mistake!"

"I know that too, Mom."

"I know you do, Isabelle. Time is the healer of all wounds."

"But what am I supposed to do in the meantime?"

"Just trust God my Dear Daughter," added her Dad, Gabe. "He will show you what He has in store for you. It might be something completely different from what you and Fallon had planned."

"I was so sure that Fallon and I would both go into the medical field. Now I'm not sure that's what I want to do. I think it would always remind me of her and our plans."

"Let God be your guide. He will show you which direction to take. Don't rush into anything."

"Well, do you guys remember when cousin Caycee was here and I said I wanted to be a fashion designer like her? That has always been in the back of my mind. Maybe I should give that some consideration. What do you think?"

"I think you should do whatever makes you happy, Isabelle," replied her Dad.

Isabelle smiled for the first time since the accident. Maybe she would consider going to a fashion design school in New York or maybe she would do something entirely different. Right now that was the last thing she needed to be concerned about.

Meanwhile, she needed to concentrate on getting through the next few days. She knew it wouldn't be easy and was so thankful for the love and support of her family. It didn't take them long to get back home on the ranch. She loved her home and would truly miss it and her family when she went off to college. At the moment she found herself wishing she was still a little girl and didn't have to face these issues. Her little sister, Rachel Rose, was only twelve so it would be several years before she would have to worry about leaving. If only she could trade places with her...

Isabelle didn't sleep well that night. She kept having nightmares about the wreck and seeing Fallon as she lay there cold and still. She wished it would all go away. She needed her best friend. They had made so many plans and now I am alone, she thought. Life is not fair. Finally, about dawn she drifted off to sleep and this time she dreamed she and Fallon were going to Heaven. She could see a bright light and a voice calling them to come on. She woke up suddenly and felt a chill. It was all so real...why couldn't it have been true? "I would gladly give my life to be with Fallon," she said aloud. "Why am I the one left?" At that moment she heard a voice so clearly, "My child I am not finished with you."

She jumped out of bed and ran downstairs. "MOM, DAD, where are you?" she sounded hysterical.

Jennifer came running, "What on earth is wrong, Isabelle?"

Isabelle ran into her mother's arms and clung to her like a baby and the tears were like a dam that had broken. She cried so hard that she couldn't talk. Jennifer just held her and told her everything would be alright. Finally, after Isabelle calmed down, Jennifer asked, "Now, can you tell me what's wrong?"

Still sobbing she answered, "I had some terrible nightmares. I kept seeing Fallon over and over and she was so cold and lifeless. In the last dream I thought Fallon and I were going to Heaven. I saw the bright light and heard a voice calling for us to come on. Then Fallon disappeared and I was left alone. I was scared and asked why I was left alone. Then I heard a voice so clearly saying, "My child I am not finished with you."

Jennifer looked at Gabe and tears filled their eyes. They knew how blessed they were to still have their beautiful daughter but their heart ached for Fallon's parents. They knew the pain that the Hollister's were feeling as they had lost a son twelve years ago. Not a day went by that Jennifer didn't think of him. She knew it would be like this the rest of her life. GONE BUT NOT FORGOTTEN! Isac had been such a free spirit, even at six years old. He and Isabelle were twins, but they were nothing alike. Isac was a little cowboy at heart and there was no doubt but what he would have taken over the ranch after Gabe got too old to run it. Isabelle was all girl and liked the fancy things of life. In fact, she was still that way. Soon she would be going to college and life on the ranch would change. Jennifer was so thankful they would still have Rachel Rose for a few more years.

"Isabelle, it was not your time to go," replied her Dad. "I am so thankful to God for sparing your life and letting us keep you."

"So am I, as we are not ready to lose you. I know you will be going off to college but that's different," added her Mom while wiping the tears from her own eyes.

They somehow got through the day. Fallon's viewing

would be tomorrow night and the funeral the next day. Jennifer took a few days off from work. Dr. Campbell said he would be glad to fill in for her. He was such a fine man and wonderful doctor. Jennifer was happy to be partners with him. He always seemed to understand her. If she wasn't married to Gabe she could see having a future with this doctor. Get that out of your mind, she told herself. You are married to the most wonderful man ever. She knew that was true. She and Gabe had been through a lot and it had brought them even closer. But she was only human and sometimes thoughts would run through her head and then be forgotten.

Isabelle seemed to be withdrawn all day and into the next day. Each of them got ready for the viewing and Isabelle had nothing to say. She seemed to be even more depressed. Gabe and Jennifer were worried about their daughter.

Finally, it was time to go. Jennifer dreaded it. They all got into the car and headed into Laurel. Isabelle lay with her head back and her eyes closed all the way to the funeral home. Once they arrived she got out and headed to the door with her family. Rachel Rose wasn't saying much either. They could all feel Isabelle's pain.

They walked into the funeral home and went straight down the aisle to the coffin. Fallon looked so beautiful... just like she was sleeping. She was wearing a beautiful pale pink dress and was holding a darker pink rose in her hand. Tears came into Jennifer's eyes. This could be Isabelle, she was thinking. She looked at her daughter only to see tears streaming down her troubled face. Isabelle leaned down close to Fallon and whispered, "This should have been me, Fallon. You are my best friend. What am I going to do without you?" The tears were coming more swiftly and she was making a groaning sound. All at once she slowly crumpled to the floor. Her eyes were closed and she lay very still.

"HELP!" Jennifer cried as she bent down over her daughter. "PLEASE...SOMEONE HELP US!"

The funeral director came immediately as well as several other people. "Everyone please sit down. We need to give her air." He took out his cell phone and dialed 911.

The ambulance arrived five minutes later. They loaded her onto a stretcher and headed for the hospital. By the time they arrived at the emergency room she was beginning to come around. "Where am I?" she asked. "What happened?"

"You were at the funeral home and passed out," said the other EMT who was riding with her. "We have to take you to the emergency room and have you checked."

"I'm okay," she said. "I don't want to go to the ER. I want to go home. Where are my Mom and Dad?"

"They're coming and should be here soon. Don't worry; we are going to take good care of you."

"I just want to go home," she said again as the tears rolled down her face.

"I know you do but we have to make sure you're okay."

They arrived at the hospital and took her to the emergency room. A young doctor came in shortly and gave her a big smile. "What are you doing here young lady?" he asked.

"I'm okay...I just passed out at the funeral home. My best friend was killed in a car wreck. I should have died with her. She was like my sister," she added as the tears started again.

"Now Isabelle," he said looking at her chart. "Don't

talk that way. You are a young girl with your whole life ahead of you. Be thankful to God for sparing you."

"In one way I am, but I am going to miss my best friend forever."

"I know you will...but for now let's examine you."

He checked her vitals and everything seemed to be normal. He realized the pressure she was under and contributed that to her passing out.

Her parents were in the waiting room when she was discharged. They looked so anxious and tired. "I'm so sorry Mom and Dad."

"Don't apologize for something you couldn't help, Isabelle. We're just glad you are okay," said her Dad. "Come on Dear...let's get you home."

It was another rough sleepless night for Isabelle. She couldn't stop thinking about Fallon. She kept seeing her lifeless body as she lay there in the car. It was a picture that would forever be etched in her mind. She would go to sleep briefly and suddenly wake up dripping in perspiration and shaking all over. She would finally go back to sleep and have the recurring nightmare. She kept thinking it should have been her and not Fallon. Finally, daylight came and she got up and went downstairs. Her Mom was in the kitchen fixing breakfast. The smell of the food made her nauseated. She sat down at the table and stared into space.

"Isabelle, are you okay?" asked her Mom.

"No, Mom! I will never be okay. My best friend is dead and I should be dead too!

"Please don't say that, Isabelle! It breaks my heart to hear you talk like this!"

"Things will never be the same, Mom."

"I know it's devastating now but time is a healer. Just think about what your Dad and I went through when

Isac died. I wanted to die too! But in time I began to feel better and realized life was worth living. I still had you and Gabe. Also, I lost my Mom and Dad. That was a very hard time too, but God helped us through it and life went on. Trust Him, Isabelle...He will see you through."

"I will try, Mom. Sometimes it's not easy."

"We'll be praying for you and ask God to lift the burden from your heart and give you peace and comfort."

"Thanks, Mom! You're the best!"

Chapter 2

The funeral was at two o'clock in the afternoon. Isabelle dreaded going but knew she had to pay one last respect to her dear friend, Fallon. The sanctuary was full and people were standing around the wall. Isabelle had never seen this many people at a funeral before. Lots of her friends from school were there. All of them looked somber and some of them were wiping tears from their eyes. She could understand that as Fallon had been the girl that everyone liked. She was Homecoming Queen this year. Isabelle had been in the running but Fallon won over her. At least she got to be on the homecoming court. Isabelle never felt jealous of Fallon.

Now her friend was gone...never to walk upon this earth again. Fallon was a wonderful Christian girl and always let her friends know where she stood. Isabelle really admired her for that. She wished she was more like Fallon. There was no doubt in Isabelle's mind; she knew Fallon was in Heaven. "What a wonderful place that must be," she thought.

Isabelle and her family left the house and arrived at the funeral home about half an hour before time for the service. She would be seeing her friend for the final time here on earth. That made her more determined to live for Jesus, so she could see Fallon again one day. Her heart ached as she walked down the aisle toward the coffin holding her best friend. As she approached she leaned over and gave Fallon a kiss on the cheek. "Goodbye my Dear Friend, I will miss you more than you could ever know! Don't worry about me; I will see you again one day. We can walk all over Heaven together, but first I want to see my Jesus." A hush fell upon the crowd. You could have heard a pin drop. Everyone had been silenced by the words spoken by Isabelle. She joined her family who was sitting near Fallon's family. John and Lynette were so distraught over the loss of their daughter. Isabelle grieved for them as well. She could not imagine how terrible it would be to lose a child. Thoughts of seeing her Mom crying so much when Isac was killed rushed back into her mind. She was really too young to fully understand the pain her Mom was going through as she was only six years old. Now at eighteen, she could understand.

The funeral was a blur. She felt so weak. Somehow her legs held her up long enough to be able to get back to the car. She crashed. Next, was the final phase. They entered the cemetery which was filled with beautiful flowers. Isabelle had never liked cemeteries. There was too much pain and unhappiness associated with them. She thought about the Parker Family Cemetery back on the ranch. She never liked passing by it as it held too many unhappy memories for her. She still felt close to the family members buried there, even though she never knew some of them.

They walked over to the green tent which was covering the grave. Fallon's family was seated under the tent, while friends crowded around on the outside. The minister was brief. He could see how distraught the family was and didn't want to prolong the service. After a brief expression of sympathy to the family and a prayer, the service was over. Each family member laid a beautiful white rose on Fallon's coffin and proceeded to walk away in tears. Isabelle looked down at the white rose she was holding. It was her turn. She walked over and laid the rose down. She was crying so hard she could barely see the other flowers. "Goodbye, Fallon." she sobbed. "I'll see you in Heaven." Those were her last words before darkness consumed her. Her parents rushed to her side. Jennifer sat down on the ground and held her daughter's head in her lap. She talked gently to Isabelle and she slowly regained consciousness. "What happened?" she asked.

"You passed out," replied her Mom. "Do you think you can get up now?"

"I think so," she said as her Mom and Dad helped her to her feet.

"We need to get you home where you can rest," said her Dad.

So they headed for the car and put her into the back seat with her sister, Rachel Rose, then headed for the ranch.

It had been a very tiring day for Isabelle. She never dreamed she would be attending the funeral of her best friend, Fallon. Why did God take her? She had been taught not to question God but for now she had to do it. Then it dawned on her... God wants the best. This made her question her own faith. She knew she was a Christian but had she done her best for the Lord? She knew she had not been as good a witness to her friends as Fallon had been. Somehow she felt she was always in the shadow of Fallon. In her heart she purposed to do better. Being a Christian meant more to her than anything else. She just hoped going away to college would not change that. She felt so safe and secure as long as she was with her parents and to be honest, she dreaded the change.

She stayed home from school the next of couple days. She dreaded going back knowing that Fallon wouldn't be there. The pain of losing her best friend was almost more than she could bear. Her life would never be the same again.

Chapter 3

Time was a healer...that's what everyone at school told her. Undoubtedly, they haven't experienced the loss of someone so dear to them. Lots of girls hung around her and she wished they would all go away. She had no room in her life for anyone else.

After school on Friday she decided to go to the hospital to visit Dustin. She didn't know if anyone had told him about Fallon. She dreaded to face him. She got on the elevator and went to the second floor. She found him in room 202 which was near the nurse station. He smiled as she walked in the door. "Hi Isabelle," he said softly.

"Hi Dustin, how are you feeling?"

"Not too well," he replied. "I've got some broken bones. They had to do surgery. I guess I'll be laid up for awhile. How are you doing, Isabelle?"

"I'm okay," she said with a tear trickling down her face.

"I know about Fallon. My heart is broken too!"

"She was my best friend!"

"She was my girlfriend!"

"I know, Dustin. It just isn't fair..."

"I know...but we don't always understand why things happen. I wish we did."

"Me too! How much longer will you be in the hospital?"

"I will be here another week or two."

"Well, I hope you recover quickly, Dustin." She leaned over and kissed him on the cheek. They had something in common. They had both lost someone they loved. "I have to go now. I promised Tracy I would go by his house on the way home."

"It sure was nice of you to come by to see me, Isabelle! Tell Tracy I hope he gets well soon. Bye, Isabelle."

"Bye, Dustin! I'll come back to see you again."

"Thanks, Isabelle."

She turned and left the room. She proceeded to the elevator and got on. She was in such a deep thought, that she was back to her car before she realized it. She drove to Tracy's house and got out. Mr. Kelley answered the door with a big smile. "Hello Isabelle, please come in. Tracy is expecting you."

"Thank you, Mr. Kelley. I am anxious to see Tracy. How is he doing?"

"Better. Seeing you should improve him even more," he said with a laugh.

She walked down the hallway to Tracy's room. He was on the bed watching TV. She stuck her head around the door and said, "Hi Tracy!"

Tracy smiled and replied, "Hello there Beautiful! I'm so glad to see you! Come on in." He turned off the TV.

Isabelle leaned over the bed and briefly kissed him on the lips.

"Is that the best you can do?" he asked teasingly.

"We're in your home...your Mom and Dad are here!"

"They won't mind," he added with a smile.

Isabelle sat down on the bed and he took her in his arms. He kissed her passionately. She could feel her face heating up and pulled away.

"What? Don't you like my kiss?" he asked with a grin.

"Of course, I do. I just feel a little uncomfortable with your Mom and Dad so nearby." She decided to change the subject. "Oh, I went to see Dustin before I came here. He said he hopes you get well soon."

"How is he doing?"

"He has quite a long way to go. He has several broken bones. He also had surgery. He will be in the hospital another week or two."

"I wish I could go see him."

"I could come by one day and take you," Isabelle suggested.

"I would like that."

So they made plans to go the following Monday after she got out of school. She stayed with Tracy for an hour, and then went home. She had homework to do which would take several hours. She was glad this was her senior year. She would be glad to get away from here and start college. She wasn't sure where she was going or what she would do. She now realized it was swiftly approaching.

Then her thoughts turned to Tracy. She liked him a lot and might even be in love with him. She kept telling herself that she would be leaving and therefore didn't let herself fall deeply in love with him. She knew what her Mom and Grandmother had gone through and she wanted to spare herself the agony of lost love.

Monday came and school seemed long. She was anxious for the school day to be over so she could go pick up Tracy and take him to see Dustin. She knew they were best friends and also knew they had missed seeing each other. She pulled into Tracy's driveway at 3:30 p.m. He was ready and sitting on the front porch. He got up and came to meet Isabelle. She got out of the car and they hugged and he gave her a brief kiss. "I sure have missed you," he said smiling.

"I've missed you too, Tracy." He opened her car door and she sat down. He then went around to the passenger side and got in.

"It feels good to get outside the house. This is my first trip out."

"I'm sure glad that you are feeling better, Tracy."

"Thanks, Isabelle. Looking at you makes me feel better." He was smiling. "I'm also anxious to see Dustin."

"I know...me too."

It was a short drive to the hospital. As they entered Dustin's room they saw that his eyes were closed. As they approached the bed he opened them. He had such a big grin on his face as he exclaimed, "Tracy, Isabelle...what a surprise!"

"How are you doing old man?" asked Tracy grinning as he shook hands with Dustin.

"Better I hope," answered Dustin. "I should get out of here in another week."

"That's great news," added Isabelle.

Looking at Tracy he asked, "Did you go to Fallon's funeral?"

"No, I wasn't able to go but Isabelle did."

"Yes, I did go and it was the saddest day of my life. I still can't believe she is gone." She was wiping the tears from her eyes as she talked.

"I don't know what I will do without her!" exclaimed Dustin. "I loved that girl so much!"

"She loved you too," added Isabelle. "She was dreading to leave you when she had to go to college."

"We had talked about that. We even talked about going to the same college, but now that dream is all gone." He was crying softly.

"I know it's hard for us to understand but God had a reason for taking her. If we could only see her now, I am sure she is enjoying herself more than we are. She's gone to a place where there is no more worry, sickness, death and heartache. Heaven is a wonderful place and I intend to live a Christian life so I can go there one day when God calls me," said Tracy.

"I wish I could be that sure," replied Dustin.

"You could be," added Tracy. "You just need to let God take control of your life."

"I am going to think about it...I promise you I am."

"When you get able, you need to start going to church. You can go with Isabelle and me. We would even come to your house and pick you up."

"I might just do that after I can walk without crutches."

They visited with Dustin until he began to get tired. A nurse came in and gave him a shot for pain. When he was beginning to feel drowsy, they said goodbye and left. Isabelle dropped Tracy off at his house and went back to the ranch. It had been an emotional visit with Dustin. Her heart went out to him, but there was nothing she could do to help ease his pain, just as there was nothing anyone could do to make her feel better. It would take time for both of them to get over the loss of Fallon. Each one loved her in a different way.

Chapter 4

The next couple of months went by fast as graduation was quickly approaching. Isabelle was resigned to the fact that Fallon was gone and she was at peace with it now. Time is a healer. She had been concentrating on trying to make a decision about college. She finally decided to apply to a Design School in New York. Somehow she wasn't as excited about this as she thought she would be. She really didn't care if she wasn't accepted. Something kept nagging at her conscience and she couldn't quite figure out what it was. She had been praying about it and asking God for His direction in her life.

She was watching TV a few weeks later and saw an ad saying there was a shortage of teachers on the Native American Indian Reservations. This is it, she thought. I am going to be a teacher and go where someone really needs me. I want to feel needed and not be just a teacher. I want to be a special teacher.

She ran downstairs to tell her parents. They were almost in shock. Jennifer had always thought her daughter would want to work in the medical field. She would stand behind her in whatever she chose to do. Actually, Isabelle had always been very caring and in lots of ways reminded her of her own sister, Miranda.

Isabelle was very excited that she finally knew what she wanted to do. She would go to Montana State University in Billings. She would be able to live at home and drive back and forth. That suited her just fine. She would take her teacher training in Early Childhood Education and get a Bachelor's Degree in four years. Meanwhile, she would be searching and praying for the perfect job. She knew if she trusted God, He would show her where she was needed the most. She felt at ease about her decision.

Little did she know that all the plans she was making were about to change. Two weeks before graduation, she, her Mom, and sister, Rachel Rose, were in a shopping mall in Billings. They were casually strolling along when suddenly a sophisticated looking man, dressed in an expensive looking suit, approached them. Isabelle and Jennifer looked at each other as he was approaching them.

"Hello Ladies," he said with a bright smile.

"Hello," they said in unison.

They started to walk away but he spoke up, "Ladies, I would like to have a minute of your time. My name is Preston Muldane and I'm from New York. I'm a talent scout for Fairmont Modeling Agency and I'm on my way to California. I stopped in Billings to visit a friend of mine and thought I would check out the mall before leaving. You never know when you will find a prospect. That's what I see in you, young lady." he was looking straight at Isabelle.

"As flattered as I am, I already have plans for college."

"What are you planning to study?"

"I want to be a teacher."

"Oh girl...you have so much more potential than that. You are beautiful and I can see you on the runway in Paris or Rome."

By now Isabelle was smiling and Jennifer was standing there in total shock.

"How do we know you are legitimate?" asked Jennifer.

The man pulled out a business card that contained his name, the name of the modeling agency and all the other necessary information she would need. He gave her the card and told her to check him out. She planned to do just that. She would call the agency and the Better Business Bureau in New York City.

"By the way, young lady...may I ask your name?"

"It's Isabelle...Isabelle Colter. My Mom is Jennifer and my sister is Rachel Rose."

"Nice to meet all of you young ladies," he said as he opened his attaché case and took out some brochures. He handed them to Isabelle and asked her to read them. "May I call you in two weeks?"

Isabelle looked at her Mom for permission. "I guess it would be okay," replied Jennifer. She took a business card from her handbag and gave it to Mr. Muldane.

"Thank you, Mrs. Colter," he said pleasantly and left.

"WOW!" exclaimed Isabelle. "Now I AM confused."

"I can understand that. I think it caught us off guard."

"What should I do, Mom?"

"What do YOU want to do, Isabelle?"

"I honestly don't know, Mom. You know I have talked about becoming a fashion designer since I was young. Maybe this is what I am supposed to do instead of being a designer."

"We'll have to discuss this with your Dad and then

we all need to pray about it. This may be your chance of a lifetime."

"I know...if I turn it down I may never get another opportunity. They say if you haven't made it by the time you are twenty, you might as well forget it. I will soon be eighteen and that leaves me two more years to get started."

"One thing I know for sure, you will make a beautiful model! With your beautiful face, your tall, slim, well built body and your long dark hair, you would be a knockout on the runway!"

"Thanks, Mom! I think I really must give this a try and see what happens. I know I have two weeks to decide but I think I already know what I will tell Mr. Muldane when he calls. Mom, I really don't think I need to pray for a decision. I have already decided I want to do this. I think we need to pray that God will be in control and direct me in this avenue of my life."

When they got home and told Gabe, he was all but excited. "Does that mean you will be leaving home as soon as you graduate? Going to New York? I thought you were going to college."

"Dad, if I don't take this chance now, there may never be another opportunity. I have to give it a try. If I don't like it or they don't like me, I can always come back home, right?"

"Of course you can, Isabelle! You will always be welcome here no matter how old you are. Don't you ever forget it my Dear!"

"Thanks, Dad and I promise I won't forget." She bent down and kissed him on the cheek.

Chapter 5

The next two weeks went by slowly for Isabelle. It was hard for her to concentrate on her school work. She was so excited. She wished she could tell Fallon...but she would never be able to share anything with her again. This brought tears to her eyes every time she thought about it.

Exactly two weeks from the day they met Mr. Muldane at the mall, he called. Jennifer answered the phone. After asking several questions she handed the phone to her daughter. "Hello," said Isabelle.

"Hello, Isabelle. How are you today?"

"I'm doing well, thank you."

"Do you have a definite answer for me?"

"Yes, I think I do. I have talked it over with my Mom and she is good with me pursing a modeling career. My Dad is not too happy about it."

"He will be fine after he sees you become a celebrity."

"I hope so. When do I start?"

"School starts in mid August. I need to come to your home and get you signed up for modeling school. May I come by later today...say three o'clock?"

"Sure, that would be great."

"I'll see you then, Isabelle."

"Thank you, Mr. Muldane."

"He's coming TODAY," she yelled as she ran through the house looking for her Mom and Dad. She was so excited! She was about to begin a whole new life. She was young and naïve and had no idea what lay in store for her.

Jennifer was more excited for her daughter than Gabe was. This was his little girl and he was very protective of her. He was not keen on the idea of her being a model to begin with. He knew bad things could happen to a young girl who left home and started another kind of life. He wished he could keep her on the ranch forever but knew that was impossible. In fact, he wished he could keep both girls here forever.

At exactly three o'clock Mr. Muldane arrived. He was all smiles and very polite. Jennifer met him at the door and invited him in. Gabe made sure he was present at this meeting. He walked over and introduced himself. "Hello, I'm Gabe Colter, Isabelle's dad."

"Nice to meet you, Mr. Colter. I'm Preston Muldane."

They shook hands as Gabe replied, "Nice to meet you, Sir."

Jennifer invited him to sit down. He walked over to a single chair, put his attaché case on the floor, and then sat down. "I guess you know why I'm here, Mr. Colter."

"Yes, and please call me Gabe."

"Okay, Gabe. I can really see a great potential in your beautiful daughter, Isabelle."

"Thank you, Sir."

"I met both of your daughters and your wife at the mall two weeks ago. Your oldest daughter caught my eye the instant I saw her. She is exactly what we are looking for in the modeling business. Give the younger one a few years and she may be what I'm looking for also."

"I am flattered but I guess the dad in me wishes you had never seen her," added Gabe.

"I think it would be a shame to hold her back and not let her explore this avenue. I think she could become a super model."

"Wow!" said Isabelle. "Do you really mean that?"

"I do. You have everything it takes in the looks department. With some runway training, I think you will be magnificent."

Isabelle was smiling from ear to ear. She couldn't believe this was happening...not to her. She had struggled for the past year trying to decide what she would do after high school and here she was having her future laid out before her eyes. She glanced at Rachel Rose who was not smiling at all. She looked worried.

"I can't believe this is happening to me!"

"I see a bright future for you, Isabelle. You will need to report to Fairmont Modeling Agency in New York City the first week in August. Here is the address," he said as he handed her a business card. "Now, if you and your parents are agreeable, we need to get you signed up. I realize your parents will want to read it before you sign. I will leave now and return in an hour. That will give your parents time to read and discuss it." He handed her the papers and left.

Gabe and Jennifer both read the papers, which sounded good to them. There didn't seem to be a hidden agenda anywhere, even in the fine print. Jennifer had already checked out the modeling agency prior to Mr. Muldane's visit. Of course she never told him. This was something she had to do. She couldn't let her daughter go off to New York without knowing something about the place she would be going to. According to the Better Business Bureau, it was a reputable agency. That sure relieved her mind. She knew she and Gabe would be going with her. The hardest part would be coming back home without her. After all, she was only eighteen.

True to his word, Mr. Muldane returned one hour later. "So what do you think?" he asked Jennifer and Gabe.

"I think it will be a great opportunity for her, if this is really what she wants. I just hate to see my baby girl leave home," sighed Gabe.

"How about you, Mrs. Colter?"

"I feel the same as my husband. I know I can't keep her at home forever, so if this is what she wants, I will stand behind her all the way."

"That's great!" exclaimed Mr. Muldane. "How does this make you feel, Isabelle?"

With a smile on her face she said, "It makes me very happy."

"Well, are you ready to sign the papers?"

"I guess so," she said.

"I will need for your parents to sign as well."

So they all signed. Isabelle was extremely excited! She looked at her younger sister, Rachel Rose, who had been sitting silent all this time. She knew this would be hard on her sister. The two of them had always been close, despite the age difference of six years.

Graduation was only a few days away. Everything was falling into place. The seniors were excited. Some would be going to college while others were trying to find a job. Isabelle just knew she had to be the luckiest girl in her class. None of them had the opportunity she had just been given. She felt so blessed.

Her thoughts turned to Tracy. They had gotten closer

since the accident. She hadn't told him about New York yet. She knew they had the next couple of months to be together. She actually dreaded talking to him about it. He was almost back to normal now and Isabelle sure was glad. She had worried so much about him. She knew that he would be leaving too, but he would still be living at home since he was going to Montana State University in Billings. He thought she was going there also. She didn't have the heart to tell him otherwise. She kept waiting for the right moment...but the right moment never came. She knew she couldn't put it off much longer.

Dustin was recovering nicely. He was back at school with only a slight limp. He was blessed to be able to walk again.

Graduation day came. All the seniors were excited. They were all dressed in their caps and gowns...looking good. The auditorium was filled with excitement. A handsome photographer was standing by to take pictures of each senior as the Principal presented them with their diploma. The photographs would be for sale at a later date.

Isabelle was among the first to graduate since her last name started with the letter 'C'. She walked so proudly across the stage as she headed toward the principal.

"Look at our daughter," whispered Jennifer to her husband. "She already looks like a model."

"Indeed she does," he answered grinning from ear to ear.

Isabelle accepted her diploma and gracefully exited the stage. She made her way to the section where the other seniors were sitting. Soon it was over. She was glad because she thought all the speeches were boring. She just wanted to graduate and get on with her life. Just two more months and she would be leaving for New York City. She was so excited and could hardly wait for the next two months to pass.

She and Tracy spent a lot of time together during those two months. She could feel they were getting closer. She never meant for that to happen, but it did. Two weeks before she was to leave, she knew she had to tell him. She had been dreading it so much. One evening they were sitting in the front porch swing and she knew this was the time. "Tracy, there is something I have to tell you."

"You're not breaking up with me, are you?" he asked with a sad look on his face.

"Of course not, what makes you think that?"

"Usually when a girl has something to tell you or says we need to talk, it means she is breaking up with you."

"Not this time, silly."

"Well, what is it?"

"Tracy, I have been accepted at the Fairmont Modeling School in New York City?"

"NEW YORK CITY!!!!" he exclaimed. "But that's a world away from home."

"I know it is, but I really have my heart set on becoming a model. If things work out, I want to be a runway model."

"WOW! I don't know what to say. I am stunned! When are you leaving?"

"In two weeks."

"TWO WEEKS?" he asked in shock. "Why did you wait so long to tell me?"

"I didn't want to ruin your summer. We've had a great time together and I hated for it to end."

"I feel like my life is ending now," he said sadly.

"You have your life ahead of you, Tracy. You're going to college and you will make new friends and meet new gorgeous girls."

"I only have eyes for you, Isabelle!"

"I know, Tracy. I love you, too! We're both young and need to get our education."

"Why couldn't we do it together?"

"Our interests are different, Tracy."

He got up from the swing and dropped to his knees. "Will you marry me, Isabelle?"

"Oh, Tracy, I do love you, but I can't marry you now. We are too young and have to get our education before we can even think of marriage."

"But I don't want to lose you, Isabelle. I know once you leave here, you will never come back. I will lose you forever." The tears were streaming down his face.

"You make me sad," she replied as she wiped the tears from her own eyes.

He kissed her goodnight and left. She could see how upset he was and knew he wanted time alone. She understood.

Chapter 6

Her suitcases were packed and she was very excited. They would be leaving in the morning. The flight out of Billings was at 9:45 a.m. so that would give them time without having to rush. Isabelle went to bed around eleven but sleep did not come easily. She was just too excited! This was the beginning of a new life for her. She was excited and at the same time a little apprehensive. She had never lived away from her parents and she knew it would take some getting used to. She had no idea how much she would miss them. Had she known, she may have changed her mind.

She knew she would miss Tracy also. He had come to see her last night and their parting had been very difficult. She hated the sadness she saw in his eyes. She loved Tracy but was she in love with him? She really didn't know. She did know that she had to pursue her dream and see where it took her. She may never get this chance again. She was only eighteen and was too young to be in love anyway, she told herself. She had to build her career first and if love came her way, then well and good. She knew what had to come first in her life. Then it hit her...God had to come first. Without Him, none of this would be possible! She made a vow right then to never forget God and to keep Him first in her life.

They arrived at JFK International Airport late in the afternoon. It had been a perfect flight. The weather was superb. This was their first trip to New York, so all three of them were excited.

"Wow," said Isabelle. "I had no idea there would be so many tall buildings. It sure is different from Montana."

"Indeed it is," said her Dad. "There is no comparison. All I know is that I wouldn't trade Montana for all of New York."

"Now Gabe..." said Jennifer."Don't discourage Isabelle."

"It's okay, Mom. I know it will take some getting used to."

They collected their luggage, left the airport and hailed a taxi. They gave the driver the address on the card Mr. Muldane had given them. About twenty minutes later they arrived at a Mediterranean style building with ornately carved pillars. They got out of the taxi and Gabe paid the driver. He pulled away as they walked toward the front door. They were anxious to see the inside. It was even more beautiful. It was furnished with the same ornately carved Renaissance furniture in shades of red and green. Isabelle thought this was the most beautiful room she had ever seen. Their thoughts were interrupted as a woman approached them.

"My name is Carol Easton. How may I help you?" she asked smiling. She was carrying a clipboard.

"I'm Gabe Colter and this is my wife, Jennifer. We have brought our daughter, Isabelle, per Mr. Preston Muldane's instructions."

"Oh, yes...Isabelle Colter," she said looking at her

clipboard. "I do have your name down to arrive today. Welcome to Fairmont Modeling Agency!"

"Thank you," replied Isabelle nervously.

"Welcome Mr. and Mrs. Colter."

"Thank you," they replied in unison.

"Please have a seat. Ms Harlow will see you soon."

They waited for fifteen minutes and finally a door opened and a middle aged woman appeared. She was dressed to the nines and was very attractive. "Hello, I'm Jean Harlow," she said as she approached them. She shook hands with Gabe as she said, "You must be the Colter family."

"Yes, we are," replied Gabe. "I'm Gabe Colter and this is my wife, Jennifer, and daughter, Isabelle."

"Welcome to Fairmont Modeling Agency, Isabelle."

"Thank you," replied Isabelle.

"Come into my office and we'll talk," suggested Ms Harlow.

They all followed her into the office and took a seat. By this time, Isabelle was really feeling nervous.

"Isabelle, can you tell me why you want to be a model?"

Isabelle looked at her Mom as if to say 'help me'. Seeing that she was on her own she replied, "I knew from the time I was a small girl that I wanted to work in the fashion industry. I was thinking about becoming a fashion designer like my cousin, Caycee Canfield."

"Caycee Canfield? I am familiar with her work. She is very good!"

"Thank you. I never changed my mind until I met Mr. Muldane in the Billings, Montana, shopping mall. I'm sure he told you how he approached me."

"Of course he did. That is how he gets a lot of our clients."

"From that day on I knew I wanted to be a fashion model. I want to learn everything about the fashion world and become a super model one day."

"I like you, Isabelle! You have set a high goal for yourself. That is what I like to see. I do have to tell you that not everyone makes it that comes here. It will depend on how hard you work and how much you want it, as to whether you make the cut."

"I understand and I will do my very best for you."

"That's my girl."

"You will have six months of training and by then you will know if this is really what you want to do and if you are good enough to make it to the next level."

"When do I start?" asked an anxious Isabelle.

"Have you found an apartment yet?"

"No, we are going to start looking today. Mom and Dad will be here with me until we find a place for me to live."

"I have a girl that is looking for a roommate. Her name is Francine Box. She is a very nice Christian girl. Would you like to meet her?"

"Sure," replied Isabelle.

"I'll call her right now and ask her to come over." She proceeded to call Francine and invited her over to meet a possible new roommate.

"She will be here in about thirty minutes, if you don't mind waiting."

"That will be fine," replied Jennifer.

So they went back out into the waiting room, sat down and waited. Finally, a dashing redhead came bouncing through the front door. She looked at them and smiled as she walked by and knocked on Ms Harlow's door.

Five minutes later they both emerged from the office and came to talk to the Colter family. "Mr. and Mrs.

Colter and Isabelle, I would like for you to meet one of our trainees, Francine Box. She has been here for two weeks and is looking for a roommate."

They all stood up and shook hands with the new girl. "Nice to meet you, Francine," replied Gabe looking her over.

"We are happy to meet you," said Jennifer. "So you are looking for a roommate?"

"Nice to meet all of you and yes, I am looking for a nice girl to share my apartment and help with the expenses." She was looking directly at Isabelle.

"Well, I am looking for a place to live, so if you'll have me, I would like to be your new roommate," added Isabelle.

"Cool!" exclaimed Francine. "You may move in any time you wish."

"Thanks, Francine. Mom and Dad are staying for a couple days and I will be with them. I will move in with you just before they leave."

"Sounds great! Well, I have to run. I have some errands to run. Oh, here is my address. You can come by later this afternoon and see the apartment."

"Thank you and bye for now, Francine."

"Bye, Isabelle. I am looking forward to having you as my new roommate."

She bounced out the door at the same speed she came in. She seemed to have a lot of nervous energy. Jennifer hoped that wouldn't be a problem for Isabelle.

"Come on back into my office," said Ms Harlow as she motioned for them to follow her. They all took a seat and waited for her to start talking.

"Again, we are happy to have you here. Your classes will start in one week, Isabelle. That will give you time to get moved in with Francine. I will get a schedule worked up for you before then."

"Thank you. It sounds great. I can't wait to get started."

"I think you will do well."

"I hope so. I want this very much and will work very hard."

"That's what it takes...along with a great physical appearance, which you have."

"Thank you, Ms Harlow."

Gabe, Jennifer and Isabelle left the office and headed for a restaurant. They were all hungry by now. They felt relief that the interview was over and Isabelle had been accepted. The women were more excited than Gabe was. He hoped and prayed everything would be okay and asked God to watch over his daughter while she was away from home. He realized the day had come when she was ready to leave the 'nest' but it still wasn't easy to let her go. She would always be his little girl.

Two hours later, with their stomachs full, they headed for the address Francine had given them. It was in a nice part of the city and not far from Fairmont Modeling Agency, which was good. Isabelle could hail a taxi to go back and forth. Gabe was looking around and thinking how different this part of the world was from the ranch they lived on in Montana. He wouldn't trade his world for this one. Not in a million years.

They pulled in at the address and parked the car. They got out and walked toward Francine's apartment. With only one ring of the doorbell, the beautiful redhead opened the door. She was all smiles. "Hello again," she said beaming. "Welcome to my humble apartment and come on in."

"Hello, Francine. Thanks again for inviting me to live

here with you. Being new in the city has to be hard and this will help me a lot. I somehow feel like I already know you."

"Great!" exclaimed Francine. "I think we will make good roomies. I'm happy to have you here and I know my parents will be glad since they are paying all of my bills."

"We can understand that," said Gabe.

"It will be much easier on them with us paying half," added Jennifer.

"It sure will," said Francine with a smile.

They looked around the apartment and were relieved to see it was nice and clean. Jennifer knew from having two girls of her own, that sometimes they don't keep their room as clean as she would like. She finally learned not to worry about it.

Her younger daughter, Rachel Rose, did not come to New York with them. She stayed with her best friend, Marla Frazier. They had been friends since the beginning of kindergarten. Marla seemed like a third daughter to Jennifer. Vickie and Bob Frazier felt the same about Rachel Rose. Jennifer was glad she could leave her younger daughter and not worry about her. With school over for the year and summer vacation beginning, the girls had made lots of plans, like shopping and going to the pool. Rachel Rose wouldn't have time to miss her family.

They left Francine's apartment and headed to the Marriott Hotel, where they had booked for two nights. They checked in and the bellman took their luggage to the room. They decided to rest for awhile before going to dinner.

An hour later, they left the hotel and drove to **Scaletta Restaurant.** It was a beautiful place which offered family friendly ambience and a wonderful selection of delectable choices all at very reasonable prices.

The hostess seated them and a smiling waitress brought the menus. "Hello," she beamed. "My name is Callie and I will be your server tonight. May I get you something to drink?"

"I'll have sweet tea," said Gabe.

"The same for me," added Jennifer.

"I'll have water," said Isabelle. The waitress left and Isabelle looked at her Mom and said, "I had better start cutting back on sugar. I can't afford to gain weight... especially now."

"I understand that."

The waitress came back in a few minutes and asked if they were ready to order.

"I'll have the **Alaska Halibut**, in Dijone and Green Peppercorn Sauce, along with the vegetables of the day," said Gabe.

"I will have the **Pollo Diavolo**, the Grilled Boneless Chicken with Mustard Peppercorn Sauce," said Jennifer.

"I'll have the **Pan Seared Beef Tenderloins** with Shitake Mushrooms and Bordolese Sauce," added Isabelle.

"Do both of you ladies want the vegetables of the day?" asked the waitress.

"Yes," they said in unison.

The waitress gathered up the menus and left. It was twenty minutes later when she returned with their food. They were so hungry and the food looked delicious. They could hardly wait to get started eating. They joined hands and Gabe said the blessing upon the food they were about to partake of. No matter where they were, Gabe always thanked God before they ate.

The food was just as delicious as it looked. They all enjoyed their meal and ate until they were about to burst. After leaving a generous tip, they left the restaurant and went back to their hotel for the night.

They were up early the next morning. Isabelle was so excited. With her parents help, she would get moved into Francine's apartment today. She was anxious to start her new life. All she had brought was her clothes and personal things. She was glad that Francine already had the apartment mostly furnished. They arrived at the apartment around eleven o'clock. Francine was waiting for them. She even helped them unload the car and carry Isabelle's clothes inside. Her room contained a bed, a chest and a desk with a matching chair. That would be satisfactory for now. She was happy to have the desk, which would be useful for doing homework on her laptop computer. Things were looking up for her.

The next day, her parents took her shopping for bed linens and towels. She wanted a comforter for the bed with matching sheets and curtains. They found exactly what she wanted in shades of blue and green with palm trees and the beach. She knew that was the one she wanted the very instant she saw it.

It was time to say goodbye the next day. Isabelle felt sad to see her parents leave, but she knew there was no other way. She had to start her new life and try to build a career. She was hoping it would all work out. She could see a bright future for herself. She just hoped somewhere along the way she would find that perfect someone to share her life with, whether it is Tracy from back home or someone new. She wasn't in a hurry...she would let God direct her. When He had the perfect man for her, she knew He would allow them to meet, if they hadn't already met.

She watched her parents drive away in the taxi and tears filled her eyes. "I sure will miss them," she told Francine.

"I know you will. I miss mine too! But it will get easier as time goes by."

"I hope so."

"Once you get started in modeling school, your days will be very busy and you won't have as much time to think about home."

"I'm ready to get started. I wish I didn't have to wait until next week."

"It will be here before you know it. We need to take a trip around the Big Apple."

"I would love that."

The next evening, the two of them hailed a taxi and did some sightseeing. Isabelle was quite impressed with New York. Everything was so different from Montana. Here in New York, people always seemed to be in such a hurry. All the hustle and bustle of the city life...it would take some getting used to.

Chapter 7

The next week went by slowly for Isabelle. Finally, the day came when she and Francine went to their first class. They were both excited and nervous. The teacher was probably around thirty and very attractive. She had blonde hair and blue eyes and was tall and thin. As Isabelle and Francine walked in the door of her classroom, the teacher met them. "Welcome, Isabelle and Francine. My name is Ms Katherine Bookman and I will be your instructor this year."

"It's nice to meet you, Ms Bookman," replied Isabelle. Francine had met the teacher earlier.

"Today is our first day and it is meet and greet. I will call the roll and I want each of you to stand up, tell your name and where you came from."

When she called Isabelle's name, she immediately stood up and replied. "My name is Isabelle Colter. I came from the beautiful western state of Montana. I live on a ranch in Laurel."

They all welcomed her with smiles and friendly greetings. She was beginning to feel more at ease now.

"Please take your seat, Isabelle."

Isabelle did as the teacher asked and sat down beside her new roommate, Francine. There were four other girls sitting at the same table. Each one gave Isabelle a welcome smile as they introduced themselves in a whispered tone, so as not to bother the teacher.

"Hi Isabelle, I'm Maggie," said a beautiful blonde with long, straight hair and dimples in her cheeks.

"I'm Crystal," said a lovely brunette, with big brown eyes and long eyelashes. "We're glad to have you here."

"I'm Noelle," added a black haired Jamaican/Chinese beauty. Her heritage gave her an alluring exotic appearance and her eyes penetrate with a startling intensity. She was breathtakingly beautiful.

"Last of all, I'm Savannah." She was another beautiful blonde with long wavy hair and eyes as blue as the sky on a bright summer day.

"Girls, I am so happy to meet all of you!" exclaimed Isabelle."I hope we can all become very good friends."

"I'm sure we will," added Francine.

"Great." replied Isabelle.

Ms Bookman started the class and everyone was listening intensely as they took notes. All the first week consisted of taking notes. All this would be very important in the months ahead, when they would be studying for exams. Ms Bookman reminded them that attitude + determination + hard work = becoming a model.

"It is important for you to understand where you fit in the modeling industry. For example, if you are 5'9", very thin, with strikingly good looks, then high fashion or runway modeling is the right option. Being able to carry oneself confidently across a ramp foes require flair and practice. A tall, thin model can carry off skintight fashion wear better than a plus-size model. You must be able to carry off a dress and make it look good at an outdoor location or within a photographer's studio. You can easily identify professional models walking the catwalk," explained Ms Bookman.

"What if we don't have all the qualities?" asked a concerned Maggie. "I am only 5'8" tall."

"I wouldn't worry if I were you, Maggie. You seem to have everything else."

"Thanks, Ms Bookman," said a relieved Maggie.

"There are other avenues open for new female models not qualifying or opting for runway modeling. The print media provides two different types of modeling assignments, advertising and editorial. You can opt to be a model for advertising wherein you take part in commercials for products of services. It could be an ad for a new hotel or promoting a new car. Some interesting opportunities present themselves to models in advertising. There are no restrictions for height or weight for this model type, though developing an outstanding personality matters. For instance, a great actor would be a better asset onscreen promoting a product or service than a runway model with the required height and body."

Ms Bookman continued, "These are usually fun projects but a bit of time consuming with the model expected to build up the right expression and attitude to carry off an item. That in essence is how becoming a model in the commercial field is conducted."

"Plus size models also have an important role to play," added Ms Bookman. "They have to be a size 12, 14, 16, or 18 and still be in shape. Editorial modeling does cater to all sections of society. A plus size model will be able to present clothes meant for oversized people. Similarly, teenagers also have a role to play when youngsters identify new trends carried off by teen models."

"Girls, the first thing you need to do is find yourself

an agent to represent you. He or she will be looking for jobs for you as you train. Be careful, as there are some unreliable agents out there. I have a list of names that are reputable agents. I will give each of you a copy. Not all girls choose to hire an agent, but I highly recommend that you do."

"Thank you, Ms Bookman."

The first day went by so quickly. Isabelle took notes until her hand was tired from writing. She tried to soak in every tidbit of information. She was so determined to make the cut. "Well, Francine, what do you think? Are we going to make it?"

"Of course we are. We are going to work hard and they will not be able to turn us down," she said with her bubbly laugh.

"Wonder how long it will be before we practice for the runway?"

"I think Ms Bookman said six months," replied Francine. "Of course we will watch and learn. She said she would bring some real models in when that time comes."

"Do you have an agent, Francine?"

"Sure I do."

"Did you get him from the list?"

"No, my parents found him. His name is Frank Holland and he is super nice. I think he will work hard for me."

"Do you think I could retain him also?"

"I feel sure you could. Would you like for me to call him?"

"Sure, if you don't mind. I would appreciate it very much."

Francine gave Mr. Holland a call that night and he said he would be happy to take on Isabelle as a client.

Isabelle felt so relieved. She called her parents that night and told them the news. They told her they would put a check in the mail for the first month's payment for him. Things were going well for Isabelle and she hardly had time to miss her family.

Chapter 8

The first month went by very quickly. Isabelle and Francine became best friends. They did almost everything together. One night while at a dinner theater, they met a couple guys who turned their heads. They were both very good looking. The guys kept looking at them while they were eating and finally one of them came over to their table.

"I'm sorry to interrupt your dinner, but I couldn't help notice how beautiful you both are."

"Thank you," replied Francine.

"Are you girls here alone, or do you have a date?"

"It's just the two of us," laughed Francine.

"My name is Brian Rutherford. May my friend and I join you?"

Francine looked at Isabelle for her approval before answering him. "I'm Francine Box and this is my friend, Isabelle Colter. You may join us if you wish."

"Thank you," replied a happy Brian as he walked away from their table. In a minute or so the two guys were back. They pulled out chairs and sat down. "This is my friend, Mike Harper."

"Nice to meet you, Mike, and you too, Brian." said Francine.

"Same here," added Isabelle.

Brian took a seat beside Francine while Mike sat down beside Isabelle.

"Where are you from, and what do you do?" asked Brian.

"I'm from Maine and I'm here in New York to become a model."

"Great! What about you Isabelle?"

"I'm from Montana and I'm also here to become a model."

"Why am I not surprised? You both have the look of a model."

"So you are from Montana?" asked Mike looking straight at Isabelle.

"Yes, I am and I love it. I live on a ranch in Laurel, Montana. The ranch was started by my grandparents, Dr. Mitch and Rachel Parker. My grandpa was killed in a car accident before my Mom was born. My grandma, Rachel, later married Grayson Sterling. He was the only grandpa I ever knew. When they both died, my parents took over the ranch. I have such fond memories of growing up there."

"Sounds like a wonderful life," remarked Mike.

"It surely is. I know I will miss it, but I have to move on with my life. I'm not a little girl anymore."

"You look little to me," he teased.

"Oh, you know what I mean! If I wasn't small, there would be no need for me to be here. Actually, they like for runway models to be a size 0."

"SIZE 0?" he asked in a stunned voice.

"Yes, they have to be very tall and thin."

"I don't mean to be forward, but are you a size 0?"

"No, I'm not. I'm a size 2."

"That's not much bigger."

"I guess you girls have to starve yourselves to stay thin, huh?"

"That's about it," she replied.

"That doesn't sound like fun."

"It's the price you pay to be a runway model, which is what I am hoping to be."

"Well, good luck!"

"Thank you, Mike."

Mike turned his attention to Francine. "Francine, are you going to be a runway model also?"

"I sure hope so," she answered.

"I wish you both the best."

"Thanks again, Mike."

The four of them sat and talked for an hour after they finished eating. "Now it's your turn to tell us about yourselves," said Francine.

"I'm from here and I'm an attorney. I just became a new partner with Williams, Shorter & Rutherford," said Brian.

"That's great," replied Francine. "How about you Mike?"

"I'm from Nashville, Tennessee, and I'm in a band called 'COUNTRY EXPRESS'. We sing Country and Bluegrass. We are on tour here in New York now. We just got here two days ago."

"How do you and Brian know each other?" asked Isabelle.

"We met a year ago when I was here in New York. We've kept in touch and here we are...together again."

"Maybe you girls could come hear my band perform," suggested Mike.

"I would love that," replied Isabelle. "I am from the country and country music is dear to me."

"How about you, Francine?" asked Mike.

"I'm a Bluegrass fan. I'm not much on country music."

"I guess I'll have to widen my horizon since I'm out in the world now," laughed Isabelle.

Mike reached into his pocket and pulled out two tickets. He handed one to each girl and said, "I hope to see you Saturday night at the concert."

"Thanks Mike. I plan to be there," said an excited Isabelle.

"I'll be with her," added Francine. "Thanks for the ticket."

"It is my pleasure girls."

"I'll meet you there," said Brian with a smile.

"Come backstage after the concert," added Mike.

"Oh, thanks...I would love that!" exclaimed Isabelle. She couldn't wait to tell her family about all this. She just knew they would be excited for her. Her Mom and Dad were big country music fans. Rachel Rose liked the more modern music. Of course she was only twelve. Isabelle was proud that she grew up hearing country music and learned to love it. Gospel music came first in all their lives. That's the way it had always been. They had been raised in a Christian home and she prayed she would never stray from her family teachings. Going to church had always been their way of life. She knew she would need to find a church nearby and start going soon.

"Earth to Isabelle," said Mike. "You seemed so far away."

"I was thinking...about home and my parents."

"I bet you miss them already, huh?"

"I do. I have to remind myself that I am grown and pursuing my dream now. It's not easy leaving the 'nest' when you live in a family as close as ours."

"You are very lucky," remarked Mike. "I left home when I was sixteen and went to Nashville to live. I worked to support myself until I got a break, which was three years later. I've been with 'COUNTRY EXPRESS' for five years. Yes, that makes me twenty-four years old."

"You look young for your age," said Isabelle.

"I thought you were about twenty," added Francine. "How old are you, Brian?

"I'm twenty-five."

"I guess you know we are fresh out of high school and that makes us both eighteen. We are just about to begin our career, that is, if we make it."

"Oh, you'll both make it. You've got what it takes," said Mike grinning. "You're both very beautiful."

"Thank you, Mike," said Isabelle. "I hope modeling school sees us like that."

"They will," added Brian.

"It's time for us to go," said Isabelle. "We will see you Saturday night."

"Great!" said Mike. "I will be looking forward to it."

The girls left and went back to their apartment. It had been a fun night. They discussed the events of the evening and decided they liked both the guys. They seemed to be very nice. They actually never tried to 'hit' on them and they respected the guys for that.

As they sat there talking, Isabelle decided to approach Francine about going to church. "Francine, were you raised in church?"

"My parents went part of the time, but never regularly. I guess they never felt it necessary. How about you?"

"We went to church every time the door was open. It was our way of life and as children, we never questioned it. It's just what we did."

"Did you ever get tired of going so much?"

"Not really. After I became a Christian, I wanted to be in church as much as possible. We had a youth group and we did lots of activities."

"We never had that at my church. Maybe that is one reason I never wanted to go."

"How would you like for us to find a good church and start going now?" asked Isabelle.

"I would go with you. I don't have a problem with that."

"Good...then we need to start looking. I guess the best thing is to look in the phone book and see what is located nearby."

"Sounds like a good idea."

Isabelle got up and went to pick up the large phone book off the table. She wasn't used to such a large phone book. Neither was she used to New York City. She hoped she would get used to it and not be too homesick. She flipped through the pages until she came to the church listings. "WOW," she said. "I didn't realize there would be so many churches in New York City."

"Do you have a map of the city, Francine?"

"I sure do." She got up to go look for the map. She sat down on the sofa beside Isabelle and they began their search. With each church they found, they would look on the map. They finally narrowed it down to a couple of churches near them. One was a Baptist and the other a Methodist. They decided to try both churches and see which one they liked best. "Let's go to the Baptist church this Sunday," suggested Isabelle.

"That's fine with me," said Francine. "We can try the Methodist the next Sunday."

They were looking forward to the concert which was only two days away. Isabelle was excited as this was the second concert she had ever attended. The other one was a

Gospel concert benefit for a child with cancer in Billings, Montana. She was only twelve at that time.

She and Francine got through the next two days of school and were glad when Saturday arrived. They spent an hour going through their clothes, before deciding what to wear to the concert. They were so excited.

Finally, it was time to go. They took a taxi to the Coliseum and arrived forty-five minutes early. They were ushered to their assigned seats on the front row. "Wow," said Isabelle. "If it wasn't for Mike, we wouldn't even be here, let alone sitting on the front row."

"I know," replied Francine. "It was our lucky day when we ran into Mike and Brian."

"It surely was."

They sat there watching the people as they filed in. Isabelle had always been a people watcher. She loved seeing what the ladies were wearing. Some were dressed up but most were casual. A few of the guys were in suits, but most were wearing casual clothes. She was glad most of them were casual. If it was the theater, it would be different.

Finally, the curtain opened. After an introduction of the band members, the music started. Mike was the lead singer and guitarist. He had only gotten started when Isabelle turned to Francine and whispered. "He has a BEAUTIFUL voice."

"Indeed he does."

"I'm so glad we got to come tonight."

Francine nodded her head and smiled.

The band played and sang for a solid hour. The time went by so quickly for Isabelle. She was thoroughly enjoying it. They had a fifteen minute intermission, and then sang for another hour, ending with 'AMAZING GRACE'. It was so beautiful and Isabelle knew she had never heard it sung better. This was a night she would never forget. In more ways than one, but she didn't know that at this point.

After it was over, the girls made their way backstage. It wasn't easy getting through the crowd, as the house was packed. They finally made it and someone stopped them at the entrance backstage. "May I help you?" asked a big guy, who was probably a bodyguard. He stood well over six feet tall and looked like a body builder.

"Yes, you may. We were invited backstage by Mike Harper."

"What is your name?"

"Isabelle Colter and this is my friend, Francine Box," replied Isabelle.

"Just a minute," he said and left. He returned shortly and told them to proceed as he opened the door for them.

Mike saw them coming and walked to meet them with a smile on his face. "Glad you got through the crowd."

"It wasn't easy, and then we had to get past your bodyguard."

Mike was smiling. "Oh, that's Rick. He is a nice guy. I know he looks intimidating because of his size, but he is harmless to my friends."

"That's good to hear," replied Francine.

"Mike, I have to tell you that I really enjoyed tonight. You have the most beautiful voice. I could have stayed another two hours and listened to you," said Isabelle.

"Thanks, Isabelle. I don't think I could have lasted that long. After singing two hours, my throat is ready for a break. I have an idea, girls. How about we go up the street to a nice little coffee shop? My throat needs something hot. Brian is meeting us there."

"Sounds great," said Isabelle.

"Give me time to change my clothes and I'll be right back."

"We'll be waiting," replied a happy Francine. She had wondered where Brian was. Now she would get to see him again and that excited her.

Mike was back in ten minutes and they left the building through the back door. The night air felt refreshing. There was a slight breeze blowing upon their faces as they walked up the street. "What a glorious night," said Mike.

"Yes, it is," added Isabelle. "I am so happy you invited us tonight. Thank you again!"

"You are very welcome. It was my pleasure to have you on the front row where I could see you." He smiled and put his arm around her shoulder. He then turned to Francine and said, "Cheer up, Francine. Brian is waiting for you."

"That's good to know. I didn't want to be a third wheel."

"Oh, you definitely won't be."

They entered the coffee shop and Brian was sitting at a table for four. He smiled and got up when he spotted them. "It's a good thing I came on ahead of you. This place was almost full when I got here. I was lucky to find this table."

"You did well, man," said Mike. "Let's all sit down. My legs need a rest."

The guys pulled out the chairs for the girls and they all sat down. They all ordered coffee and a donut. Usually, the girls never eat dessert, but decided to make tonight an exception. After all, Mike would be leaving soon. Isabelle figured she would probably never see him ever again. Their lives were too different and would take them in different directions. She was living in the moment.

"Isabelle, do you have plans for tomorrow?" asked Mike.

"Francine and I had planned to go to church in the morning. We have nothing else planned. Why?"

"I thought we might go to the park and have a picnic, if you want to."

"That sounds great. What about Francine and Brian?"

"Oh, they can come too."

"Sounds good to me," responded Francine.

"Me too," added Brian.

"How about one o'clock?" asked Mike.

"Sounds great," said Isabelle.

"Brian and I will pick you up at one o'clock. We will have the food ready."

"Thanks guys, that sure is nice of you," said Isabelle smiling.

The continued to sit and talk long after their donuts were gone. Mike had several cups of coffee to soothe his throat. He probably would have a hard time sleeping tonight. The same thought was running through Mike's head. It wasn't the coffee he was worrying about keeping him awake. It was this beautiful girl sitting beside him. He had met lots of girls, but never anyone like Isabelle. She was very unique for this day and age. Most girls were so loose with their love and that was not what he was looking for. He knew Isabelle was one in a million. But what was he going to do about it? What could he do about it? He was going one way and she was going another. This made him feel sad. He couldn't see a future for them, but he knew she would remain in his heart forever. She had touched his heart like no other girl had ever done. She had no idea how he was feeling and he couldn't tell her. It wouldn't be fair to her. She was just starting her career and had years of modeling ahead of her. It was uncertain where her career would take her. He would never try to stand in her way. He did want to keep in touch with her, if she would allow him to.

Two hours later, they walked out of the coffee shop. They loaded into Brian's car and headed to the girl's apartment. The girls offered to take a taxi, but Brian wouldn't hear to that. "We need to know where to pick you up tomorrow."

"I guess you do," said Francine laughing.

Mike and Isabelle were in the back seat and he had his arm around her. He suddenly leaned over and kissed her briefly. "I hope you don't mind," he said softly.

She shook her head and said she didn't mind. He leaned over again and this time he gave her a passionate kiss, which left her breathless.

"Whew," she said after he withdrew from her lips. "I guess I wasn't expecting that."

"I hope you're not mad at me!" he exclaimed.

"Of course not. I just wasn't expecting that kind of kiss."

"You didn't like it?"

"It's not that...I did like it, in fact, I loved it," she said shyly as she moved a little closer to him. She was in Heaven on the ride home. She wished it had been a longer ride. When they reached the apartment, Brian parked the car and they all got out. The guys walked them to the door, gave them a brief kiss and reminded them to be ready at one o'clock tomorrow. They each kissed their girl goodnight and walked toward the car.

After they were inside the apartment, Isabelle was the first to speak. "What an incredible evening!"

"It surely was. I really like Brian. I am so glad he lives in New York City, because I plan to see more of him."

"You're lucky. I guess tomorrow will be the last time I will see Mike, since he is leaving on Monday morning."

"I know that is a shame. To meet someone you like and only get to see them a few times is rotten luck."

"Even though our time will be short, I am still glad we met. I will miss him! People enter our lives, some for just a short time and I think it makes us a better person by knowing them. This is how I feel about Mike. To know him for a short while is better than not knowing him at all."

"That is a great way to think, Isabelle!"

"We had better try to get some sleep tonight so we can get up early and go to church. I am really looking forward to going."

"It will be the first time I have been in a long time."

"Then it's good that we are going," teased Isabelle. "I can't imagine not going to church."

"You were blessed with parents who took you. That makes a difference!"

"I know it does. It's never too late to start on your own."

"I'm so glad you are my roommate! I think you will be a positive influence on my life."

"I hope I can be, Francine. With God's help, I want to be the kind of Christian I need to be and let my light shine in front of you and others."

"Goodnight, Isabelle."

"Goodnight, Francine."

They each went to their own bedroom and slipped off their clothes and got into a nightgown. After their nightly routine, each one climbed under the covers of their own bed. Isabelle lay there and reflected over the happenings of the night. She had a great time with Mike and found herself wishing tomorrow would hurry up and get here. On the other hand, she knew it would be their last day together...maybe forever. That was a somber thought. She also knew if she told her parents how old Mike is that they would not be happy. They would say he was too old for her. Six years did not matter to her. In fact, she enjoyed him being older. Boys her age were usually immature. Her thoughts turned to Tracy Kelley, back home in Montana. He was her age and seemed immature after being with Mike. She loved Tracy, but was it puppy love? At this point she really didn't want to think about it. Her head was full of thoughts of Mike. She was glad that Tracy didn't know...

Chapter 9

Sleep overtook her around midnight. When she woke up the sun was shining through the shade. She got up and walked over to the window. She pulled up the shade and looked out the window at the glorious day God had made. "Thank you, God, for this beautiful Sunday morning. Keep us in your care and give us a good service at church. In the name of Jesus I pray. Amen."

She made up her bed and got into the shower. She decided to skip breakfast today since they were having a picnic. She continued to get ready for church. She put on a pretty royal blue fitted dress with pleated ruching around the waist and bodice. It was very figure flattering. She looked stunning, only she didn't know it. Her long, dark hair was flowing down her back. She didn't realize her beauty and that was one of the things that made her extra beautiful.

She came out of her bedroom and found Francine sitting on the sofa. She was dressed in an emerald green dress, which made her look stunning as well, with her red mane flowing down her back. Memories of Isabelle's Aunt Miranda came flooding into her mind when she saw the green dress. That was Miranda's best color. She was so beautiful with her long, flowing, golden hair. When she wore emerald green, she stood out in a crowd. Isabelle never knew her Grandma Rachel, who died before she was born. She had seen pictures of her and knew she was a very beautiful lady. In fact, Miranda was almost a carbon copy of her. On the other hand, her own Mom was completely opposite from her sister Miranda. Jennifer was a beautiful woman with long dark hair like Isabelle. Of course, Gabe had dark hair too, so Isabelle was like both of her parents. She was glad. She loved her parents so much and was missing them more than she realized.

"Good morning, Francine," said Isabelle as she approached.

"Good morning. Did you sleep well?"

"In fact, I did...that is, after I finally got to sleep. I was doing a lot of reminiscing."

"Oh?"

"I had a lot on my mind. I was thinking about Mike and about my friend, Tracy, back home."

"That's the first I've heard about Tracy."

"We were double dating with my best friend, Fallon, and her boyfriend, Dustin, when we were hit head on by a drunk driver." Tears welled up in her eyes. "My best friend was killed that night."

"Oh, I am so sorry, Isabelle. I didn't know."

"Of course you didn't. I find it very hard to talk about."

"I won't ask anymore. If you ever want to talk about it, just know that I am here for you."

"Thank you, Francine. That means a lot to me."

"Let's get out of here and go to church," suggested Francine.

"It sounds good to me."

They left and hailed a taxi to take them a few blocks to church. It was a beautiful old Baptist church that had been built many years ago. Isabelle loved these old churches. The taxi let them off in front of the church. They walked up a few steps to the front door. As they entered, a nicely dressed man met them with a church bulletin and welcomed them. They smiled politely as they thanked him. They walked down the aisle and sat down on the fifth row from the back. Several people were already gathered there. Isabelle noticed that most of them were dressed up. She was glad she and Francine had chosen nice dresses to wear. Back home, it was more casual. She knew that being in the big city meant a lot of things would be different. She would get used to it.

The Pastor came in and stopped by their pew. He introduced himself as Pastor Bill. He was very tall and good looking with salt and pepper hair. He looked to be somewhere around fifty. He welcomed them to the church and asked if they were originally from New York. Isabelle was sure her accent gave her away.

"I'm from Montana," she replied.

"What brings you to New York?"

"Modeling school."

"Oh, a model in our midst, huh?"

"I'm only in school now. Time will tell...My friend Francine is going to the same school."

"Where are you from, Francine?"

"I'm from Maine," she replied.

"Well, good luck to both of you. I'm happy to have you with us this morning and hope you will come back."

"Thank you," they replied in unison.

Church started shortly and they both enjoyed the congregation singing. It was very uplifting. After the pastor prayed, the choir sang a special. They had such good harmony. It reminded Isabelle of back home. Later in the service, there was special singing by a husband and wife. They were really good and blended so well together. Then it was time for the Pastor's sermon. He took his text from Luke 15: 11-32. He preached about the Return of the Prodigal Son. Every now and then, Isabelle glanced over at Francine, who had her eyes glued on the pastor. She was taking in every word. Isabelle could tell this message was touching her new friend. She was happy about that. She could see that Francine's eyes were brimming with tears.

The pastor closed with an alter call. One young man responded and an older man went to pray with him. The young man rose to his feet with a smile on his face. You could tell he had given his life to Jesus. It showed on his face.

The service was dismissed with a prayer and it was over. Isabelle and Francine left the pew and started up the aisle toward the door. Several people stopped to talk a minute to them and invited them back.

As they walked down the outside walkway, they could see several taxis heading their way. They hailed the third one and went back to their apartment. Isabelle could hardly wait to get Francine's opinion of the church service. "Well, Francine, how did you like the service?"

"I thought it was very interesting. I heard things today from the Bible that I don't remember ever hearing before."

"Really?"

"Yes, it makes me realize how much I have missed by not going to church."

"We can remedy that. I think we need to purpose in our hearts to go every Sunday."

"I agree," replied Francine.

"Do you still want to check out the Methodist church next Sunday?"

"I really don't think it's necessary. I would like to go back to the same one we went to today."

"That's fine with me. I have always gone to a Baptist church anyway."

"So did I...what little bit I went," added Francine. "That's going to change now."

"I'm glad to hear that."

"We had better get our clothes changed so we'll be ready when the guys get here."

"You're right."

Each one went into their bedroom and changed. They came out about the same time wearing jeans and a T-shirt. They were anxious for Brian and Mike to get there.

Chapter 10

At exactly one o'clock, the guys appeared. Isabelle answered the door and invited them in. They stepped inside for a few minutes. They left shortly and headed for the park. Once they got there, the girls took over. They spread the tablecloth on a table and took the food out of the picnic basket. Something sure smelled good. They guys had outdone themselves. They had bought fried chicken, ham, potato salad, macaroni salad, rolls, tea and a chocolate cake for dessert.

They enjoyed the meal together and the girls momentarily forgot about their diets. The food tasted so good. Normally they ate light, so this was a real treat for them. After they finished eating and had everything cleaned up Mike asked Isabelle if she would like to go for a walk in the park. It was a big park with trails leading through some trees.

"I would love to go," she answered him.

So they started walking. Just as they entered the tree area, Isabelle felt a tug on her handbag, which was hanging from her shoulder. Then she felt nothing. A thief had cut the strap and ran off with her handbag. Isabelle screamed.

Seeing what had happened, Mike ran after the thief. He caught him and knocked him to the ground. He was able to grab the handbag and was starting to get up, when the thief pulled out a knife and stabbed him in the chest. Mike screamed, "HELP!!!" The thief then grabbed the handbag again and ran away.

Isabelle heard Mike and went running to him. When she saw he had been stabbed, she almost passed out. She sat down on the ground beside him to regain her composure. "I am going for help, Mike!" She took his cell phone from his pocket and dialed 911. She ran as fast as she could to find Brian and Francine. They were still at the picnic table. They knew something was wrong when they saw Isabelle running toward them. They could see the fear in her eyes.

"What's the matter?" asked Brian, dreading to hear her answer.

"It's Mike...he has been stabbed! Please hurry and come with me."

"Did you call 911?" asked Francine.

"Yes, I called from Mike's phone. The police and ambulance will be here soon."

"Tell us what happened," requested Brian with much concern.

"A thief cut my shoulder strap and stole my handbag. Mike ran after him. They fought on the ground and Mike ended up being stabbed in the chest."

"IN THE CHEST?" asked Brian with fear of what was to come.

"Yes."

"Which side of his chest?"

"I don't know."

"Oh Dear God. We need to get to him quickly."

They all ran as fast as they could to where Mike lay

upon the ground. He was lying very still and they were about to panic. "MIKE!!!" yelled Brian. "CAN YOU HEAR ME?"

Two policemen got there just before the ambulance. They took a statement from Isabelle. They leaned over Mike and said his name. He groaned and opened his eyes momentarily. At that moment they heard the sound of a siren. "I'll run out to the clearing and let them know where to come."

A few minutes later the EMT came rushing to Mike's side. They checked his wound and started an IV before loading him onto the stretcher. Brian bent down over him and said, "Don't worry Mike; you are going to be okay. We'll all be there with you."

The EMT left with him and loaded him into the ambulance. It was a short trip to the nearest hospital. Brian and the girls pulled in just behind the ambulance. They all jumped out of the car and were right behind the EMT as they wheeled Mike into the hospital emergency room. They were in the waiting room and finally a doctor came out and told them Mike was being taken into surgery. He had damage in his chest that needed to be repaired. The next forty-eight hours would determine whether he would make it or not.

Isabelle looked at Brian and Francine. "Let's join hands in prayer for Mike." So they extended their hand to Isabelle and she started to pray. "Dear Heavenly Father, we come to you with humble hearts. Please, Dear God, in the name of Jesus, I ask you to touch Mike's body and restore him back to normal. Please be with the doctor and guide his hands during the surgery. We know Mike's life is in YOUR hands. We ask this in the precious name of your son, Jesus. Amen."

Sudden relief passed through Isabelle's body. She had

done all she could do. She would continue to pray for him. She knew that God's will would be done, no matter what the outcome was.

Four hours later, a nurse came out and told them the surgery was over and that Mike was in recovery. A half hour later the doctor emerged from the operating room and headed their way. "I wanted to let you know that your friend came through the surgery. It wasn't quite as bad as I had anticipated. The knife barely missed a main artery. Should that artery have been cut, he would have died before you could have gotten him here."

"Thank God for answered prayer!" exclaimed Isabelle.

"It was a higher power," stated the doctor. "It will take Mike several days to recover. Does he have family nearby?"

"I'm afraid not," answered Brian. "He is a member of the band 'COUNTRY EXPRESS' and they performed here last night. They were supposed to be leaving in the morning for another gig."

"Mike won't be going anywhere for quite some time. He is going to need time to heal and someone to take care of him." The doctor looked at all three of them.

"I guess it will be me," said Brian. "I do have a guest bedroom."

"That's good. Mike is going to need it."

"Don't worry, doctor, I will take good care of him."

The doctor left and went to the recovery room to check on Mike. He came back out and told them he was resting nicely and was not fully awake yet. He would be taken to the Intensive Care Unit as soon as he woke up.

"When can we see him?" asked Brian.

"Not until they get him moved to the ICU and then only one at a time. Limit your stay to five minutes."

"Thanks, doctor. We can do that."

The doctor left and they kept waiting...

"Brian, maybe we can help some when Mike comes home," said Isabelle.

"Thanks, Isabelle. All help will be appreciated."

"We can fix some food and bring over," added Francine.

"Now that sounds like a winner. I think Mike will appreciate that and I know I will."

"That's the least we can do. Don't expect a miracle though. I am not a great cook. I don't know about Isabelle, but I have a feeling she's a good cook."

Isabelle laughed, "I did learn to cook from my Aunt Miranda. She was the cook in our family. They say she took after her mom, Rachel, who was also a great cook. My Mom can cook when she has to. While Aunt Miranda lived on the ranch, she did about all the cooking."

"I'll be anxious to sample some of your cooking," said Brian smiling.

Isabelle smiled, "I hope you won't be disappointed!"

"I have a feeling I won't be. Anything will be better than what I can do."

The nurse came to the waiting room and told them Mike was awake. "Only one at a time and only five minutes each," she reminded them.

"Thank you," replied Isabelle. "May I go first?"

"Follow me," replied the nurse.

As Isabelle walked into the room and saw Mike, she felt a chill run up her spine. He was lying there with his eyes closed and looked so helpless. She walked over to the bed and took his hand. "Mike," she whispered softly. "It's Isabelle."

He opened his eyes and looked up at her without

speaking. She leaned over and gave him a kiss on the cheek. He smiled at her. "Thank you," he whispered.

"How are you feeling?" she asked.

"Not too good," he replied in a soft tone.

"Don't talk, Mike. Save your energy. I just wanted to see you for a few minutes. The others are waiting to see you also."

He smiled and answered, "Good."

"I will go now and let someone else come in to see you."

He squeezed her hand and said a soft, "Thank you for coming."

"I'll see you again soon." She walked out the door and as she looked back his eyes were glued on her.

Brian went in next and told Mike not to worry about where he would go once the hospital released him, because he had a guest room prepared for him. Mike seemed surprised and tears welled up in his eyes. He thanked Brian and told him he owed him one.

"The good part is this; the girls are going to do some cooking for us. So you can relax, you won't have to eat my cooking all the time."

Mike smiled and said, "That sounds good."

"I have to go now and let Francine come in to see you."

"Okay and thanks."

By the time Francine got in to see him, he seemed to be tired out. She just said hello and wished him a speedy recovery and left.

The three of them left and Brian took the girls to their home. Tomorrow was a school day, but Isabelle was going to have to go to the DMV and get a new driver's license. She had no hope of getting her handbag back. She was so glad she didn't have any credit cards. She hated that her cell phone was gone. She would have to get another one. She would have to wait until her parents could send her some money. She had over one hundred dollars in her billfold, which was gone with the wind. She had no money at all. She found herself wishing she hadn't carried it all with her and had left some at home.

After Brian dropped them off, Isabelle asked Francine if she could use her cell phone to call home. She dialed the number and waited. After three rings, a chirpy voice said "Hello."

"Rachel Rose, is that you?"

"Of course it's me, who else do you think it would be?"

"Is Mom there?"

"She's downstairs somewhere."

"Well, go get her for me."

"Say please," she teased.

"Rachel Rose, I don't have time for foolishness. This is a serious matter."

"Oh...okay." It was only a few minutes until her Mom was on the phone.

"What's the matter, Isabelle? Are you okay?"

"I'm fine, Mom. My body is okay but my spirit is broke."

"What do you mean? What is going on?"

"I was robbed, Mom. A man cut my handbag strap and ran off with it."

"Oh, my goodness Isabelle! How awful! Are you sure you're okay?"

"Yes, Mom, but my friend, Mike, is not okay. He ran after the thief and they had a confrontation. Mike is in the hospital in serious condition. He was stabbed in the chest."

"Oh, no... Is he going to be okay?"

"We hope so. He had surgery to repair a lot of damage. The doctor said the next twenty-four hours would be crucial. I did get to see him for five minutes today."

"When did it happen?"

"This afternoon around two o'clock."

"Where were you?"

"We were in the park having a picnic. After we ate Mike and I went for a walk. Francine and Brian were in the park with us. I ran back to get them and called 911."

"I sure am glad you are okay and hope Mike recovers quickly. Now tell me, who is this Mike?"

"He is a member of the 'COUNTRY EXPRESS' band from Nashville."

"How on earth did you meet him and how old is he?'

"I met him in a café and he is twenty-four."

"TWENTY-FOUR??? He is too old for you."

"Mom, I am not dating him. He gave Francine and me a ticket to his concert on Saturday night. He was supposed to be leaving in the morning and I probably would never see him again. Anyway, he is very nice. So is his friend, Brian."

"Who is Brian?"

"He's an attorney here in New York and he and Francine are kind of together."

"Be careful, Isabelle."

"I will, Mom. I hate to ask you, but I don't have any money at all. All I had was in my wallet when my handbag was stolen. I'm broke."

"Don't worry; we will wire some money to you in the morning."

"Thank you so much, Mom. Thank Dad for me, too! I don't know what I would do without you."

"You're our daughter and we will always be here for you!"

"That warms my heart so much. Thanks again. I will talk to you after I get a new cell phone. Love you! Bye Mom."

"Bye Isabelle and I love you, too!"

"Thanks for the use of your phone, Francine. My parents are wiring some money to me in the morning."

"You're welcome and that's great. It sure makes you feel better if you have a little money in your pocket."

"Tell me about it!"

Chapter 11

Mike got out of the hospital two weeks after the accident. He was doing much better but still needed someone to take care of him. Isabelle and Francine did all they could do to help. They cooked or baked something almost every day and took over to Brian's house. The guys were always happy to see them, especially when they were carrying food. The four of them became close friends. They all knew this was only temporary and agreed not to get serious, knowing that would only bring heartache later on when they went their separate ways.

School was going well for Isabelle and Francine. They were really enjoying it. Ms Bookman was a great teacher and wanted her students to do everything perfect. "That's the way you learn," she told them one day. "Do it right the first time and you will prevent a lot of frustration for me and yourself."

Today they were going to do their first trial run. They would walk down the long hallway at the school.

"Girls," said Ms Bookman. "Posture is very important in being a model. Keep your back straight and your head up, looking straight ahead. If you make a mistake, keep going. Don't be afraid to flash a smile, but don't over pose, just act naturally. Keep your hair off your face. The judges want to see your face. If it's covered, that can ruin an otherwise positive impression."

Ms Bookman continued, "Keep your legs straight and cross one foot over the other as you walk. This will take some getting used to, especially walking in four-six inch heels. This takes lots of practice. In walking this way, it tends to make your hips sashay naturally. Keep your arms at your side and don't fling them back and forth. Sometimes you may have on an outfit with pockets and it is permissible to walk with your hands in your pockets. When you arrive at the end of the runway, pause, put your hand at your waist and thrust your hips the other way. If you are wearing a jacket, you may remove it and fling it over your shoulder just before you turn and walk back up the runway. Any questions before we get started?"

No one seemed to have a question so Ms Bookman had them line up at the far end of the hallway. Isabelle was third in line. She didn't want to be first. She was nervous and wanted to watch a couple of girls before trying it herself. When it came her turn, she looked straight ahead and walked as she had been instructed. That hallway seemed to be a mile long. She finally reached the other end without making a mistake, she hoped.

"Well done, girls," said Ms Bookman, after all the girls had walked the walk. "I am very proud of you! For your first try, you actually surprised me. Each time will be easier for you. Before long you will feel like a professional."

"Thank you, Ms Bookman," said a delighted Isabelle. "I think I am going to love this. I think it will be more like fun than an actual job."

"Don't get too comfortable. Modeling is a lot of hard work, if you want to become great at what you do."

"Well, I am willing to do what I have to do to become a super model."

"Me, too!" exclaimed Francine. All the other girls agreed.

Isabelle and Francine cooked dinner for Mike and Brian. They cooked enough so that they could all eat together. Francine had called Brian to let him know. At six o'clock the girls went to Brian's house with the food.

After they had eaten, Mike spoke up, "I don't know how to tell you this but I will be leaving next week. I am going back home to Nashville. My Mom wants me to come home where she can take care of me. I want to thank all of you for the many things you have done for me. I couldn't have made it without you!"

"You're welcome, Mike. I sure will miss you," said Isabelle. "It has been wonderful knowing you. Maybe our paths will cross again someday."

"I sure hope so. I wish you the best in your modeling career."

"Thanks Mike!"

"You too Francine."

"Thanks," she replied.

"Brian has been wonderful to me by allowing me to stay in his house and taking care of me when I couldn't take care of myself. I thank you for that, Brian!"

"You are very welcome, Mike. I only did what any good friend would do."

The next week seemed to go by quickly. Isabelle dreaded for Mike to leave, but she also knew they had no future together. He would be back on the road when he was well enough to start traveling again with the band. God only knew where she would end up if she made it in the modeling world. She and Mike did plan to keep in touch.

The girls cooked their final dinner for Mike and went over to Brian's house at six o'clock. They had cooked an extra special meal for tonight. They spread all the food out of the table and Mike gasped. "Look at all that food, Brian!"

"Wow," said Brian. "Are you feeding an Army?"

"No, we just wanted to give Mike an extra special send off. Of course, we were thinking of you, too, Brian," she teased.

"It sure looks wonderful and I thank you so very much," replied Brian.

"So do I," said Mike. "I don't know if my Mom will cook like this for me or not."

"I bet she will," added Isabelle. "She will be so happy to have you home that your wish will be her command."

"I don't know about that."

They all enjoyed dinner and ate until they were extra full. Two hours later the girls said their goodbyes to Mike. He took Isabelle in his arms and kissed her like she had never been kissed before. He held her in a long kiss, which left them both breathless.

"WOW," she said. "One would never know you have been sick."

"It doesn't take a lot of energy for a kiss," he answered back smiling. "I may never see you again, so I had to leave you with something you won't ever forget."

"I don't think I could ever forget that kiss," replied Isabelle looking at him with tears in her eyes. "I am going to miss you, Mike."

"I'll miss you, too! Best of luck to you wherever you go and whatever you do. I won't ever forget you, Isabelle."

"I feel the same and I wish you all the best with the band. I will look forward to hearing from you after you get to Nashville."

"You will, you can count on it," he said smiling. "We will be 'Forever Friends'!"

"You have been a bright spot in my life, Mike and I will never forget you!"

"Nor I you! Goodbye, beautiful Isabelle!"

Chapter 12

School was getting harder as time went on. Francine was still seeing Brian from time to time. She wasn't sure where that relationship was going.

They were halfway though their school now and Mr. Holland called and set up an appointment with both of them for new headshots and body shots. He was going to send them to various modeling agencies. He told them they needed to start getting their name and photos out there. He said the agencies were looking for the very best and only a few would make it. This made them wonder if they were pretty enough and had enough talent to make it. Only time would tell.

The photo sessions went well. A week later, Mr. Holland called and told them their photos were ready to be picked up. They went that afternoon to get them. Both girls were very pleased with their photos. The photographer had done a wonderful job. Mr. Holland would be sending their photos to various modeling agencies in the United States and abroad. Isabelle was hoping she would be picked up by an agency abroad, either Paris or Rome. This would give her a chance to see the world. Francine was hoping to go to Paris. Meanwhile, they would have to wait and see what the future held for them.

Back home in Montana, Isabelle's family was getting ready to drive to New York for her graduation. She was so excited! She hadn't seen them for six months and that was a long time to someone who had never been away from home before. She felt like this time away from home had really made her grow up. She felt even older than her eighteen years. Even though this had been an exciting six months, she was glad that she would be going back home with her parents and sister. She would go back home and wait.

The trip to New York was a long one for Gabe, Jennifer and Rachel Rose. They did some sightseeing along the way. This broke the monotony of the five day trip. They were so excited at the thought of seeing Isabelle again. Rachel Rose was very excited that Isabelle would be going back to the ranch with them. She had missed her sister terribly.

Isabelle's family arrived the day before graduation. They checked into the Marriott Hotel where they had previously stayed six months ago. As soon as they checked in and got their luggage taken to their rooms, they gave Isabelle a call. She was so excited they were in New York. "Hello, Isabelle," said her Mom.

"Hi Mom!"

"We finally made it."

"That's great. I hope you had a safe trip."

"Everything went well. We want to take you and Francine out to dinner in about an hour."

"Sounds wonderful," said a delighted Isabelle. "I can't wait to see all of you!"

"I know. We'll be over in an hour."

"Thanks, Mom. See you then."

Gabe, Jennifer and Rachel Rose arrived exactly one

hour later. They were all so excited and kept hugging and kissing each other. Finally, they settled down and headed toward the car.

Francine spoke to Isabelle, "You have such a nice family."

"Thank you. They are the best."

"I can see how much they love you. I am very happy for you, but it makes me see how much I have missed."

"What do you mean?"

"My parents divorced when I was small and my Mom remarried several times. She never could seem to get it right, until after I was grown. I'm happy to say that now she has a wonderful husband who is very good to me. I wish she had found him when I was small. It would have made my life more pleasant and hers too."

"We have to accept what God has in store for us. Some people are more blessed than others. Sometimes I think that the hard times make us grow. I am so thankful I never had to go through any of that. I know I am very blessed to have such wonderful parents."

"You surely are!"

They all got into the car and Gabe asked, "Where would you like to eat?"

"If no one else has an idea, I would like to eat where we ate six months ago," suggested Isabelle.

"What was the name of it?"

"It's the Scaletta Restaurant," answered Isabelle. "You know that is the only time I have eaten there. It is too expensive unless someone else is paying for it." She smiled at her Dad.

"I think we can handle that today, Isabelle."

"Thanks, Dad!"

They got to the restaurant and finally got seated. The waiter brought menus to them. After much concentration, each one was ready to order. It was another wonderful meal. They were full when they left.

"I hope I can get into my dress tomorrow," said Francine rubbing her stomach.

"So do I," added Isabelle.

"Tell us about the graduation ceremony. How many will be graduating?" asked Jennifer.

"There are twenty-two of us. We will be doing a fashion show for you. Ms Bookman always does this on graduation day."

"That sounds exciting!" exclaimed her Mother.

"I can't wait to see that," added Rachel Rose. "Seeing my sister on the runway will be very exciting."

Isabelle laughed and added, "The best is yet to come, little sister. I hope."

"Oh, it will happen for you, Isabelle. I know it will."

"Thanks for your confidence in me, Rachel Rose."

Graduation was at eleven o'clock in the morning, so they all turned in early. Jennifer knew the girls needed a good night's sleep so they would look fresh tomorrow. She couldn't believe her daughter was graduating from modeling school. She wondered where this would take her. She was hoping it wouldn't be too far away. Isabelle had hinted that she would like to go abroad. Jennifer hardly knew how to pray. She wanted her daughter to be happy, but the mom in her was being selfish. She would never let Isabelle know how she felt.

Gabe, Jennifer and Rachel Rose were at the girl's apartment at ten the next morning. They all left shortly and headed for the school. Ms Bookman wanted them to be there an hour early. Isabelle's family stayed in the waiting room at the school. Since it was December, it was too cold to sit in the car. Jennifer was glad that Isabelle would be home with them for Christmas. She was thinking and planning, as she sat there. She planned to invite Isabelle's friend, Tracy Kelley. She hadn't mentioned this to her daughter yet but she was sure it would be fine with Isabelle.

Ms Bookman came to get them fifteen minutes before time to start. They followed her into an auditorium. It was beautifully decorated for this special occasion. She seated them near the front where they would be able to see well. Jennifer was glad.

At exactly eleven o'clock the curtains opened and the show began. One girl after another came on the stage and walked down the runway. They were dressed in casual apparel. Some beautiful outfits, thought Jennifer. Next they came wearing swimsuits. WOW, some of them were skimpy. Jennifer and Gabe were anxious to see what their daughter would be wearing. She entered so gracefully, wearing a red, one piece swimsuit that was tastefully done. It was much better than some of the others. They let out a sigh of relief. She was extremely beautiful with a perfect body. Her long, lean legs were perfectly shaped and she carried herself like a true model. She was at ease with herself and one would think she had years of experience.

Ms Bookman continued, "Next we have Isabelle Colter, from Laurel, Montana. She is wearing a chic one piece swimsuit in Lipstick Red by Zeurgari called a twisted Monokini. Crystal embedded silver sliders at each strap add shine to this monokini. Four straps come together for a twisted middle. Ties at neck and back. Matching hardware at each hip. Tie side bottom sits low on the hips and provides less than moderate coverage. This is a beautiful swimsuit that flatters a perfect figure like Isabelle has."

"She will make it," whispered Jennifer to Gabe.

"I think you're right. I am very proud of our daughter!"

The final performance was the evening gowns. "This is the best one of all," said Jennifer.

"I kind of like the swimsuits," Gabe teased his wife.

"You would. You're a man!"

Isabelle was the fifth one to enter. Ms Bookman continued, "Next is Isabelle Colter, our little girl from the west. She is wearing a Sweet Heart Neckline Dress in Lavender by Tony Bowls Le Gala. Wrapped up in ribbons of light, this Tony Bowls Le Gala gown radiates élan. Fabulous jewel embroidery adorns one side from the strapless neckline to the upper thigh, gathering curve-conforming radiant tucks from the bodice, waist and hips. Offset gathers expand from the thigh to floor length for a fashionably flared finish. This one is a winner. Isabelle accents the gown perfectly."

"She is breathtakingly beautiful," said an overwhelmed Jennifer.

"Indeed she is. That's our daughter," replied Gabe proudly.

"Her long dark hair looks stunning against that lavender gown."

"Yes, it does."

The rest of the girls modeled their gowns. After the last one finished, they all returned to the stage. A magnificent rainbow of colors adorned the stage. They were all breathtakingly beautiful. Ms Bookman had a big smile on her face. One could tell she was very proud of her girls. "Thank you, girls for a job well done. I couldn't be more proud of you!" She turned to the audience and continued, "Thanks to each and every one of you parents or friends who came for this special occasion. It means a lot to me and I'm sure it means even more to your daughter or friend to have you here. Now we will continue by presenting the diplomas." She started at the beginning of the line and hugged each girl as she presented her with the diploma. She told each they had done a superb job.

Finally, it was over. Isabelle made her way to her parents and sister. "I am so glad you could be here," she said.

"We wouldn't have missed it for the world," said her Mom.

"That's right, Dear Daughter!" exclaimed her Dad.

"You look pretty," said her sister, Rachel Rose.

"Thank you so much for being here for me. I love all of you very much!"

"Are you ready to go back home to Montana?" asked her Dad.

"Yes, I think I am. It will be good to get back to my roots and out of this rat race."

Isabelle gathered all her belongings from the school, said goodbye to her friends, wished them well, then left with her parents. They got back to the apartment just before Francine and Brian arrived. This would be her last night in New York, as far as she knew. She would be leaving with her family in the morning. She was excited. The six months in New York had been a learning experience for her. She felt as if she were much older than eighteen. She had learned so much. She never realized how naïve she was.

Gabe took them out for a late lunch around three o'clock. Brian and Francine joined them. Of course, Isabelle wanted to go back to Scaletta's Restaurant. They had such a wide variety of food to choose from. She felt a little sad that this would be her last time to eat there.

Afterwards, her parents took her back to the apartment.

They told her to pack and they would pick her up around eight in the morning. They left and headed back to the hotel for some much needed rest before starting the long journey in the morning.

Chapter 13

Isabelle was up and ready when her parents arrived at the apartment the next morning. She hugged her new friend and told her she would miss her. They had gotten close.

"I'll miss you, too! We will keep in touch. I will want to know where you go from here. I hope that both of our dreams come true."

"Me, too," said Isabelle with a smile. "I will call you as soon as I get an offer."

"I will do the same."

"Goodbye, Francine and good luck."

"Goodbye and all the best to you, my friend."

Isabelle walked to the car and got into the back seat with her sister. Gabe was carrying her suitcases. After he loaded them into the trunk, he took his place in the driver's seat and started the car. They were beginning their long journey back home to Montana.

Isabelle fell asleep almost instantly. She was so tired from the previous day. It was a day she would never forget. She couldn't believe she had just graduated from Fairmont Modeling Agency in New York. It seemed more like a dream. It had been a wonderful time in her life. Not only did she love the school and her new friends, but she had met Mike. She wondered how he was doing. He said he would keep in touch, but so far she hadn't hear one word from him. Then she started to dream..."Isabelle, where are you?" she heard Mike say. She wanted to tell him she was right there, but somehow the words wouldn't come. It was as if her throat was paralyzed and she couldn't speak. She was trying so hard to speak. Then she heard her Mom call her...she still couldn't speak. She felt herself falling in a downward spiral, down, down, down...there seemed to be no end. She started to moan and then she felt someone touch her arm. She abruptly opened her eyes to see her sister shaking her arm.

"Wake up, Isabelle! Were you having a bad dream?"

"Yes, I was falling and kept going down. I couldn't see the end. I am so glad you woke me. I heard Mike's voice asking me where I was, and then I heard Mom calling my name. I couldn't speak at all. I wanted to answer them but I just couldn't."

"You're okay now, Isabelle," said her concerned Mom. "We're taking you back home to the ranch and you can get settled in and relax. You might want to help Rachel Rose and me get things ready for Christmas."

"Of course I will, Mom. I am excited that I will get to spend this Christmas with you. You know, it could be my last one for awhile."

"I don't even want to think about that," said her sister.

"I don't either. I want us to have the best Christmas ever and not worry what will be next Christmas. We have no way of knowing what the future holds; we only know WHO holds the future."

"Amen to that," replied Gabe. "Let's just enjoy the present time and take it one day at a time."

"Sounds good to me," replied Isabelle. "I'm just happy to be going home!" She took out her cell phone and selected a number.

"Hello," said a familiar voice.

"Tracy, it's Isabelle."

"Hi Isabelle. How are you? Did you graduate?"

"I am fine and yes, I did graduate yesterday. We're on our way home."

"YES!" he exclaimed excitedly. "I can't wait to see you!"

"So how are you doing, Tracy?"

"I am doing well, thank you. It took some time to get over the accident, but it hurt me even worse when you left."

"I'm sorry, Tracy. I never meant to hurt you."

"I know," he laughed. "Even though I missed you terribly, I'm glad you are pursuing your dream."

"Thanks! How is your school going?"

"Good. I'm off for Christmas now. This will work out quite well for us."

"It will," she replied. "It will be nice to spend time with you again. We have been through some rough times."

"Indeed we have. Dustin is finally doing better. His bones have healed and he is walking again, but with a limp. It may take a year or more for him to be back to normal. I'm just thankful to still have my best guy friend."

"I know...I wasn't that lucky with my best friend."

"I'm so sorry, Isabelle. I shouldn't have said what I did. Forgive me."

"That's okay, Tracy. I know you never said it to hurt me. You were just speaking what was on your heart and that is good. As far as Fallon, I keep telling myself it was her time to go."

"As much as it hurts you, I know you are right. God said it was time for her to come home to be with Him.

When I think about Heaven and all I have read in the Bible, it makes me know she is the lucky one."

"I know you are right, Tracy...but I miss her so much!"

"I know you do. I thought getting away for six months would help you."

"Oh, it did! I made another best friend, Francine Box. We hit if off instantly, but NO ONE will ever take Fallon's place. Francine and I plan to stay in touch."

"That's great. I love you, Isabelle, and I want you to be happy. No matter where you may go or whatever you may do, I will always love you. Don't ever forget that."

"Thanks, Tracy, I won't. I love you, too! There will always be a bond between us."

"I hope so."

"I will see you soon. I will give you another call when we get home tomorrow."

"That sounds great!"

"Bye for now."

As soon as Isabelle was off the phone she asked her mother, "Mom, do you care if Tracy joins us for Christmas?"

"Of course not, Isabelle. I was thinking of inviting him myself."

"Good, then I will ask him the next time we talk."

"I think that's a wonderful idea. I'm sure you two have a lot of catching up to do."

"We do and it will be great to see him again."

Chapter 14

The Colter family drove several hundred miles before stopping for the night. It would be at least a four day trip, since it was a little over 2,000 miles. They were driving on Interstate 90-W. Their first stop was in Cleveland, Ohio. After getting a bite to eat, they retired for the night.

They were up early and started another day of driving after eating a light breakfast. Their destination was Chicago, Illinois. It was another tiring day. They would have liked to do a little sightseeing along the way but were afraid to waste time, not knowing what was ahead of them. Being December, you never knew what to expect.

Day three was on to Sioux Falls, South Dakota. It was a rough, snowy day. The snow was accumulating fast. It took them longer to reach Sioux Falls, due to hazardous driving conditions. They were thankful to be driving a SUV. They saw many stranded cars along the way and several wrecks.

When they got up the next morning and looked out the window, they were in for a big surprise. There was at least a foot of snow on the ground. "Ladies," he said to his three 'girls'. "I think we will be here for a couple more days. We have a deep snow."

"Oh no," moaned Isabelle. "I want to go home."

"Not in this weather," replied her Mom. "We would be risking all our lives to get out in this."

"I know..." Isabelle sighed.

They next two days went by slowly as there was nothing much to do, except watch TV. They were lucky that the power hadn't gone off. They ate all their meals at the hotel restaurant and never ventured out into the snow.

Finally, a couple days later, they were able to continue their journey. They were planning to spend the night in Rapid City, South Dakota that night. It snowed all day as they traveled. They prayed each morning before starting the day and asked God to protect them as they traveled and take them home safely.

Gabe hoped everything would be okay at the ranch. He put his top hand, Clark Morrison, in charge while he was gone. Clark had been with him since right after Miranda's husband, Mardi, was killed. He had proven to be very trustworthy in everything he was asked to do. Gabe knew he was very blessed to have found Clark.

When they reached Rapid City, Gabe called Clark, who told him they had more than a foot of snow. He advised Gabe to drive carefully; that he had everything under control at the ranch. This relieved Gabe's mind.

After breakfast they left Rapid City and headed for home. That was such a good sounding word, HOME! It was later in the afternoon when they reached their ranch in Laurel, Montana.

"It sure is good to be home," said Isabelle before even getting out of the vehicle. "The way I feel right now, I never want to leave the ranch again."

"I like the sound of that," said her Dad. "You might decide modeling is not for you after all."

"I wouldn't go that far," piped up Isabelle. "I just don't want to think about a job or leaving this soon. Can you understand, Dad?"

"Of course I can, Dear Daughter. Everything changes when you leave here. Right now I don't think you want a change."

"You are so right, Dad. Is this childish of me?"

"No, Isabelle. After all, you are only eighteen and I feel you are too young to be out on your own."

"But Dad," she started. "If I am to become a model, I have to do it now. If I wait until I'm older, I won't stand a chance. They told us if you don't make it by the time you are twenty, it is almost impossible. So you see I only have two years."

"Well, I am praying for God's will to be done in your life!"

"Thank you, Dad. I need your prayers."

The main road had been scraped and when they came to their driveway, they saw that it had been scraped as well. Gabe was sure Clark was responsible for this. They unloaded the SVU and walked in the path that Clark had made for them. That sure was better than walking through knee deep snow. The house was cozy. Clark had made a fire in the fireplace and had turned up the heat. They were dreading coming home to a cold house, but Clark had made sure that never happened.

The Christmas tree was already up, but not decorated. Jennifer was waiting so that both of her daughters could help, as well as Gabe. They always did this as a family. This was one of their family traditions. It was only a week until Christmas. Jennifer had a lot to do. Miranda, Eli, Savannah, Taylor and little Tommy were coming from

Medicine Bow, Wyoming, for Christmas this year. Jennifer was so happy that her sister and family would be with them this year. She missed her sister so very much. Things were not the same since she moved away. But Miranda had found a wonderful husband. Eli Warren had been an answer to prayer for Miranda. Not to mention that he was the stranger dressed in black that they saw in the shadows when Mardi was being laid to rest in the Parker Family Cemetery on the ranch. "It's strange how things happen," said Jennifer to herself. "Life has so many turns and we never know what to expect next. I sure am glad to know that God is in control."

Jennifer unpacked for herself and Gabe. The girls did their own. While they were working, Jennifer went downstairs to the kitchen and fixed some sandwiches. It was getting late and she was too tired to cook.

After dinner she gave Miranda a call. Miranda was happy to know they were back safely. "I am so glad you are back home. We will be leaving in two days," she said.

"I know and I can hardly wait to see you."

"Jennifer, I miss you as much as you miss me!"

"I know you do, Miranda. It's not like we live so far away that we can't visit. Five hours is not that long, especially after the long trip we just made."

"Winter time is not a good time to travel across the country."

"Tell me about it. It just happened to be the time we needed to go. I am glad it's over."

"Wonder where Isabelle will be going next?"

"It's hard to tell. She is hoping to go abroad."

"ABROAD?"

"Yes, that is what she wants."

"I think she will get homesick if she goes that far from home. It's not like you can come home that often."

"I know and it's about to kill her Dad and me. I try not to let on though...it's her life and she has to make her own way now. She really does have her heart set on becoming a runway super model."

"If that's what she wants, I hope she makes it. She has the looks and personality, that's for sure."

"Thanks. She and her new best friend, Francine, are both reaching for that goal."

"I hope they both make it."

"Me, too, even though I hate the thought of her being so far from home."

"You have to let her go. She is a young lady now, in search of a new life."

"I know that, but it doesn't mean I have to like it."

"Dear Sister, hang in there. We'll see you in a couple days."

"I can't wait, Miranda!"

Jennifer was in a very cheerful mood after talking with her sister, Miranda. She hadn't seen her since last Christmas. They had so much to catch up on.

The next morning after breakfast the family started decorating the tree. It looked very beautiful after they finished. "I do think this is the prettiest tree we've ever had," remarked Jennifer.

"I can't remember any prettier than this one," added Gabe. "What do you think, girls?"

"I love it," said Isabelle with a big smile.

"So do I," added Rachel Rose.

"This could be our last Christmas together," said Jennifer.

"Now, Mom," said Isabelle. "Don't start thinking about that. Just take one day at a time. We have no idea what next Christmas will bring."

"I was just thinking if you go abroad, it won't be as easy to get home."

"I guess it depends on how much money I make," laughed Isabelle.

"It will also depend on how busy you are."

"Don't start worrying now, Mom!"

"I don't have time to worry now. We need to start baking the cookies. Who wants to help?"

"I do!" exclaimed an excited Rachel Rose. "I love baking cookies."

"We need some cakes, too. How about it, Isabelle? Do you want to help?"

"Sure, I will make a Red Velvet Cake. They are always appropriate for Christmas and besides, it's Tracy's favorite cake."

"I knew there was some reason in you volunteering so quickly," said her sister.

"So?"

"We will be here, too, you know!" exclaimed Rachel Rose.

"Now girls..." said their Mom."We need to get busy."

So, the three of them worked together the rest of the day. They baked several batches of cookies and four cakes, which included the Red Velvet, German Chocolate, Rum Cake and a Coconut Dream Cake.

They spent the next day making some appetizers which they could put in the freezer for a few days.

On the day Miranda and her family were due to arrive; Jennifer and the girls spent the day cooking. Jennifer boiled a country ham, baked a turkey, and fixed a pot roast with veggies in the slow cooker. "I couldn't have made it without you girls!" she exclaimed. "Thank you so much for your help!"

The girls told her they were happy to help her. After

all it was Christmas and she shouldn't have to do all the work.

Jordan and his family would be there. They were still living in Billings, so that was not far for them. Rob, Kati and Grayson III were still living on Prince Edward Island, so they would not be able to make it. They tried to come for a visit once a year but they preferred to visit in the summer time when the weather was warm. Jennifer could understand that, although she always invited them. She wasn't sure about Jordan's twin brother, Blake. He was in the middle of a new movie and doubted if he could make it this year. Hollywood had been good to him. He was a well known actor now and got lots of lead movie roles. The name 'Blake Parker' was a household name now. Jennifer was very proud of her brother.

Chapter 15

Later that afternoon, Miranda, Eli and their three children arrived. The house was beginning to fill up and Jennifer loved it. It brought back memories when they were all children. Their mom, Rachel, always loved cooking for a crowd. She seemed to be the happiest when her family was gathered around her. Jennifer had many happy memories of her Mom and missed her very much. Time does lessen the pain but you never get over the death of someone so dear to you.

"Hello Miranda," said Jennifer as she gave her sister a big hug. "It's so good to see you. I have missed you very much."

"I've missed you, too. Thank you for having us again this Christmas."

"Well, it sure wouldn't be the same without you!"

"Hello Eli," she said as she hugged him. Then she hugged the children and remarked, "You guys have grown so much. Look how big little Tommy is getting. I can't believe he is two years old. He looks just like you, Eli."

"Thanks, that's what I hear all the time."

"You should be proud."

"Oh, I am!"

"Savannah looks a lot like you too, but not as much as Tommy."

Eli grinned as he took off Tommy's coat.

"That leaves Taylor...of course she looks a lot like her Mother. She has the same beautiful, long, golden hair. She looks like a little angel. Miranda, you and Eli are truly blessed with beautiful children."

"I know," said Miranda. "We are so thankful for our children. Not only are they beautiful, they are good as well. We have very little trouble with them."

"That's great," replied Jennifer. "I hope it continues through adulthood."

"So do we!"

The Warren family got settled in and all of them seemed happy to be there. Rachel Rose took charge of the children. She loved babies and was more than happy to help. Miranda and Eli were thankful...it gave them some time to rest and talk to the grownups.

Gabe came in from the barn around five o'clock. It was almost dark. He was checking on the horses. He knew Clark had already checked on them, but he wanted to see them for himself. He had missed his horses while they were in New York. He was thinking to himself how happy he was to be back home on the ranch and how city life was not for him. He knew Jennifer felt the same and he sure was glad.

He greeted their visitors as he came in the back door. Since Eli was a rancher, the two of them had a lot in common. He was so happy that Miranda had found Eli. He was a great guy and loved Miranda so much. She had her glow back and he was happy to see that she had gained a little weight. Of course you never tell a woman she has gained or she automatically thinks you are telling her she is fat. You just don't go there!

"It's so good to have you here," he said to both of them. "You're looking well."

"Thanks," said Eli. "It's good to be here. I know how much the sisters miss each other. I am glad they can be together for Christmas. By the way, something sure smells good."

"Yes, it does and I'm starving," added Gabe.

Jennifer and Miranda were in the kitchen working on the finishing touches of dinner. The tantalizing aroma of ham, turkey and beef filled the air. Everything was cooked and ready to be served. Jennifer and Miranda placed the food on the table, and then went to look for the children. They were upstairs playing with Rachel Rose. She was a good baby-sitter. They were all sitting in the floor and she was reading a story to the children. Even little Tommy was listening as he sat on his sister, Savannah's lap. When they saw Jennifer and Miranda, they jumped up from the floor. "We'll finish this later," Rachel Rose told them.

"It's time to eat now," said Jennifer. The children followed them downstairs and sat down where their Mom directed. The table was full of delicious looking food and there were nine people sitting around it. Jennifer loved this!

"Your food is delicious, Jennifer," spoke up Miranda with a smile.

"Thank you. Are you surprised that I learned to cook?" she asked laughing.

"I guess you had to after I left, didn't you?"

"I sure did. I didn't want my family to starve." She was smiling at Gabe.

"Actually, Jennifer is a great cook," added Gabe. He

patted his stomach and said, "See this shows she can cook."

"I'm proud of you, Jennifer," said her sister.

After dinner was over, Jennifer brought out the Coconut and Rum cakes. She was saving the other two for Christmas day. They had dessert, and then settled in the den while that Isabelle cleaned up the kitchen. Rachel Rose took the children back upstairs to finish the story she was reading to them.

Jennifer and Miranda sat on the sofa where they could talk. The men were on the other end of the room. "Jennifer, I have something I would like to discuss with you. How would you like for both our families to take a vacation together?"

"What's on your mind?"

"I thought we might all go to the Yellowstone National Park. My children have never been."

"That sounds like a great idea. Our children have never been either. Of course, Isabelle may not get to go. It depends on whether she has a job by then. When are you thinking about going?"

"Oh, not until warm weather, it will probably be in July."

"That would be a good time to go. Have you discussed this with Eli?"

"Yes, and he is all for it. The children are excited too!"

"I know Gabe will go along with whatever I want, so YES, go ahead and get reservations at a nice hotel for all four of us. Just let us know how much we owe you and I will send you a check."

"I can do that. In fact, I will do it as soon as we get back home."

The next few days went by quickly. Jennifer and

Miranda were having such a grand time together. They dreaded for Christmas to be over because that meant they would be separated once more.

Today was Christmas Eve. They had been busy the last couple of days, fixing food for Christmas Day. Miranda was such a wonder in the kitchen. It brought back memories to Jennifer, as to how it used to be before Miranda moved away.

Isabelle called Tracy and invited him over for their Christmas Eve dinner. He had already been invited for Christmas Day. He was thrilled to get the extra invitation. He showed up fifteen minutes early. Isabelle was excited to see him. She met him at the door and gave him a big hug. "I'm so happy to see you, Tracy!"

He had a big grin on his face as he replied, "It sure is good to have you home. I missed you more than you know."

"I missed you, too."

"Come on in and join the others. Let me take your coat."

He pulled off his coat and handed it to her, "Thank you."

He went into the den and joined the others. Jordan and his family were already there. Isabelle introduced Tracy to her Uncle Jordan and his wife, Haley.

"It's nice to meet you both," said Tracy with his beautiful smile and showing his perfect white teeth.

"Nice meet you, too," said Jordan as they shook hands.

Dinner was served shortly. "What a feast!" exclaimed Tracy as he looked at the kitchen counters covered with food.

"My Aunt Miranda LOVES to cook. I think she helped get Mom in the mood too."

"No one will leave here hungry, that's for certain."

After the blessing was said they all lined up and filled their plates. It was a joyous occasion for all of them. Family was so important to all of them.

After dinner they all settled in the den and enjoyed the cozy fire that was roaring in the fireplace. Decorations filled the room and candles burned brightly in the windows. The Christmas tree was brightly lit and covered with unique decorations. Some were from the childhood days of Isabelle and Rachel Rose. Each one was very special to the family. Many of them had a special meaning.

They were relaxing and talking when the phone interrupted them. Jennifer got up to answer it. "It's for you Isabelle," she said as she handed her the phone. She rolled her eyes at Isabelle.

"Hello, this is Isabelle."

"Hi Isabelle, this is Mike."

"MIKE?"

"Yeah, it's me. I wanted to call and wish you a MERRY CHRISTMAS. How are you doing?"

"I'm fine, Mike. MERRY CHRISTMAS to you. So, how are YOU doing?"

"Much better, thank you. I think I just needed to get home."

"There's no place like home. I found that out."

"I feel like a little boy again, the way my Mom treats me," he said laughing.

"I know they sure like to baby us, don't they?"

"Yes, but I must admit...I have been enjoying it."

Isabelle laughed, "Enjoy it while you can."

"I plan to. Take care of yourself and call me and let me know when you get a job."

"I'll do that. You take care and I hope you will soon be able to return to your band."

"Me too! I sure miss it. I will call you again sometime. Bye for now."

"Sounds great. Bye."

Isabelle hung up the phone and went back to sit down with Tracy. She knew he was wondering about the call, so she decided to just tell him.

"Did you date this guy in New York?"

"We went out a couple times and that's it." She proceeded to tell him about the attack and how Mike was stabbed.

"That's too bad. So where does he live?"

"Nashville, Tennessee. He is at his Mom's house now."

"That's a long way from here."

"Yes, it is. He travels with his band most of the time. He is with the 'COUNTRY EXPRESS'.

"I have heard of them. They are very good."

"Yes, they are. Mike got tickets for my friend, Francine and me. We went to hear him the night before he was stabbed."

The conversation about Mike came to an end. Isabelle was glad. She felt a little uncomfortable talking about him. She somehow sensed a little jealousy in Tracy. He had no reason to be jealous; she would probably never see Mike again. Mike was just a friend. Their lives were too different for anything to ever be between them.

Chapter 16

Christmas morning came with more snow. It measured eighteen inches. Isabelle was glad her Mom invited Tracy to spend the night or he probably wouldn't have made it back today. They had plenty of bedrooms in their big two-story log home, so there was plenty of room for everyone.

Miranda insisted that she cook breakfast for all of them. Jennifer didn't interfere. In fact, she was happy with the arrangement. Miranda was a better cook and they all knew it.

After breakfast they opened their gifts. There was much excitement and squealing as the children opened their gifts. Jennifer was so pleased and wished her Mom and Dad were here to join in the fun. She missed them so much!

Tracy gave Isabelle a 14k gold, beautiful dove necklace with a small diamond for the eye. It was on a delicate gold chain. "Oh, thank you so much, Tracy. I love it!" She was so excited and asked him to fasten it around her neck. She gave him a blue cashmere sweater that matched his beautiful blue eyes.

"Thank you, Isabelle. I love the sweater."

"I can't wait to see you wear it."

"On our next date, I promise."

"Okay, I'll hold you to that."

Christmas Day was always a joyful occasion in the Colter household and today was no exception. Jennifer was thrilled to see Isabelle looking so happy with Tracy. He was a good boy and the two of them seemed to love each other, but she planned to keep out of it. She thought back to how her Mother reacted to Gabe. It was not a good thought.

She knew that once Isabelle left on an assignment, things would change between herself and Tracy. She remembered how it was with Gabe. Distance is hard on any relationship. She knew it was very easy to get caught up in the moment and forget the one back home. She had been there.

After dinner was over and they had gathered in the den, Gabe picked up his Bible from the coffee table. He turned to Luke 2 and began to read the Christmas Story, as he did every year. The children all gathered around him and listened intensely. Even baby Tommy sat down in front of Gabe with the other children and listened. This was always a sacred time in the Colter household. This year was no different. It made them realize the true meaning of Christmas. *'Jesus is the Reason for the Season'.*

The snow lingered for the next several days. Miranda and Eli had planned to leave the day after Christmas but the snow changed their plans. Jennifer was secretly glad for the snow. It gave her more time with her sister.

The sun came out three days after Christmas and the snow began to melt. The highway department was able to plow the snow from the roads. Tracy decided to leave that day. He felt he had overstayed his welcome. Isabelle tried to tell him differently. She made him promise to call her when he got home and let her know he was okay.

Jordan and his family left the same day.

Miranda and Eli waited a couple more days, and then they started their journey back to Medicine Bow, Wyoming. Jennifer was so sad to see them leave. Miranda promised she would call as soon as they reached home. It was a five hour drive but would take longer in this weather.

By the end of the day, everyone was safely home and had called the Colter house as they had promised. It seemed so quite now, with all the children gone. Jennifer had forgotten the cheerful sounds of a baby in the house. It had been so long. Somehow she felt sad. She knew she needed to cheer up and concentrate on her own family. This could be the last year they would all be together. She had no idea where Isabelle's career would take her. She decided to put that thought out of her mind. That was depressing and she didn't need that right now.

In a few days it would be New Year's Day and the beginning of another year. Jennifer wondered what the New Year would hold for them. Only God knows...

They celebrated New Year's Day quietly, with only the family there. Jennifer had thought about having a party, but that would have to wait until next year. With the bad weather and all the company she had for Christmas, it was just too much on her. She felt exhausted. She needed to get some rest before she had to go back to work. Even though she knew it was tiring; she would have it no other way. Family was so important to her.

Chapter 17

The New Year brought newly fallen snow. Isabelle looked out the window and saw the sun glistening upon the pure white snow, which looked like diamonds dancing around in their best array. It was truly a beautiful sight. She loved this time of year when the ground was covered with a blanket of fresh snow. It reminded her of a bridal gown, all pure and white. She seemed to remember that Jesus referred to his church as the bride. That meant only the pure in heart would be allowed to attend the wedding supper with Him. She was so glad that she was among the pure in heart. She had become a Christian several years ago. She was trusting God to take care of her, no matter where she might go. She asked for His guidance in making the right decision.

Time passed and the winter was over. It had been a rough one with much snow and cold temperatures. Isabelle loved the snow but was also happy to see spring approaching. The flowers were beginning to bloom and the trees were budding. Spring was her most favorite time of year. It reminded her of the birth of a baby, a new beginning.

She still hadn't heard anything about a job prospect. That was okay with her. She was enjoying this time at home with her parents and sister. She also spent as much time as possible with Tracy. She could feel they were getting closer. This bothered her to some extent, knowing that both of them would be parting one day soon. Tracy knew it too. They often talked about it. In the meantime, they were enjoying the time they had left.

The last day of April, Isabelle received a phone call from her agent. He had gotten her a modeling job in Rome. The agency would be contacting her in a few days. Isabelle didn't know whether to be excited or to cry. This is what she had longed for, so why did she feel a little sad? The thought of leaving her family was the big issue. She knew this might be her once in a lifetime chance to make it in the modeling world.

Two days later, Glamour Model Agency called her from Rome. They were very interested in her. After seeing her portfolio, they knew she would make a perfect runway model. Now the decision was hers. They told her they would send her a contract and after carefully reading it, she could make her decision. This sounded fair to her.

Later that afternoon she received an email containing the contract. She printed it and began to read. It sounded great to her. She wanted her parents to read it also before making her final decision.

When her parents came home from work she had to tell them as soon as they walked in the door. "I received a contract from Glamour Modeling Agency today!"

"That's wonderful," said her Mom. "I know it's what you have been waiting for."

"Yes, it is."

"Are you sure you want to go that far from home?" asked her Dad looking very solemn.

"It's not that I want to go that far away from home, Dad. This is a once in a lifetime opportunity for me."

"I know," he said. "It's just that I will miss you so much."

"I will miss all of you too, Dad. I want you and Mom to read the papers before I sign and mail it back to them."

"Of course we will," answered her Mom.

After dinner Gabe and Jennifer read the contract. Everything sounded solid to them. "I guess the ball is in your court now, Isabelle," said her Dad. "I must admit, this sounds like a great opportunity for you."

"Thanks, Dad, I'm glad you feel this way."

"I can't believe our little girl is all grown up."

"Dad, you can't keep us children forever."

"I know, but I would if I could," he said smiling.

"When I get famous, will you and Mom come to Rome to see me on the runway?"

"We may not wait for you to get famous. I think your Mom should fly over with you the first time."

"That would be great! I must say I was dreading the thought of going alone."

"Don't worry about that. One of us will go with you. I think your Mom would be the best one to go. She can find you an apartment and get you settled in before she leaves."

"Wonderful! Now I can quit worrying. Will you go with me, Mom?"

"Of course I will, Isabelle. You don't think we would allow you to go alone, do you?"

"I didn't know," said Isabelle smiling. "Since this is all settled, I am going to sign the contract and get it in the mail tomorrow. I am excited!"

A week later, Isabelle received a call from the Glamour Modeling Agency in Rome. She was so excited! They asked her if she could be there to start work on the first day of June. She told them she would need to discuss this with her parents. They agreed and told her they would call back the next day.

Jennifer said she would need to clear her work schedule for the entire month of June. She wasn't sure how long it would take to get Isabelle settled. So when the agency called the next day, Isabelle told them she could be there as they had requested. She also told them that her Mom would accompany her. They understood. She was to report to the agency as soon as she arrived in Rome. They would make plane reservations for her and her Mom. They would be flying Delta. Isabelle was so excited. This would be her first trip abroad.

The next thing on her list was to call Francine in New York. She waited until around eight o'clock that night and gave her a call. "Francine, it's Isabelle."

"Hi Isabelle, how are you?"

"Great," answered Isabelle. "I'm going to Rome soon."

"Wow, congratulations! I'm still waiting to hear something."

"Sorry about that. Time seems to drag by when you're waiting."

"It surely does. I'm not giving up though."

"Never give up. Let me know when you get a job. I'll have my cell phone with me."

"Sure, I will do that. Best wishes to you in your new venture."

"Thanks, Francine. I need all the luck I can get. Are you still dating Brian?"

"As a matter of fact, I am."

"How are things with you and him?"

"Great. We have even talked marriage."

"Marriage? What if you go abroad?"

"We're waiting to see what happens."

"If you leave, what then?"

"We'll stay in touch and he said he would come to visit me."

"Wow, he must be in love!"

"I really think he is. I know that I am very much in love with him."

"Then I wish you the best. Long distance relationships are hard, but not impossible."

"We're just taking it one day at a time."

"That's what Tracy and I are doing."

"Tracy?"

"Yes, he is my boyfriend here in Montana. I was seeing him before I left for New York and now we are closer than ever."

"Now you are leaving..."

"I know. I haven't told Tracy yet. I actually dread telling him."

"You had better go ahead and tell him. Don't wait until the last minute."

"I know you're right, Francine."

"Have you heard anything from Mike?"

"Yes, I heard from him on Christmas Eve," said Isabelle. "Tracy was here when he called. Mike seems to be doing better and I think he loves having his Mom spoil him."

"Who wouldn't?"

"I know. I have been enjoying the attention I've been getting since I came back home but it will soon be over."

"Good luck on your new venture. Thanks for letting me know. Keep in touch."

"I will. I hope you get a job soon and I hope things work out for you and Brian. Bye for now, Francine."

"Goodbye, Isabelle."

Chapter 18

Their bags were all packed and they were almost ready to leave the house. Jennifer and Isabelle said their tearful goodbyes to Gabe and Rachel Rose.

"Have a safe trip," said a tearful Gabe as he hugged and kissed both of them. "I will miss you both. At least one of you is returning." He smiled through the tears.

"Mom, Isabelle, I am going to miss you both. I wish I was going with you," said a sad Rachel Rose.

"Then Dad would be alone. He needs someone to take care of him."

Rachel Rose looked at her Dad and said, "Sorry Dad. I want to take care of you while they are gone."

"That's my girl," said Gabe.

Gabe loaded the luggage in the back of the SUV and the four of them climbed in the front. The ride to the airport in Billings was mostly silent. There didn't seem to be anything left to say. All four of them were sad. Each one in a different way.

The plane was on time. Gabe and Rachel Rose watched as Jennifer and Isabelle boarded. They watched the plane take off and stood there until it was out of sight. Gabe turned to his daughter and said, "It's just you and me kid."

"I know, Dad. We will be okay."

"I know we will. We're tough," he said smiling. Inside he was torn up. Just thinking about his older daughter leaving home was almost more than he could bear. All he could do was ask God to take care of her while she was in a foreign land.

The plane ride was a smooth one with no turbulence. They were thankful for that. They had several stopovers before reaching Rome the following evening. Both of them were very tired. They hailed a taxi which took them to the Rome Marriott Grand Hotel Flora, where they would be living for the next few weeks. What a beautiful sight to behold! It was right on top of the noble Via Veneto and next door to the Villa Borghese gardens. This gracious edifice with the stylish decor capturing the grandeur of Neoclassicism was exclusively designed for those looking for refined luxury in an atmosphere of sophistication and the highest level of welcoming hospitality every need of today's business or leisure traveler.

As they approached the reception desk, a beautiful young girl with coal black hair and olive skin gave them a smile, showing her perfectly even teeth that were sparkling white. "Welcome to our hotel. My name is Adriana. How may I help you?"

"I'm Dr. Jennifer Parker. My daughter and I have reservations for two weeks."

Adriana looked on the computer and found their reservation. She asked for a credit card. After finishing the paper work, she handed Jennifer two keys. "Are you here on business or pleasure?"

"I guess you could say both. I brought my daughter

who is beginning a new job with Glamour Modeling Agency."

Adrianna's eyes widened as she spoke, "That is wonderful! Congratulations! What is your name?" she asked looking at Isabelle.

"Isabelle Colter."

"Where did you get your training, Isabelle?"

"New York City."

"That is impressive. I wish you the best and maybe I will see you on the runway sometime."

"Thanks, I hope so."

Adrianna spoke to Jennifer again, "Enjoy your stay here. Just sink back in the timeless elegance of the superbly appointed room and relax, or delight in the culinary highlights of the Mediterranean cuisine at the restaurant *The Cabiria*. The adjoining bar is the ideal place to meet, to see or be seen, or to take in the flamboyant atmosphere of Via Veneto. The rooftop Ailanto is the perfect setting for exclusive celebrations, or simply for admiring the enchanting view over the roofs of the eternal city."

"Thank you for your help, Adrianna."

They headed toward the elevator. They had reserved a suite on the fourth floor. Staying as long as they were, Jennifer knew they needed more than just a room. She wasn't prepared for the breathtakingly beautiful view as she unlocked the door, stepped inside and walked over to the window. Their room was overlooking a large garden filled with an array of rainbow colored flowers. It was breathtaking! She couldn't wait to explore the garden.

"Mom, I need to call the modeling agency before I do anything else. It is too late to go there now. I will just have to leave a message and tell them I will be there in the morning after breakfast."

"Go ahead and take care of business. Then we will go to dinner."

Isabelle made the call and left a message. She was glad they weren't there. She was too tired to think of business tonight. She was glad her Mom mentioned dinner, as she was starving.

"I think we will try ***The Cabiria*** restaurant tonight. Are you ready to go?"

"Sure Mom."

The restaurant was rather crowded. They were met by a friendly host who seated them shortly. They waited only a brief time. "Hello, my name is Alanzo. I will be your server tonight." He handed each of them a menu. "What would you like to drink?"

"Water for both of us," replied Jennifer. They had discussed this earlier.

"I will be back with your drinks," said Alanzo as he left.

Five minutes later he returned. "Are you ready to order?"

"Yes," replied Jennifer. "We will both have the Paccheri Pasta."

"This comes with 'Aubergines' (eggplant) sliced into thin strips and fried until they are golden brown, 'Pachino' (cherry) tomatoes dried, Salted 'Baccalà' Cod and Gaeta (black) Olives."

"That sounds wonderful," replied Jennifer.

Alanzo left and returned in twenty-five minutes with their dinner. After he left Isabelle spoke, "I hope this is good, because I am starving."

"It looks delicious. I guess if you are hungry enough, you can eat anything, even if you don't like it."

The food turned out to be delicious. They didn't realize just how hungry they were until after they had eaten. They went back to their suite for the rest of the night. Jennifer decided to call Gabe again. "Hello Rachel Rose. How is everything at home?"

"Fine, Mom. How are you and Isabelle?"

"We're good. We just had a wonderful dinner at **The Cabiria** restaurant."

"I wish I was with you," sighed Rachel Rose.

"I know, honey, it just isn't the right time for you. Maybe one day..."

"How long do you think you will be gone, Mom?"

"Just as long as I need to be. After we go to the modeling agency in the morning, we are going to start looking for an apartment."

"I hope you find one soon so you can come home."

Jennifer never commented on that. "Is your Dad nearby?"

"Yes. Hold on and I will get him. Bye Mom, I love you!"

"Bye Sweetheart. I love you and will see you soon."

"Hello, Jennifer. How are things going?" asked Gabe.

"Great. We just had a wonderful dinner. I wish you and Rachel Rose were with us. I miss you both."

"We miss you, too. Someone has to stay home and work."

"I know. I will be home as soon as I can. We are going to start looking for an apartment in the morning."

"Good luck with that. I'll see you soon, Babe. I love you!"

"I love you, too!"

It had been a long day, so Jennifer and Isabelle went to bed early. Both of them slept well and were up early the next morning. Isabelle was excited and a little nervous about going to the agency. She hoped she had learned all she needed to know at the academy in New York. Of course, she was sure they would do things differently in Rome.

After she and her Mom ate breakfast, they hailed a taxi and went to the Glamour Modeling Agency. It was located about a mile from where they were staying. The receptionist was very friendly and told them to have a seat as she paged the owner.

Five minutes later the door opened and in walked a strikingly handsome man of about forty. His black wavy hair, dark skin and brown eyes made him very appealing. "Hello, I'm Sergio Lombardi, owner of the agency," he said in his distinct Italian voice.

Jennifer and Isabelle stood up. Jennifer extended her hand, "I'm Jennifer Parker and this is my daughter, Isabelle Colter. We're pleased to meet you."

Taking Jennifer's hand and kissing it lightly he replied, "So nice to meet both of you and welcome. What do you think of our fair city?"

"What we have seen so far is very beautiful!" exclaimed Jennifer.

Sergio turned to Isabelle. "So this is the beautiful Isabelle Colter, who is to become our famous model?"

Isabelle smiled and replied, "I sure hope so."

"I'd like for you to report to work on Monday at ten o'clock. We have some things to go over with you. Momma, you can come too."

"Thanks," said Jennifer. "We need to find an apartment for Isabelle before I go back to the states. Do you know of any available?"

"Actually, I have a studio apartment for rent. In fact, it will be available in about a week. The girl who lives there is moving out this weekend. I will need to have some maintenance work done before it will be ready. Would you be interested?"

"How close is it to the agency?"

"It's within walking distance. I can show it to you after Anita moves out."

"I would like that."

"Where are you staying?"

"We're at the Rome Marriott Grand Hotel."

"I will give you a call."

"Thanks, Mr. Lombardi."

"Call me Sergio."

Jennifer smiled and said, "Sergio."

"I will see you Monday morning, Isabelle."

"Thank you, Sir."

Chapter 19

Jennifer and Isabelle did some sightseeing over the weekend. They saw places they had only read about and others they had never heard of. They visited some landmarks of Rome.

They visited 'Victor Emmanuel Monument' which was a gigantic building located on Capitoline Hill in Rome. It had beautiful sculptures, statues and fountains which contributed to the elegance of the fine building. It was built in honor of the first king of a unified Italy.

They made the trip to see the 'Trevi Fountain', which is one of the most famous landmarks in Rome. The fountain featured a statue of Neptune which was completed in 1762. They were told it was beautiful both day and night. They also found out that it was featured in the 1954 movie entitled *'Three Coins in the Fountain'* starring Dorothy McGuire and Rossano Brazzi. The theme song for the film won the Academy Award for the best original song that year.

Of course they had to see the 'Spanish Steps' which were located on a hillside at the Piazza di Spagna. The steps led up to a beautiful 16th century church called

'Trinita Del Monti'. The view from the summit of this hill was wonderful. The 17th century 'Spanish Steps' were located in an exclusive district of Rome. Fashionable Italian shoes, suits, and dresses could be purchased in the many high-end shops located near Piazza di Spagna. Of course Jennifer and Isabelle had to check out the shops. Jennifer ended up buying a couple dresses for Isabelle, one for Rachel Rose and one for herself. She also bought high heel shoes for Isabelle to match each dress.

The weekend was over and Monday morning arrived. Isabelle was up early and excited about her first day at work. She arrived at the agency fifteen minutes early. Anita greeted her with a smile. "Mr. Lombardi is waiting for you. Follow me."

"Thank you," she replied and followed Anita down a long hallway and turned right. Mr. Lombardi's office was on the left. Anita knocked and waited for the door to open. "Hello ladies," he said as he opened the door. Thanks, Anita. Come on in Isabelle."

"Thank you, Sir."

By this time Isabelle was feeling fairly nervous. She didn't know what to expect next. She took the chair that he offered.

"Isabelle, I am very happy to have you here and wish the very best for you. I must admit, I have a good feeling about you. Fairmont Modeling Agency in New York gave you an exceptionally high recommendation."

Isabelle smiled at him and said, "Thank you, Sir. That is nice to hear."

"You may not know this, but they rarely rate a recommendation as highly as they did yours."

She smiled at him again. She was thinking to herself, "Am I really that good? I had no idea, but I like the sound of it."

"Isabelle, I want to start with some glamour shots today. Paolo (Pow-low) De Luca is our photographer and he is very good. The wardrobe crew will supply your clothing. All you have to do is look pretty," he said laughing.

"I'll do my best."

Mr. Lombardi took her into a large room where Paolo was photographing another model. He told Isabelle to watch and learn. They sat down and waited until Paolo finished. He walked over to where they were sitting. "Hello, Sergio. Who is this beautiful young girl?"

"This is Isabelle Colter from Laurel, Montana."

Paolo took her hand and kissed it, "So nice to meet you, Isabelle. Welcome to our fair city of Rome."

"Thank you, Paolo. Rome is a beautiful city." She was thinking, "And so are you." He was over six feet tall with black straight hair that was perfectly styled. He had olive skin like all of the Italians. His chiseled Roman nose and his dark brown eyes was an asset to his good looks. He had a smile which would make a girl melt. His white teeth were perfect when he smiled. She knew she had to come back to reality as she heard him speaking to her.

"So you have done some touring?"

"My Mom and I toured some places over the weekend. I hope to see many more landmarks while I'm here."

"You will, my love."

Isabelle didn't know how to take that statement, but was sure he talked to all the girls that way.

"Are you ready to do some glamour shots? We will do head and full body shots. Go over to the wardrobe set and they will fix you up."

"Okay, thanks Paolo."

She went over to the wardrobe set and introduced herself. Angelo introduced himself and told her, "We will start with the full body shots. What size dress do you wear?"

"Size two."

He picked out a long dress in flaming red and showed it to her. "After you get your hair and makeup done, come back here and you can change into this dress."

"What size shoes do you wear?"

"Size six."

So she left and went to the makeup crew who gave her a nice welcome. It took about twenty minutes there and then it was on to the hair expert. Franco was the hairdresser who took care of her. He used the straightening iron until her hair was completely straight with a little tease on the top so it wouldn't be flat to her head. After he finished with her, he let me look in the mirror. She was surprised at how different she looked after her makeover.

Then it was back to the wardrobe crew. Angelo had the dress ready and she went into the dressing room and changed into the flaming red 'Jovani Couture' evening dress. The bodice was square with off the shoulder sleeves, with embellishment beads on the left side. The long, floor length skirt was A-line with drape side details and elaborate train. The fabric was a beautiful Satin.

Angela was there to help her get dressed, especially to zip the back. The dress fit like a glove and that's what they wanted. She slipped into the size six matching red six inch heels. She sure felt tall. She was already 5'9" tall. She had already mastered six inch heels in New York, so she felt comfortable walking in them now. At last, she was ready.

She walked back to where Paolo was waiting for her. His eyes widened and a smile graced his face as she walked toward him. She could tell he like what he saw. "Wow!" he exclaimed. "You look amazingly beautiful!"

Isabelle smiled her sweet innocent smile, "Thank you, Paolo.

Her shiny, dark hair was cascading down her silky, smooth, tanned back. She was standing in front of a huge fan that was giving her hair the wind- blown look.

He took dozens of shots in every imaginable pose you could think of, including headshots. He also shot a lot of videos. Isabelle was having the time of her life. She felt like a Fairytale Princess, swirling around and around.

After he finished, he told her to go change and he would take more photos. Her adrenalin was high. She was on cloud nine. She went back over to wardrobe and they handed her a Mac Duggal Evening Dress to put on. She was making a fashion statement by showing off a little skin with this gorgeous Lilac dress. The Cocktail dress had a beautiful tulle train that fell to the floor behind her and trailed along behind her as she walked. Stunning flower appliqués, beads, jewels and sequins covered the strapless, sweetheart bodice. She was wearing matching lilac high heels with sequins on them. She was also wearing lilac flowers in her hair. As she walked out on stage, Paolo gasped. He was watching her long, tanned legs as she headed toward him. This girl is a beauty, if I have ever seen one, he thought.

"Absolutely gorgeous!" he said. "That dress is perfect for you."

"Thank you, Paolo. I feel like a Princess at a ball," she said laughing.

After dozens of full body shots and many headshots, he told her they would do one more shoot, and then call it a day.

She hurried back to wardrobe and changed into another beautiful gown that they had waiting for her. She had never had so much fun. She was wearing another

Mac Duggal evening dress in Mocha. This sexy but elegant dress was perfect to show off all of her curves. The beautiful strapless, sweetheart bodice was completely covered with large mirror-like sequins, beads and jewels. It was all shine and glitter. The fitted mermaid gown flared at the bottom of the skirt.

She could tell that Paolo was very pleased as she walked toward him. Once again she stood in front of the fan as he took dozens and dozens of body and headshots, along with lots of videoing. She had never felt so glamorous in all her life. Once they finished she headed back to wardrobe to change into her own clothes. She was so excited! When she returned, Paolo was waiting for her.

"A job very well done Isabelle. You are a natural."

"Thank you, Paolo. I had so much fun. It's hard to imagine this as work."

"I will see you day after tomorrow. I will give you one day to rest or go sightseeing."

"I'm sure that's what my Mom and I will do. She wants to see all she can before returning to the states."

"By the way...we are having a runway fashion show at the end of this month. Do you think you are up to participating in it?"

"I would love to be a part of it."

"Great. I will tell Sergio and welcome aboard!"

Thank you!"

Isabelle could hardly wait to get back to the hotel and tell her Mom about her wonderful day.

Chapter 20

Isabelle was still on a 'high' the next morning when she awoke. The sun was shining brightly through her window and she could hear the melody of the birds singing. It took her a minute to realize she was actually in Rome, fulfilling her dream. She still couldn't believe this was happening to her. God certainly had blessed her.

"Do you feel up to touring some more today?" asked Jennifer.

"Sure Mom. We need to take in as much as we can while you are here."

After they showered and got ready for the day; they went to have breakfast. They were excited to be seeing more landmarks.

The first place they went was to 'Ponte Vittorio Emanuele' which was a lovely bridge that spanned the Tiber River in Rome. It connects with central Rome to an area located just west of Vatican City. The dome of St. Peter's Cathedral could be seen in the background.

They enjoyed their visit to 'Palazzo Senatorio' which was a large palace situated at the top of Capitoline Hill in Rome. This Renaissance building is the home to the city government. In ancient Rome, the Tabularium was located at this magnificent hilltop location. Statues of Romans Castor and Pollux can be seen at the top of the staircase. This was truly magnificent to see. The Capitoline Museums were located next to the Palazzo Senatorio. That would be their next place to visit.

The 'Piazza del Campidoglio' was designed by Michelangelo in the 16th century and that is the home of the Capitoline Museums. Located on this picturesque piazza, they contain some fine paintings and sculpture. Great views of the city of Rome and the Roman forum can be enjoyed from the viewpoints near the Piazza del Campidoglio. They spent two hours going through the museum and still never saw everything. This was such an interesting place to visit.

The 'Palazzo di Giustizia' was a gorgeous structure located on the south side of the Tiber River just west of 'Castel Sant'Angelo' and the 'Vatican'. Gorgeous did not describe the beauty this large landmark held.

Next it was on to the 'Castel Sant'Angelo' which was a huge fortress built in 139 AD as a mausoleum for Emperor Hadrian. The castle has been used for different purposes over its long lifetime. It was once a prison, a refuge of the pope from his enemies and is now a museum. A tunnel connects Castel Sant'Angelo to the Vatican.

"Wow," said Isabelle. "We are getting a history lesson for sure."

"Indeed we are and I love it," said her Mom.

"So do I. You will have so much to tell Dad and Rachel Rose when you go back home."

"I know. I think we need to wait and visit the 'Vatican' another day. My feet are burning from so much walking. We will start afresh on your next day off work."

"That sounds good to me."

When they reached their hotel, the phone was blinking. Jennifer retrieved the message, which was from Mr. Lombardi. The apartment was ready for them to see. Jennifer returned his call and he asked them to meet him in one hour at the modeling agency. Isabelle was very excited. They were there a few minutes ahead of time. He came in exactly on the hour.

"Hello ladies, are you ready to go?"

"Yes," replied Isabelle.

So they followed him down the street to a large apartment building. It was not in the best condition, but maybe the inside will look better, thought Jennifer. As they walked up the steps to the second floor, Jennifer was not impressed. The walls needed painting and looked so old. She was beginning to get worried. My Lombardi unlocked door # 20 and they entered the one room studio apartment. Jennifer and Isabelle were both surprised how much better it looked than the rest of the building.

"This has just been remodeled. Take a good look around and see if this will fit your needs Isabelle."

They looked at the place thoroughly and talked between themselves. "What do you think, Mom?" asked Isabelle.

"It looks okay but I want to see how much rent he is asking."

Jennifer approached him and asked the amount of rent he would be charging. He studied for a moment and replied, "I normally charge $700 for a studio apartment, but since Isabelle is new here, I will let you have it for $500 a month."

"We'll take it," added Jennifer. "I need to get her moved in before I return home."

"I understand that," he replied.

So Jennifer wrote him a check for the deposit and the

first three month's rent. That would give Isabelle time to start making money and take over her own bills. She looked at Isabelle and asked, "Are you happy?"

"Extremely!" she exclaimed. "Thank you, Mom!"

The next afternoon Isabelle returned to work. Paolo was there taking pictures of other models. She had an appointment with him at 1:00 p.m. She was glad it was that late, so she could sleep in. She was tired. He finished with the others and told her to get ready. She headed to wardrobe wondering what beautiful gown she would be wearing today.

They selected a dress from the 'Johnathan Kayne' collection. It was a romantically beautiful long dress that flattered her figure as it molded her slim body. The royal blue gown featured silver stars on the long skirt as well as the bare-shouldered bodice. The empire waistline was embellished with a silver metallic sequined trim and featured a split in the center of the bodice, attached to a silver sequined collar around her neck. She was a raving beauty in this dress.

If she had any doubts, they were put to rest when Paolo saw her. He just couldn't hide his emotions. It made Isabelle smile.

"Wow! You are a knockout in this one!" he exclaimed.

She smiled as she thanked him. Then it was down to work. He shot photo after photo of her, from headshots to body shots. She felt like she was in another world. She was so happy that she never thought about the pain her feet were in with those six inch high heels.

After two more sessions, they called it a day. "Would you like to go out to dinner with me tonight?" he asked as they were leaving.

Isabelle smiled and replied, "As flattered as I am, I

have to turn you down this time. May I have a rain check? I feel that I need to spend my time with Mom while she is still here. Ask me again, after she leaves."

"I sure will, you can count on that. I do understand. Perhaps I could take you and your Mother to dinner one night."

"I'm sure she would love that and so would I."

"How about tomorrow night?"

"I will have to ask her and I will call you. That is, if you want to give me your number."

"Certainly," he said as he took out a business card and handed it to her.

"Thanks and I will call you tonight."

"I'll be waiting."

She walked to the hotel and her Mom was waiting. "How was your day?" she asked.

"It was great!" exclaimed Isabelle. "Paolo asked me out."

"WHAT?"

"He asked me out. I told him I couldn't go until after you leave. Then he asked both of us out to dinner tomorrow night. Will you go?"

"I don't see why not. I would be delighted to get to know your Paolo."

"He is not my Paolo, at least not yet," she said with a smile.

"We will go shopping tomorrow and buy the things you need for your new apartment. We will just buy the basic things, like towels, bed linens, dishes and of course food and cleaning supplies. Let's make a list tonight so we won't forget anything. We need to get up rather early in the morning; so we can get finished in time to get ready for our date," she said laughing.

"Our date? It's only dinner, Mom."

"Well, I can't wait to meet Paolo."

"You will like him. He is very nice. I need to call him before I forget it."

"I don't think you could forget," laughed her Mom.

"Paolo, this is Isabelle," she said when he answered his phone.

"Isabelle, it is good to hear from you so soon. Is the answer good or bad?"

"Good. My Mom will go. She is anxious to meet you."

"I had better be on my best behavior."

"That's a good idea as I'm sure she will be watching you."

"In that case, I will be a perfect gentleman," he said laughing. "I will come to your hotel at seven o'clock. See you then."

"Sounds great. Thanks!"

Jennifer and Isabelle went to get some dinner. They decided to use the hotel restaurant. They ate and retired back to their suite to relax. Isabelle was glad to relax after the long day of strutting around in six inch heels. She loved modeling but never realized how exhausting it would be and she was just beginning. She was excited and also a little nervous about the fashion show coming up soon.

Isabelle and her Mom were up early the next morning and got ready to go shopping. They were both anxious to go. Both were relieved that they had found a place for Isabelle to live. It was small but it would do for now.

Six hours later they were finished shopping and went to the apartment to unload their purchases. They made up the bed with the pretty multi floral sheet and comforter set. The flowers were bright and intermingled with pastel rainbow colors. The moment Isabelle saw it in the store she knew it was the one for her. They also found curtains and throw pillows to match. She was very excited as they worked and she saw it all coming together.

Once they were finished with the bed, they started in the kitchen washing dishes and placing the food in the pantry. They had already loaded the refrigerator with staples. It was looking more like a home to Isabelle. Jennifer was glad to see how happy Isabelle was but she also worried about leaving her alone in the big city. They quit early and went back to the hotel to get ready for their date with Paolo.

He arrived on time with a big smile. Isabelle was wearing one of the new dresses they had purchased since coming here. Jennifer was wearing her new dress also.

"Wow, ladies!" he exclaimed. "You both look amazing!"

"Thanks," they said in unison. Isabelle introduced her Mom and Paolo to each other and they exchanged greetings with him kissing her hand. Then it was time to leave.

They followed Paolo to his flaming red Lamborghini Aventador. Isabelle gasped for breath as she looked at the expensive spots car they were about to climb in to. Paulo opened the passenger door. "Sorry, ladies...I think you can both squeeze into the seat since you're small. This is the best I can do," he said smiling.

"Of course we can fit into one seat," replied Isabelle. "We have never ridden in a Lamborghini or least I haven't."

"I haven't either. It sure is a beautiful car."

"Thank you. It is fast too!"

"We will take your word for it. Frankly, I would just as soon not find out for myself," added Jennifer.

Paolo laughed at that remark as he closed their door and went around the car and let himself in. It wasn't far to the restaurant. He decided to take them to a new one where they hadn't been to yet.

They pulled into the parking lot of the *'La Cabonara'*. They went inside and were seated by a handsome Italian boy of about eighteen. Isabelle gave him a second look. He was staring at her also. They followed him to a table near the window. "Your waiter will be with you in a moment," he said in his Italian accent.

"Thanks," replied Paolo as he seated Isabelle and her mother. Shortly, a pretty young girl appeared and handed each of them a menu, "I am Angelina and I will be your server tonight." She took their drink order and returned shortly with the drinks.

As Jennifer looked at the menu she asked, "Paolo, what do you recommend?"

My favorite is the 'Fiori di Zucca' which is fried zucchini flowers, and the 'Saltimbocca alla Romana' which is veal with proscuitto (thin sliced, salted and air dried ham) and sage. That is a delicious meal.

"I think I will try it," said Jennifer.

"Me too," added Isabelle. "It sounds delicious."

"Shall I order for you ladies?"

"Please do and thank you," replied Jennifer.

Angelina returned shortly and Paolo gave her the order. It was thirty minutes before she returned.

"Thank you. This looks very good!" exclaimed Jennifer as Angelina set her plate down.

"Yes, it is excellent," replied Angelina.

Jennifer and Isabelle were surprised how good the food was. Paolo had made an excellent choice. "You made a fine choice, Paolo," said Jennifer as she finished her meal.

"Thank you. I thought you would like it. How about you, Isabelle?"

"It was great."

They left the restaurant and Paolo took the long route home. He drove around and showed them some places of interest that they might want to visit later.

"Paolo, tell us about your family," requested Jennifer.

"There's not a lot to tell. My family owns a large vineyard just outside of Rome. It has been in the family for several generations."

"You never told me that," said Isabelle.

"You never asked me," he replied laughing.

"I guess I didn't. I had no idea your family was in the wine making business."

"That's all my family has ever known. Of course, we do have several horses. Do you ride, Isabelle?"

"Oh yes, I love to ride. We have several horses on our ranch."

"Great! I will take you out to meet my family and take you for a tour of the vineyard and our winery. We can also go for a ride."

"That sounds wonderful! What breed of horses do you have?"

"We have several different breeds. We keep some just for pleasure riding but we have Arabians for breeding stock."

"Tell me about the Arabian horses."

"They are good-natured, quick to learn, and willing to please. The Arabian also developed spirit and alertness needed in a horse used for raiding and war. This combination of willingness and sensitivity requires modern Arabian horse owners to handle their horses with competence and respect. The Arabian is a versatile breed. Arabians dominate the discipline of endurance riding and compete today in many other fields of equestrian activity. They are one of the top ten most popular horse breeds in the world. They stand between 14.1 to 15.1 hands (57 to

61 inches) tall. They are noted for both intelligence and a spirited disposition."

"Interesting," said Isabelle. "What about their color?"

"The Arabian Horse Association registers purebred horses with the coat colors bay, gray, chestnut, black, and roan. Bay, gray and chestnut are the most common; black is less common. One thing I find interesting is that all Arabians, no matter their coat color, have black skin, except under white markings. Black skin provides protection from the intense desert sun."

"I have never heard that. Thanks for enlightening us. Did you know this Mom?"

"No, I didn't," replied Jennifer. "We don't have Arabians horses on our ranch."

They discussed horses the rest of the ride home. Paolo walked them to their suite and left after they had thanked him for the wonderful evening. He told Isabelle he would see her the next morning.

Chapter 21

Isabelle was up early and ready for another day of work. Paolo was already there when she arrived. "Good morning, Isabelle."

"Good morning."

"Today I think you will be modeling lingerie. I will take some photos as well as videos. I heard that Victoria's Secret is looking for some new faces and this may be your opportunity to get your foot in the door."

Isabelle's eyes widened, "Are you serious?"

"Indeed I am. Wardrobe has already picked out your lingerie, so we need to get started. It may be a long day, depending on how well the shots and videos go."

She walked over to the wardrobe department with a smile all over her face. She could not believe this was happening to her. She knew that Paolo liked her and she wondered if that had anything to do with him wanting to help her. She hadn't heard any of the other girls talking about it. Perhaps the information had just been released. She looked at the bikini and bra sets they had picked out for her. They were a little more risqué than what she normally wore. She sure was glad she had gotten a bikini wax yesterday while she and her Mom were in town.

She picked up the first black lacy set and changed into it. She put on the matching six inch heels. It was really hard for her to walk out on the stage where Paolo was waiting. As she crossed the stage, his eyes were glued on her. She felt so self-conscience. She thought she would be modeling 'clothes' and not underwear. She didn't dare say no, as she reminded herself this was the life she had chosen. Then her mind turned to her Dad. He would have a fit if he could see her. She knew he would be very disappointed in her. This made her feel disappointed in herself. She knew if she continued this way of life, she would have to get over it. Suddenly she thought of Jesus. How would he feel? She knew the answer before she even asked herself the question.

As she reached Paolo, she told him she needed to talk to him. "Paolo, I am very uncomfortable like this. First of all, I am a Christian and I know God is not pleased with me exposing my body for the world to see. My Dad would also be very disappointed in me. I just cannot do this. If Victoria's Secret would like a model for their 'clothes', then I am willing to do that. I am going to have to leave the lingerie modeling to someone else."

She thought Paolo might get mad, but he didn't. "I understand, Isabelle. If that's the way you feel, then you shouldn't do it."

"Thank you, Paolo. I thought I could do it until I actually walked out on the stage."

"I must say you have a beautiful body, Isabelle. If you don't want everyone seeing it, I understand, but you could be giving up a lot of money if you choose not to do this."

"Money is not everything. I have to be able to live with myself."

"Okay, if that is how you feel. I will contact them and see if they need a model for any of their other clothes." She could tell he was disappointed.

"Thanks, Paolo."

She went back to wardrobe and told them she was not going to model lingerie. So they picked out some beautiful gowns for her. She changed into a Ruby Red Organza Ball Gown. It was sleeveless with only one shoulder embellished with beading. The beading and sequins continued down below the fitted waistline. The embroidery on the dress was hand sewn. The pick up skirt had side draping. Isabelle felt much more comfortable as she walked back out onto the stage. She saw Paolo give her the 'I like it' look.

"You look amazing!"

"Thanks. I feel better in this," she said laughing lightly.

After many photos and lots of video filming, she went to put on another gown. This time it was a strapless Sweetheart gown in a beautiful Turquoise color. The bodice consisted of beading and ruching with cascading ruffles down to the floor in Organza and Taffeta.

Next she modeled a Trumpet/Mermaid Strapless Court Train Tuelle Evening Dress, with crisscross ruching and cascading ruffles in a beautiful shade of purple. It fit her like a glove and accented her perfect figure. She was amazed how transparent Paolo was. She could read him like a book but she would never let him know.

"I think we will call it a day," Paolo told her. "We will add these to your portfolio. You are getting quite a collection."

"Yes, I am, thanks to you."

"Don't forget, Isabelle, next Saturday is the fashion show in Milan. I will be there photographing all the models. Would you like to ride with me?"

"I would love to. I was wondering how I would get there. My Mom is leaving this Saturday morning, so she won't be here for the show."

"I will make sure that I get you on film so you can send her a copy."

"That would be wonderful."

"How would you like to go meet my parents on Sunday?"

"I would like that. How do I need to dress? Will we go riding this time?"

"No, I think we will wait until the next time to go riding. So wear semi-dress clothes. A nice pair of pants and a silk blouse would be fine."

"I can do that."

Isabelle was sad to see her Mom leave but knew she needed to get back home to Gabe and Rachel Rose. Paolo drove them to the airport in his other car so they would have more room for all three of them, plus Jennifer's luggage.

Isabelle waved goodbye to her Mom as she boarded the plane. She was glad Paolo was with her. It would have been much harder for her if she had been alone.

"Let's go get something to eat," he suggested.

"That sounds like a good idea."

He took her to a quaint little pub nearby. They ordered a cheeseburger, fries and a drink. The food was delicious. Isabelle was glad to get a cheeseburger again. It had been a long time since she had eaten one and it tasted delicious. Just as they were about to finish eating, a shadow crossed the table. Isabelle looked up and there stood a beautiful olive skinned, Italian girl with long black hair. She did not look happy.

"PAOLO," she said in a loud tone of voice. "What are you doing here and who is SHE?"

Paolo looked up and Isabelle could tell he was uncomfortable. "This is Isabelle, a client of mine. Isabelle, I would like for you to meet Gabriella, who is a friend of mine."

"Do you always take your clients out to lunch?" asked an unhappy Gabriella.

"Not really. Isabelle is new here and I am showing her around."

"I JUST BET YOU ARE!"

"Would you like to join us, Gabriella?"

"NO, I WOULD NOT!" she exclaimed as she walked away.

"I am so sorry about this," Paolo said to Isabelle.

"It's okay. I can tell she likes you."

"I have dated her a few times but she doesn't own me."

"That's good to know," said Isabelle in a soft voice as she smiled at him.

"Don't let this ruin your day, Isabelle."

"I don't intend to. I have too many other things to think about without wasting my time thinking about her."

"That's my girl!"

They left as soon as they finished eating. Isabelle invited Paolo to come in when they got to her apartment. He accepted. "I can't stay too long. I need to let you get your beauty sleep, not that you need it. We will leave around ten in the morning."

"I'll be ready. Would you like a glass of lemonade? I don't drink so I have nothing else to offer except coffee and water."

"Lemonade would be fine. It's too late for coffee."

"I can't drink it at night either. It keeps me awake."

She fixed both of them a glass of lemonade and they

sat and talked as they drank it. Isabelle was feeling more comfortable around him. She knew he liked her but wasn't sure how deep his feelings were. She hoped he couldn't tell, but she was liking him more every day. She hadn't thought much about Tracy lately and this made her feel guilty. She knew he would be going to college soon and as handsome as he was, she knew the girls would be after him. He wouldn't be lonely for very long. She was sure of that.

Isabelle woke up early the next morning. The sun was shining brightly through her window near the bed. She looked at the clock and jumped out of bed. Then she remembered...this was the day she would be meeting Paolo's parents. She was excited and a little nervous at the same time. She hoped they would like her.

She ate a piece of toast and then got into the shower. Two hours later she was completely ready. She was wearing black satin pants and a royal blue silk blouse. Paolo had told her to wear flats since they would be walking a lot. She didn't realize how stunning she looked. She had straightened her long dark hair and her makeup was perfect.

When Paolo arrived, his eyes showed approval at how she looked. "You look beautiful," he told her.

"Thank you, but I am a little nervous."

"Don't be. My parents will love you."

Forty minutes later they arrived at Paolo's parent's home. It was a huge two-story white house with burgundy shutters. To the left of the house was a beautiful flower garden with an array of rainbow colors. To the right was a rose garden. Isabelle had never seen so many beautiful roses. There were so many different colors.

"The flower gardens are beautiful. Does your Mom tend to them?"

Paolo laughed, "No, I'm afraid she is not much of a gardener. We have a full time gardener who works here. Dino is responsible for all the beauty you see around the house."

They got out of the car and walked up to the front door. Paolo opened the door before his Mom could get there. "Hi Mom," he said as he hugged and kissed her. "I would like for you to meet Isabelle Colter. Isabelle, this is my Mom, Nicola De Luca."

Mrs. De Luca took a step toward her and gave her a hug as she replied, "I have heard a lot about you, Isabelle. I am so happy to finally get to meet you."

"Thank you, Mrs. De Luca. It's nice to meet you as well."

"Oh, please call me Nicola."

"As you wish, Nicola," said Isabelle with a smile.

"Let's go find your father, Paolo."

They followed her through the house until they located him. "Dad, this is Isabelle Colter. Isabelle, my Dad, Franco De Luca."

Mr. De Luca eyes showed that he approved of Paolo's choice. He gave Isabelle a hug and said, "It is very nice to meet you, Isabelle."

"It's nice to meet you also, Mr. De Luca."

"We'll have none of the Mr. De Luca in this house," he said smiling. "It's Franco to you, my dear."

"Whatever you say, Franco." She gave him a sweet smile. She was feeling more at ease now. Paolo was right. They really did seem to like her. She was glad.

"I hope you had a light breakfast because Nina is cooking an extra special lunch for us today."

"That's great, Mom. I never ate breakfast. I was waiting to eat here. I never miss an opportunity to eat Nina's cooking."

An hour later they all sat down in the spacious dining room. The table was huge and would seat twelve people. She had never asked Paolo about his family. Now she wondered how many siblings he had. There was time for that later.

Nina had cooked a wonderful lunch for them. There were so many dishes that Isabelle had never heard of. She decided she must taste a little of everything. She liked some of it better than others. She couldn't let them know. She pretended to like everything she tasted, but that actually wasn't true. It would take some getting used to.

After lunch Paolo asked her if she was ready to take a walk. They left the house and walked through the Rose Garden. She stopped to admire them. She had never seen such a beautiful garden. How proud Paolo must have been to grow up in a place like this. It was all he ever knew until he moved into the city. Isabelle loved country living. It was all she had ever known. She hoped someday that she would be able to move from the studio apartment and get a house in the country. Only God knew what was in her future, because it was all in His hands.

They walked out to the vineyards which were as far as the eye could see. "How many acres is this?" she asked.

"Fifty acres."

"I guess you employ a lot of people."

"We do. We are fortunate to have the people we do. They are hard working people and always get the job done."

"That's what counts."

After they had walked around some of the vineyard, they went to tour the winery. It was a large building with many barrels of wine. They watched as the grapes were being processed before making the wine. In another section of the building, they watched as the wine was being bottled, labeled, and packed ready to be shipped. "This is the first time I have ever seen this process. I had no idea what all was necessary before the bottles were ready to be shipped. It is all so very interesting."

Paolo laughed, "Most people don't realize all that is involved in wine making. There is a lot of work that goes into it from planting the grapevines to the finished product."

"Thank you for sharing this with me, Paolo."

"It was my pleasure."

They headed back to the house and said their goodbyes to his Mom and Dad.

"Come back anytime, Isabelle," said his Mom with a lovely smile as she hugged her. "Our home is always open to you."

"Thank you, Mrs. or I mean Nicola." Isabelle laughed.

"Bring this lovely girl back to see us Paolo," said his Dad smiling. He walked over and gave Isabelle a brief hug.

"I will, Dad. You can count on it. We will be back soon. I want to show Isabelle the horses and take her for a ride."

Franco turned to Isabelle, "Are you a horsewoman?"

"Indeed I am. I love to ride. We have horses on our ranch. I started riding when I was very young."

"That's great. Paolo has been riding forever also. He rides like the wind."

Suddenly a cloud came over Isabelle's face and Franco knew he had said something wrong. "What is it, Isabelle? Did I say something wrong?"

"I'm sorry, Franco. When you said 'ride like the wind', it brought back a painful memory."

"I am so sorry. Please forgive me."

"It's okay, you didn't know. I had a twin brother, Isac, who was killed at the age of six, when he was thrown from his pony. His last words were that he was going to 'ride like the wind'. Our Grandpa tried to stop him but it was too late. When I heard you say the same words, it all came back so intensely in my mind."

"I would never have said that if I had known," expressed Franco.

"It's okay. There was no way you could have known. I have never spoken to Paolo about it. Even after twelve years, it is still painful to talk about it."

"I am so sorry, Isabelle. I can't imagine what your parents went through. I have never lost a child, so I really don't know the pain," said Nicola.

"It was a very tough time for all of us."

"I guess we had better get going, Isabelle. Tomorrow is another work day."

They left the house and started the drive back to the city. Isabelle was quiet on the ride back. As they got out of the car at her apartment, Paolo spoke, "I am so sorry Isabelle. My Dad would never have said anything had he known."

"It is okay, Paolo. I know he wouldn't. Let's just forget it."

"See you in the morning," he said as he hugged her goodnight. He gave her a brief kiss on the lips.

Sleep did not come easily that night. As she lay there wide-eyed, she couldn't help but think about Isac and how much she missed him. She wondered what he would be like if he had survived. As much as she missed him, she knew that he was in God's care.

Chapter 22

The following week seemed to fly by. Isabelle worked Monday, Wednesday and Friday. On her days off, she did some sightseeing on her own. She missed her Mom. They had visited several places and had such a good time together. They had a very special Mother/Daughter relationship.

Saturday finally got here. Isabelle was very excited and nervous at the same time. She knew there would be buyers from all over the world attending. The Milan Fashion Show was the big event of the year. It started at two o'clock, so she and Paolo left early. He needed to be there in time to get all his camera equipment set up.

Isabelle had no idea what she would be modeling. She could hardly wait to see the fashions. Wow! Her head was spinning. Never in her wildest dream did she ever think she would be modeling in a fashion show in Milan.

At one o'clock, Isabelle went backstage and joined the other models. She introduced herself and told them where she was from. There were eleven other models from various places. Watching them made Isabelle realize how naïve she actually was. She was thinking how sophisticated all of them looked. She felt like the smallest fish in the sea. Then it occurred to her that she was here to do the same thing they were, so she held her head up and walked tall.

Every seat was filled in the audience. The curtain opened at exactly two o'clock. Isabelle was the third model to walk out. She was wearing a bright red, strapless, Sweetheart Full Length Taffeta Ball Gown with silver appliqués, beading, and embroidery on the front and back bodice and the pick up skirt. She was wearing an updo hairstyle with a silver, diamond lined tiara on the right side of her head. She was wearing matching diamond earrings and necklace.

She walked slowly to the end of the runway, turned, paused for a moment and then walked back behind the curtain. She listened at the crowd's applause. She felt good. They continued one after another, modeling an assortment of high-end clothing. Two hours later, the show was over. Isabelle was so glad and relieved.

She had seen Paolo filming as she walked the catwalk. She was sure he had filmed the entire show. She would be anxious to see it.

She changed back into the clothes she wore and headed out to look for Paolo. He was packing his camera equipment. She helped him carry it to the car and they started their five hour journey back home. Isabelle lay her head back and relaxed.

"Are you okay?" asked Paolo. "You're very quiet."

"I'm just thinking. Today seems unreal. I still can't believe I was on the runway in Milan."

"But you were, and will be many more places. I believe in you."

"Thanks, Paolo. I need that."

They stopped on the way home and had dinner. It would be bedtime by the time they reached home. It had been a great, but tiring day for both of them. He walked her to the door of her apartment and after a brief goodnight, he left.

Isabelle was glad the next day was Sunday. She slept in until nine o'clock. She felt refreshed when she finally crawled out of bed. She fixed herself a cup of coffee and decided to call her parents. "Hi Mom," she said.

"Hello, Isabelle. How are you?"

"Great, Mom."

"How did things go yesterday? I have been dying to know."

"They went great. I was a bit nervous, but I soon got over it. There were twelve of us modeling. Paolo did all the videoing. I can't wait to watch it. He said he would make a copy for me to send you."

"Oh, that would be wonderful. Tell Paolo I am very grateful."

"I will. Have you seen Tracy lately?"

'No, we haven't. Has he called you?"

"No, I haven't heard a word from him. I guess what we had is over. Even though I am having a great time with Paolo, I somehow feel sad when I think of things ending with Tracy. He is a very special person to me and will always have a place in my heart."

"I understand, Isabelle. I've been down that road too."

"I know, Mom. I am so glad that love brought you and Dad back together."

"So am I."

"I'll call you again soon and I love you, Mom. Tell Dad and Rachel Rose that I love them too."

"I'll do that. Goodbye, Isabelle."

Just as she had finished her coffee and was heading to

the shower, her cell phone rang. It was Paolo. "What are you up to this morning?"

"I just had a nice talk with my Mom."

"Was she excited for you?"

"Of course she was. I told her you were going to make her a DVD of the fashion show. She was very excited and said to thank you."

"Anything for the mother of my beautiful Isabelle."

Isabelle smiled to herself at his remark.

"What are your plans for today?" he asked.

"I have no plans."

"How would you like to go back to the country and go horse riding? Since Mom doesn't know we are coming, we will stop and eat lunch before we get there."

"Sounds like a great plan to me."

"Can you be ready by eleven o'clock?"

"I can if I don't wash my hair. Since we are going horseback riding, I will wear my hair in a ponytail."

"That sounds good. I'll be there around eleven."

"Thanks, Paolo."

She was ready when he arrived. She was wearing jeans and a lavender t-shirt. No matter what she put on, she always looked beautiful. She could tell she met his approval when he first saw her. "You look gorgeous," he said.

"Even in a ponytail?" she asked laughing.

"It makes you look younger than ever. So far my Mom hasn't asked how old you are. I am only seven years older than you."

"That's not enough to matter, as far as I'm concerned. I am surprised that my Mom hasn't asked your age, Paolo."

"Age is just a number, you know."

"I think you are exactly right."

It was a beautiful Sunday morning as they started their trip to the country. Paolo seemed to be in a very happy mood. Every now and then he would look over at her and smile. They stopped to eat in the town just before they reached Paolo's parent's home.

When they pulled into the driveway at his parent's home, they both came running out of the house. They were very surprised to see him and Isabelle again this soon.

"Paolo, my son, it is so good to see you!" exclaimed his Mom as she hugged him tightly. Then she walked over and hugged Isabelle, "I'm so happy to see you too! Come on in."

They followed Nicola and Franco into the house. "How are things with you, Dad?" asked Paolo.

"Going well and how about you?"

"Things couldn't be better," he answered looking at Isabelle.

"That's good. I'm happy to hear it," replied his Dad.

They sat and talked for half an hour. Isabelle told them about her first fashion show. Nicola soaked in every word. She had wanted to be a model when she was young, but she was not tall enough; so she settled for getting married and raising a family.

"I brought Isabelle out for some horseback riding?"

"Great," said Franco. "Nicola and I ride sometimes. We find it very relaxing."

"Do you want to ride with us?"

"Oh no, you take Isabelle. I think Cianna or Charo would be good for her to ride. Both of them are gentle."

"Okay, Dad. We will take both of them. I don't want to ride one that has more spirit than hers. These mares are the best for gentle riding."

They walked out to the stable, which was almost as

nice as the house. Several horses were in the stalls. Paolo brought out Cianna and Charo. Isabelle helped him with the saddles. She chose to ride Charo, who was a beautiful Palamino. She was gold in color with a white mane and tail.

They rode for two hours. Isabelle was drinking in the beauty of this wonderful place. She hadn't ridden for quite some time and she could feel the effects as she dismounted Charo. What a nice gentle mare she was. "Thank you for taking me riding, Paolo. I enjoyed it immensely."

"It was my pleasure and I'm glad you enjoyed it. The next time we come, I will take you for a ride on my Harley. Have you ever ridden a motorcycle?"

"No, that's one thing I haven't done. I think I would like it though. Do you ride a lot?"

"Every chance I get, which isn't very often. I love to ride."

"How long have you been riding?"

"Seven years. I got my first bike when I was eighteen. My Mom wasn't too happy but she finally resigned herself that I would always be a bike rider."

"Interesting! I never thought about you being a biker."

"Why not?"

"I don't know. You like expensive sports cars and horses. I guess I thought that might be the extent of your hobbies. With your photography job, I don't imagine that leaves you a lot of time for horse riding or biking, does it?"

"Not really, but it is very relaxing when I can find time to do either or both of them."

"Interesting."

After they said goodbye to his parents, they left for home. Isabelle was so happy. She loved being with Paolo and she found herself liking him more all the time. Of course she didn't want him to know yet. It was still too early. For now she was happy with the close friendship they shared. She enjoyed doing things and going places with him. She really liked his parents, too. But she had her career to think about. She didn't want to get serious with any guy. She needed to see where modeling would take her. She decided to have a talk with her boss, Sergio Lombardi. She wanted some answers to questions that kept popping up in her mind.

Monday morning she asked the receptionist if Mr. Lombardi would see her.

"I can ask," she replied as she paged him. She talked briefly with him and told him that Isabelle Colter wanted to speak with him. He said to send her in.

"Mr. Lombardi will see you now, Isabelle."

"Thank you so much."

She went down the hall and knocked on Mr. Lombardi's door. "Come in," said a pleasant voice.

"Hello, Mr. Lombardi. Thank you for seeing me on such a short notice."

"That's quite alright," he replied. "How may I help you, Isabelle?"

"I have some questions that I need answers to. I have been wondering what I need to do to try to become a supermodel."

He rolled his eyes at her and smiled, "Young lady that is a big question. First of all there are ten tips to becoming a supermodel." He took a paper out of his desk. "Here are the tips."

"#1. You need to weigh 110-120 pounds and be at least 5'9" tall.
#2. Be photogenic.

#3. Get signed with a big modeling agency.

#4. Be quiet.

#5. Don't party. Don't be a Diva. Attitude is important.

#6. Befriend powerful people.

#7. Date Celebrities

#8. Expand your Brand - clothing or lingerie line

#9. Now you can talk - TV Talk Shows, Actress

#10. Don't gain weight...Ever."

"WOW!" exclaimed Isabelle. "I didn't realize they were that strict."

"Oh yes, but it's worth it if you can make it to the supermodel level, which very few girls do."

"Well, Mr. Lombardi that is my dream!"

"I hope you make it Isabelle. If I can help you in any way, I will be glad to."

"Thank you very much and thanks for all your help."

"You're welcome, Isabelle. You are a very beautiful young woman and I have a feeling you will make it."

Chapter 23

Isabelle decided to start sending pictures to upscale modeling agencies like IMG, Elite, and Next, in New York. She knew she needed to get her pictures out there. Two months later she received a call from Elite Modeling Agency. They asked her to come to New York for an interview in two weeks. She was very excited and couldn't wait to tell her family. She called them later that night. They were very excited for her and wished her the best. Hoping that this might mean her return to the USA was enough to excite them. They missed her so much.

She called Paolo later and he wasn't as excited. "I am happy for you, Isabelle, but I am hoping you won't leave Rome. I was hoping we would have a future together one day."

"I'm sorry, Paolo. I have my career to focus on now. I can't let my personal life interfere."

"I realize that, but it doesn't mean that I want you to go."

"I don't have a job yet, so don't worry until that time comes."

"I know we need to make the best of the time we have at the present time."

"You are exactly right, Paolo. Anyway, I have two weeks before I go to New York."

The next morning she received a call from the *'Sophia Cosmetics'* in Milan. The President of the company had been at the fashion show two months earlier looking for the perfect girl to become a spokes model for their company. After much thought, she decided that Isabelle was the perfect choice. So she gave her a call.

"Isabelle Colter speaking."

"Hello Isabelle. This is Sophia Lazio with *'Sophia Cosmetics'* in Milan. How are you this morning?"

"Fine, thank you, how are you?"

"I'm doing great. I was at the fashion show a couple months ago and saw you on the runway. I understand that you're a beginner."

"Yes, Ma'am that is correct."

"From what I saw, I think you are a natural. I am looking for that special someone to become a spokes model for my cosmetic company. I would like to interview you."

"Wow, thank you."

"Can you come to Milan next week on Tuesday at two o'clock?"

"I'm sure I will be able to do that as I only work on Monday, Wednesday and Friday."

"Wonderful! I will be looking for you." She gave Isabelle the address and her cell phone number.

As soon as they hung up, she called Paolo. "Paolo, I have some exciting news!"

"What?"

"I just had a call from Sophia Lazio who owns *'Sophia Cosmetics'* in Milan. She wants me to come for an interview next Tuesday. She is looking for a spokes model for her cosmetic company."

"That is exciting news! I hope you told her you would be there."

"I did. I have a favor to ask you. Could you take me?"

"Of course, I will take you! We will take some of your favorite outfits in case she doesn't furnish your clothes."

"Thank you very much, Paolo! She never mentioned clothes."

"We'll go prepared."

"Good idea. You are so thoughtful, Paolo! I think I need to talk with Mr. Lombardi also."

"I think that is a good idea. I don't think he will object, but it's a good idea to run it by him."

The next morning Isabelle went to see Mr. Lombardi. He sat there with no expression on his face as she explained everything to him. That made her very nervous as she wondered what he was going to say when she finished talking. "I think that sounds like a wonderful opportunity for you, Isabelle. I know Sophia personally and she is a great lady. If she decides to hire you, I think you will be in good hands. She can make you into a supermodel."

"Really? That is what I have been dreaming about."

"Then go to see her next week. Go with my blessing."

"Thank you so much, Mr. Lombardi." She was very thrilled as she walked out of the door and couldn't wait to call Paolo.

"I knew Sergio would give you his blessing. He is a great guy to work for; he won't hold you back if you can move up."

Next Isabelle called her Mom. Jennifer was very excited for her daughter. "Will you be moving if you get the job?"

"I'll probably have to since it's a five hour drive and I don't have a car yet. Paolo is taking me next week."

"He is a great guy. Don't let him slip away," said Jennifer with a laugh.

"Now, Mom...I'm not ready to marry anyone yet. I have my career to focus on and that's what I intend to do."

"I'm only teasing, Isabelle. I want to see you make it as a model before you think of getting married and raising a family."

"I'll have plenty of time for that later. I have to go now. Give my love to everyone. I love you, Mom!"

The next few days seemed long, as all she thought about was going to Milan. Finally, Tuesday came and they left early since it was a long drive. Paolo had picked out four outfits from the wardrobe. Isabelle had told him to choose his favorites. He knew what she looked the best in. Today she was wearing a lavender silk blouse with black silk pants and flats. She brought her high heels for the interview.

Paolo had entered the address into his GPS and they drove straight to the company after eating a light lunch. They approached the receptionist's desk and she greeted them. "Hello, my name is Olivia. How may I help you?"

"I'm Isabelle Colter and I have a two o'clock appointment with Ms. Lazio."

"Oh, yes, she is expecting you. Have a seat and I will let her know you are here."

In five minutes the door opened and there stood a lovely black haired lady in her mid forties. She smiled and said, "Come on in, Isabelle."

Isabelle got up and followed her while Paolo waited in the reception area. Thirty minutes later, Isabelle came through the door with a huge grin on her face. Paolo knew she had gotten the job. It showed in her face. She thanked the receptionist and they left.

"I GOT THE JOB! I signed a contract for the next two years," she exclaimed with joy. "I can't believe this is happening to me."

"Congratulations! I'm sure they picked the right girl for the job. When do you start?"

"In three weeks. I don't know whether I will have to move there or not. We never discussed that."

"Don't worry about getting back and forth. I will be glad to drive you."

"Thank you so much, Paolo. I don't know what I would do without you."

He grinned and responded; "Now I like to hear that."

"You have been so good to me and I appreciate it very much!"

"You're a very special lady to me, Isabelle. I think you know that by now."

She turned and smiled at him, "You're very special to me too. I think God brought you into my life at the perfect time when I desperately needed someone."

"I'm not very religious, but I think you could be right."

They enjoyed their time together on the five hour trip back to Rome. Time seemed to pass quickly since they continued to talk all the way home. Isabelle was so excited and could hardly wait to call her parents and tell them her good news.

Later that evening she made the call. Her Dad answered the phone and she got to tell him first. Since he hardly ever answered the phone when her Mom and sister were home, Isabelle was delighted to hear his voice. "Hi Dad, how are you?"

"I'm fine and how are you my Dear Daughter? It is so good to hear your voice. It seems forever since you left. I miss you very much! I know your Mom is going to be unhappy that she missed your call. She and Rachel Rose went grocery shopping."

"I guess this is your time to talk with me since they are not home. I have some good news to tell you. I got a job in Milan as a spokes model for **'Sophia Cosmetics'.** I went there for an interview today and Sophia hired me. I still can't believe it's true. I'm afraid I will wake up and find it was only a dream."

"Congratulations, Isabelle! I am so proud of you! When do you start this job?"

"In three weeks. My friend, Paolo, is going to drive me there."

"Who is this Paolo that I have been hearing so much about?"

"He is a great guy, Dad. He has been my photographer as well as my friend. He took me to meet his parents and to tour their vineyards and winery."

"I'm sure you enjoyed that."

"I really did, Dad. He took me horseback riding and soon we are going motorcycle riding."

"It sounds like you are having a great time. Just be careful."

"We will, Dad. It's good to talk with you again. Tell Mom and Rachel Rose hello and I will talk to them soon. I love you, Dad!"

"I love you, too. Take care and stay in touch. Bye now."

"Bye Dad."

She was so excited that she hardly slept any that night. Every time she woke up, the reality of the day came rushing back into her mind. She had to thank God for His blessings upon her. Without Him, she could do nothing!

Chapter 24

She spent a lot of time with Paolo over the next three weeks. Since she had signed a contract with **'Sophia Cosmetics'**, she was not allowed to model for anyone else. Mr. Lombardi had been so gracious to let her out of the contract she signed with him. He knew he was only a stepping stone to bigger and better things for her and he didn't want to hold her back. He really liked Isabelle and knew she had great potential.

Paolo only worked when he just had to. He wanted to spend as much time with Isabelle as possible. He took off work the next day and they drove out to his parent's home in the country. It was time to take Isabelle for that motorcycle ride. He called his Mom and told her that they would be there and she had lunch ready when they arrived. It was good to see Nicola and Franco De Luca again. They were so nice to her and treated her like the daughter they never had. Paolo and his older brother, Mario, were the only children they had. Mario was five years older than Paolo and married to Danielle. They had two boys, Marco and Roman.

"I have a surprise for you!" exclaimed Nicola with

a huge smile on her face. "Mario and his family will be here for lunch. In fact, I think they have arrived." She hurried to the door to see. "Come on; let's go outside to greet them."

They all went outside as Mario and his family exited the car. Paolo had his arm around Isabelle. "Hello, big brother. How have you been?"

"Great! How about you?" They hugged instead of shaking hands. This pleased Isabelle to see that they were a loving family.

"I'd like for you to meet my friend, Isabelle."

"Hello Isabelle," said Mario as he gave her a hug. "It's so nice to finally meet you. I have been hearing a lot of nice things about you."

"Thanks," replied Isabelle. "It's very nice to meet you."

"This is my lovely wife, Danielle, and our sons, Marco and Roman."

Danielle gave Isabelle a friendly hug and they exchanged greetings. Isabelle stooped down and said hello to the small boys. They grinned as she talked to them.

Then they went into the house and had lunch. Conversation flowed as they ate. It was very enjoyable. "I hear you landed a big job as a spokes model," said Mario. "Congratulations! That is a big step for you."

"Thank you. Indeed it is a big step. I am very excited about it."

"You should be," added Danielle. "Not many girls get this opportunity."

"I am very thankful to God for allowing me this opportunity. I have been praying for God's guidance concerning my future."

"That's good," replied Danielle. "Will you be moving to Milan?"

"I'm not sure yet. I may have to since it's a five hour drive from Rome and I don't own a car. Paolo has graciously offered to take me there in two weeks."

Mario looked at his brother and rolled his eyes. Isabelle saw it and wondered exactly what he meant. Did he think she was taking advantage of his brother? This made her feel a little uncomfortable. She decided to ignore it.

After lunch was over, she and Paolo went to the garage where he kept his motorcycle. It was the first thing she saw when they entered the door. It was white metallic and silver and about the shiniest thing she had ever seen. He sure did take care of it. "Wow, your bike is beautiful! It looks big too. What kind is it?"

Paolo laughed. "It is big, but very easy to ride. It's a Harley Davidson."

"You mean they have Harley Davidson motorcycles in Rome?"

"Absolutely! I bought this one in Via Pinciana."

She looked amazed as he opened a cabinet door and took out two shiny white helmets that matched the bike. "Here, put this on," he said as he handed her the smaller helmet. She proceeded to put it on and fasten the chin strap.

"This feels so heavy."

"It is heavy but you will get used to it. Wearing a helmet could be the difference in life and death, should we crash. I never ride without one."

"That's good to know."

He helped her on the bike and then he got on and started the motor. It was loud. She wasn't used to this kind of noise and was wishing she had some ear plugs. She wouldn't dare let him know what she was thinking. He was so excited about taking her for a ride and she surely wouldn't spoil his day by complaining about the noise. She assumed she would get used to it after awhile. At least she hoped she would.

They drifted out of the garage. When they got to the road, he slowly gained speed and they were off on a joyful ride, or so he thought. She had her arms around his waist, holding on for dear life. This was her first ride and she felt nervous. Although she was excited, it was hard for her to relax. He had already explained to her about curves and how she needed to lean as he leaned. She kept thinking about that and hoped she would not lean too much and cause them to wreck. She was conscious of this the whole time they were riding. She felt as stiff as a board. They rode for an hour and then stopped and both got off the bike. "How are you doing?" he asked with a smile.

"Okay," she answered. "Am I doing okay on the curves?"

"You're doing fine. Just keep doing what you've been doing."

"Sure, I will try." She was thinking...I'm so stiff now I can hardly move.

"Do you like riding?"

"Yes, it's fun." If he only knew how scared she was. "I can see why guys and even girls love to ride a motorcycle. It gives you the feeling of being free, doesn't it?"

"Indeed it does. It makes you feel as free as the wind. I have been riding since I was eighteen. Mom and Dad bought my first bike for my high school graduation. That was the only thing I ever wanted; even as a small boy I dreamed of owning a motorcycle."

"Have you ever wrecked?"

"I had a couple fender benders not long after I got my first bike. You have to learn to ride. I guess I thought I already knew how and that was a mistake."

"Were you hurt when you wrecked?"

"I had a broken arm the first time. The next time it was all bruises and no broken bones."

"You were lucky, or I should say blessed."

"I know that."

After they rested for awhile, they resumed their ride. Isabelle seemed to loosen up some this time. She was beginning to enjoy it and not think so much about when she needed to lean with Paolo. It was beginning to come natural, as he said it would. She was actually having a good time now. He was very patient with her and she loved that about him. She had never seen him get angry at all. This told her a lot about him. She was sure he wasn't like this all the time, or he wouldn't be human. There are things in life that upset us and things that make us angry. The most important thing she had learned in her life was not to act on her anger and to think before she spoke. Words of anger spoken in haste cannot ever be taken back or be forgotten. She prayed daily for God's wisdom in her life and to let her be a witness for Him.

They rode for another hour and then headed back to Paolo's home. His parents, along with Mario and his family were waiting. "How was the ride, Isabelle?" asked Mario.

"It was wonderful...after I got used to leaning with Paolo. I have to admit I was nervous at first. Paolo is a good rider and I felt secure with him. Do you ride, Mario?"

"I used to. I sold my bike after I got married. Danielle wouldn't ride, so I decided to devote my time to her."

"That sounds like a caring husband."

"I found out that I loved my wife more than my bike. I haven't regretted the decision. Then the boys came along. We have a busy life and I don't even miss my motorcycle."

"I know that makes you happy, Danielle."

"It truly does, Isabelle. I am afraid of motorcycles. I had a cousin who was killed on one. He was only twenty years old. It was so sad," she said as the tears welled up in her eyes.

"I'm so sorry."

"Thanks. That was ten years ago. He was an only child and his mother about lost her mind."

"I can't even imagine. Although I did see some of what my Mom and Dad went through when my six year old twin brother was killed in a riding accident."

"Oh my goodness, that is so sad. I'm sorry Isabelle," said Danielle as she hugged her.

"Thank you. My Mom says you never get over it; that you just have to pick up the pieces and move on."

"It sounds like you have a wise and wonderful Mom."

"I do. I feel that I have the best parents in the world, no offence to any of you. They raised me in a good Christian home and taught me the ways of the Lord. I am so thankful for my upbringing."

"You should be," answered Danielle.

"I guess it's time we get back to the city," interrupted Paolo. They said goodbye to the family and left, promising to come back soon.

"Thank you for a wonderful day, Paolo," said Isabelle as she smile at him.

"You are more than welcome. I was honored to show you off to my brother and sister-in-law." He laughed and reached over and took her hand. "Isabelle, I think I am falling in love with you."

"Oh, Paolo. What am I going to do? Here I am starting a new job in a new city and will probably eventually be moving. Where does that leave us?"

"I have a car, you know."

"It's a long drive though."

"Let me worry about that, my dear."

They had small talk the rest of the way home. He walked Isabelle to her apartment and gave her a smoldering kiss before he left, leaving her breathless. She was trying to fight the feelings she was having for him. She knew she had her career ahead of her and after all she was not even nineteen yet. She was too young to think about marriage anyway. She knew they had plenty of time and if it was meant to be, then it would happen, but just not now. She knew she would meet other guys when she went to Milan. She wanted to make sure she would choose the right man when she chose to settle down and get married. She was depending on God to guide her in the right direction. She also was asking Him to provide her husband when the time was right. She had no doubts, she knew that He would.

Chapter 25

Three weeks had passed and they were on their way to Milan. Isabelle was very excited. After five hours of driving they reached their destination. They drove straight to **'Sophia Cosmetics'** and pulled into the parking lot. They got out of the car and walked to the door. Paolo opened it and they both walked in. Olivia greeted them with her pleasant smile and asked them to have a seat. She paged Sophia, who appeared shortly.

"Welcome to Milan, Isabelle."

"Thank you, Ms. Lazio."

"Call me Sophia."

"Okay, Sophia."

"Come on back to my office."

Isabelle followed her. She noticed how dressed up she was and how perfect her face was done. Isabelle had never worn much makeup, except for when she was modeling but she knew that was about to change. Her makeup would have to be perfect for close up shots of her face. She was sure they had all that under control and there was no use of her worrying about it.

"Have a seat Isabelle. There are a few things I need

to discuss with you. First of all, you will need to move to Milan, so you will be available at a moment's notice, should the occasion arise. Is there a problem with that?"

"No, Ma'am, it will just take a little time. I will need to find a furnished apartment and get my things moved from Rome."

"I have an extra bedroom which I will allow you to stay in until you can find an apartment."

"Oh, that is so kind of you!"

"You're my girl now, so I will help you in any way I can."

"Do you have someone who can help you get moved?"

"I am sure my friend and photographer, Paolo, will help me."

"Great. See to it as quickly as possible."

"I sure will."

They finished their discussion and Isabelle went back out to where Paolo was patiently waiting. "What are your plans?" he asked.

"She wants me to move here as soon as possible. She has an extra room that I can use until I find an apartment. I hate to ask you, but do you think you can borrow your Dad's truck and help me move after I find a place?"

"No problem," he replied with a smile. "Dad would be happy to help you in any way he can. He really likes you, Isabelle and so does my Mom."

"I'm glad and thank you!"

"So I'm assuming you will be staying here tonight."

"Yes, that is correct. I'm glad I brought some extra clothes and my personal toiletries. I had a feeling I might be staying."

"I sure will miss you, but I will come to see you as often as I can."

"Please do!"

She said goodbye to Paolo and watched him drive away. Her heart went with him. She felt so alone knowing he was leaving. She had to remind herself this was what she wanted...a career and not marriage. She knew Paolo would marry her now if she would consent. She truly hoped she was not making a mistake.

Isabelle waited until Sophia was ready to leave and they left together. It felt strange going to live with someone she really didn't know. She hoped she wouldn't disappoint Sophia.

They drove a couple miles to Sophia's beautiful Mediterranean style house. It looked like something out of a magazine. Isabelle was very impressed with the exterior of the house. She could hardly wait to see the interior. It was even more beautiful than she could imagine. The foyer was large with a high ceiling which had inlays of gold in an intricate design around the top of the walls. This led into a large living room with the same design continuing. Gold, plush velvet curtains graced the long windows. It was breathtakingly beautiful! Isabelle had never seen anything this elaborate. She gasped. Sophia turned and asked if anything was wrong.

"No, Ma'am. I am just in awe of your beautiful home. I have never seen anything this beautiful."

Sophia laughed. "One day you may have a home more beautiful than mine."

"I doubt that. I don't think there is one anywhere prettier than yours."

"You're too kind, Isabelle. I hope you will enjoy your stay here. It will be nice to have a young person in the house again. I had a daughter and she was the light of my life. She was killed in a car accident when she was sixteen.

She had just gotten her driver's license two months before she was killed."

"I am so sorry! I didn't know."

"How could you? I rarely talk about her. It is too painful. My husband left me after our daughter died. I don't blame him. I withdrew from him and he moved on."

"Again, I am very sorry."

"That's when I decided to start my own cosmetic company. I have devoted my life to it and have never dated another man."

"But Sophia, you are a very beautiful woman. I know there are many men who would be honored to have you."

"That is so sweet of you. The truth is, when Oliver left me, anything that was left in me died. He watched me mourn the loss of our daughter and he did everything he could to help me, but I didn't want to be helped. I wanted to wallow in my own self pity. He took all he could take and then he left. I have never blamed him. He was the love of my life and no one could ever replace him."

"That sounds like true love. Have you ever seen him again?"

"No, and I think it's better this way. I heard he had remarried and had a couple of children. I hope he is happy. I know I failed him."

"I am so sorry. This makes me sad."

"Let's not talk about this anymore. I wanted you to know because you would be wondering about all the pictures I have throughout the house."

"Thank you for trusting me enough to share your life story."

"I have to admit, there is something about you that reminds me of my daughter. I saw it the first time I met you. You and Adriana are similar in so many ways. You have the same long, dark hair and brown eyes that sparkle when you speak. She had a gentle spirit just like you."

"I have to ask you a question. Did the resemblance to your daughter have anything to do with you hiring me?"

Sophia smiled. "I want to say no, but I'm not sure I can. I just knew you were the one the moment I saw you."

"That was good for me, but I'm not sure if it is good for you. I hope it won't make things more difficult for you."

"Actually, I find myself more at ease knowing that you are here."

"What a nice thing to say!"

"In fact, I have been thinking. How would you like to live here with me permanently?"

"Sophia, I am stunned!"

"I must admit, this is a hasty decision. It would mean a lot to me to have a young girl in the house again. I know you are not my daughter, but I would treat you like you were. What do you say?"

"Anyone would be crazy not to accept your invitation. You are very generous, Sophia!"

"Then you'll do it?"

"I accept. I want you to know that I greatly appreciate this and I will help you as much as I can with the chores around the house."

"Honey, I don't do chores. I have a maid, a cook and a gardener. They take care of everything. Rosa is the maid, Nikki is the cook and Dino is my gardener. I pay them well and they serve me well. I am so lucky to have all of them."

"Wow!"

"I don't want you to do any work around here. I just want you to get plenty of rest, so you will look fresh in the mornings when we do our taping. You are going to become a supermodel. You mark my word!"

"I am thrilled and excited beyond words. Thank you so much for believing in me!"

"Come on, I want to show you the rest of the house."

"I can't wait to see it!"

She followed Sophia into the huge kitchen where Nikki was preparing dinner. She was about forty and had a great personality. She was happy to meet Isabelle and excited that she would be staying at the house.

Rosa had already gone home for the day. She would meet her the next day. Dino was still in the garden working. Sophia had introduced them on the way in. Dino was very pleasant and she could tell he liked her by the admiring look he gave her. He was probably in his mid thirties and ruggedly handsome with his olive skin and black hair.

Next they went upstairs. She followed Sophia down the hall to a large bedroom decorated in shades of green with just a touch of red. It was the most beautiful bedroom Isabelle had ever seen. On the wall above the bed hung a huge picture of Scarlett O'Hara from '*GONE WITH THE WIND*'. She was wearing a red dress and was descending the stairs. She looked very beautiful. In reality, it was the actress, Vivian Leigh who portrayed Scarlett in the movie, which was made in 1939. There were several dolls of Scarlett and Rhett sitting on the dresser and more pictures hanging on the walls. A lamp with Scarlett and Rhett kissing graced the bedside table. The beautiful quilted comforter and matching curtains had a picture of the '*Tara Plantation*', Scarlett's home. Sophia must have a fortune invested in this memorabilia. Sophia was watching Isabelle's face as her eyes went from one thing to another. "Well, Isabelle, how do you like this room?"

"It is absolutely breathtaking! It is the most beautiful bedroom I have ever seen."

"My daughter loved **'Gone With The Wind'** and I did this room in her memory. I didn't have the money to do it when she was alive. This was her room, but it was decorated entirely different. No one has ever stayed in this room since she died, but I want you to take this bedroom and enjoy it."

"Are you sure? Will it not bother you to see me in here?"

"No, my child. In fact, I think it will be just the opposite. I have dealt with my grief in losing my daughter and have tried to put the past behind me. I think you will help me in more ways than you can ever know."

"I sure hope so. But remember, I am not trying to replace your daughter."

"I know that. I am just grateful to have you here. I hope you will be happy."

"I'm sure I will be. What girl wouldn't be?" she asked smiling.

"I'm glad to hear that. I want you to make yourself at home. The entire house is open to you. Nothing is off limits."

"Thank you so much for your generosity!"

"I will leave you alone to unpack. I know you need to go back to Rome soon and get your things, so whatever you work out is fine with me."

"Paolo is going to help me move. I need to let go of my apartment and settle up with my landlord."

"Take whatever time you need. I will be waiting. Dinner will be ready in an hour."

"Thanks, I will be there."

Chapter 26

Later that night when she retired to her room, she gave her mom a call. "Hi Mom," she said as Jennifer answered the phone.

"Hi Isabelle. What a nice surprise! Where are you?"

"I'm in Milan. My boss invited me to stay at her house. Oh, Mom...you should see the house. It is unlike anything I have ever seen."

"Do you mean you are staying there until you find a place?"

"That's what I thought at first, but Sophia has invited me to live with her."

"Isabelle, this worries me. I'm not sure this is the correct thing to do. After all, what do you know about this woman? Is she married?"

"No, she is not married. She is divorced. She had a daughter named Adriana, who was killed in a car accident when she was sixteen."

"I'm so sorry to hear this."

"She withdrew from her husband while she was grieving for her daughter, so he left her. She has never dated another man. She told me he was the love of her life."

"That is so sad. Is she trying to replace her daughter by having you move in?"

"She said she is not. She gets lonely by herself and she knew I was all alone so it seemed the right thing to do."

"Just be careful, Isabelle."

"I will, Mom. Sophia said she will make me a supermodel. I honestly think my looks influenced her when she chose me. Mom, it is uncanny how much I look like her daughter, Adriana."

"Now I think I am beginning to understand."

"She even gave me Adriana's bedroom. You should see it, Mom. It is decorated with lots of **'GONE WITH THE WIND'** memorabilia. She said this is all new since Adriana's death and she did it in honor of her daughter who loved Scarlett O'Hara and Rhett Butler."

Isabelle, promise me that you will call us every night. I have to know you are okay."

"I promise, Mom. I will talk to you tomorrow night. I love you!"

"I love you too!"

As soon as she hung up, she dialed Paolo. "Hi Isabelle. How are things with you?" he asked.

"Hi Paolo. Things are going well. You are not going to believe what has happened to me. Sophia has invited me to live with her."

"LIVE WITH HER?"

"Yes, she said she gets lonely all alone." She proceeded to tell him the story that Sophia had told her.

"Are you sure this is what you want to do, Isabelle?"

"It is for now. It will make things much easier for me."

"It sounds like she is using you to replace her daughter."

"Even so, what does it hurt? If I can comfort her then what's the harm? It not only benefits her, but me as well. She will try harder to make me into a supermodel. So you see, this could mean the difference of making it or not making it in the world of modeling."

"I guess that's one way of looking at it. When do you want me to move you?"

"As soon as possible. Sophia is going to loan me a car to drive back to Rome to get everything packed."

"That sure is nice of her. You know I would have come to pick you up."

"I know that, but this will be easier on you."

"Dad said I can borrow his truck anytime, so do you want to get moved this weekend?"

"That sounds great. The sooner the better. Thank you, Paolo!"

"My pleasure, Dear Sweet Isabelle!"

"I will be there on Friday and get things packed so we can leave on Saturday. I will call Mr. Lombardi and make arrangements to give him the apartment key before we leave. I will call you when I get to the city."

"I'll be waiting!"

Isabelle was so excited that she slept very little her first night in Sophia's beautiful home. As she turned down the covers, she saw the most beautiful red silk sheets adorning her bed. She had never slept on silk sheets in her life. All of this was overwhelming. She felt like she was in another world and was another person. It would be impossible to explain this feeling to anyone. She told herself that she was the luckiest girl in the world. What she didn't know was that Sophia was having much the same feelings. Her spirit had been lifted since Isabelle had moved in. She felt as if she was getting her life back. She knew that Adriana was gone, but Isabelle was surely filling a void in her life. She had never thought much about God, but she realized that He must have something to do with this. It had been so long since she had been to Mass. Being a Catholic was not as strongly inbred in her as it was most people in Italy.

The next morning when Isabelle woke up she smiled to herself. She lay there looking at this beautiful room and at Scarlett and Rhett. She knew they weren't real people, but Vivian Leigh and Clark Gable were. She had never watched **'Gone With The Wind'** but she intended to put that on her 'to do' list. Being in this room made her curious to find out what the movie was about.

She put on a pale pink robe and went downstairs. Sophia was sitting at the dining room table sipping coffee and reading the morning paper.

"Good Morning!" exclaimed Isabelle in a cheerful voice.

Sophia looked up from the paper. Her black rimmed reading glasses were on the end of her nose. "Good Morning, Isabelle. I hope you slept well."

Isabelle smiled, "I think I was too excited to sleep. It takes a few nights to get adjusted to a new bed, although the bed was very comfortable."

"Would you like a cup of coffee?"

"Yes, please and I will get it."

"Rosa is preparing a light breakfast. You know we have to keep our trim figures," she laughed.

"I've never had a weight problem. I have been a size two for a long time."

"That's great. I have to really watch what I eat or I gain. The older you get the harder it is to get off the weight."

"I've heard that. My Mom and Dad are both slim, so I guess I have good genes."

"Do you have any siblings?"

"I have one sister, Rachel Rose. She is going on thirteen."

"Does she look like you?"

"No, we are completely opposites. She is extremely gorgeous! She has beautiful, long, golden hair that looks like pure silk. She looks a lot like our Aunt Miranda and our Grandmother Rachel, for whom she was named."

"Interesting. It's funny how siblings can be so different. Do you think she will become a model also? I might be interested in her as well. I am always looking for beautiful faces to advertise my products."

"I have no idea. She has been a tomboy growing up. She says she is going to be an FBI agent."

"I am amazed! It seems such a waste for a beautiful girl to be a cop. Let the ordinary ones do that job."

"She may change her mind by the time she graduates from high school. I sure hope so, because being a police officer is a very dangerous job."

"Yes it is. I know several policemen who have been killed in the line of duty."

"Sophia, I talked with Paolo and he is willing to move my things this Saturday. If it's okay with you, I need to go home on Friday and get everything packed."

"Sure, that will be fine. I will be glad when you get everything moved here and can start calling this home," she said with a big smile.

Chapter 27

Isabelle left on Friday and headed back to Rome. She was excited about moving and worked steadily to get everything packed. Paolo had gotten some boxes and brought them over. He got there just after she arrived. He offered to help her pack but she declined saying that he was doing enough. She wanted to pack and label each box so she would know exactly what was in it. She was finished before bedtime. She grabbed a bite to eat and went to bed early.

Paolo arrived early the next morning. He loaded all the boxes for her and she took her clothes in the car. They started on the five hour journey stopping only once to buy gas and to eat. They arrived at Sophia's around three o'clock. She met them at the door with a huge smile on her face. "Sophia," said Isabelle. "I would like for you to meet my good friend, Paolo, who was also my photographer."

"Hello Paolo. It's very nice to meet you. I think I saw you when you brought Isabelle for the interview, but I never actually met you."

He kissed her extended hand and replied, "It's nice to

meet you too, Sophia. I feel that I already know you from hearing Isabelle talk about you."

"Great! I hope she said something good."

"She did and she is very excited about living in your beautiful home."

"I'm excited to have her. Come on in. Where are my manners?"

Paolo and Isabelle followed Sophia into the living room. "You house is magnificent!" exclaimed Paolo.

"Thank you. For many years it has just been a house, now that Isabelle is here, it will become a home once more," she said with tears brimming in her eyes.

Paolo looked at Isabelle and saw tears in her eyes also. He could see the two of them had already started bonding and that was good. He was happy that Isabelle had someone who cared about her besides him. He knew she missed her family and Sophia would become her new family. He was glad things turned out this way. He loved Isabelle and hoped that one day she would agree to marry him. He had never met anyone like her. Gabriella thought he was going to marry her and he must admit the thought had crossed his mind, that is, until he met Isabelle. He hadn't told Isabelle, but it was love at first sight. She was everything he could ever want in a woman. He knew she was young and he was willing to wait. He hoped she wouldn't meet someone else in Milan and forget about him. He knew that was always a possibility.

Sophia invited Paolo to stay for dinner and he gladly accepted. A very delicious dinner was served in two hours. Paolo was starving and one could tell that by the way he ate. "Thank you so much, Sophia. The meal was wonderful."

"My pleasure, Paolo. It's nice to have a gentleman in the house once more. I would like to invite you back any time you want to visit Isabelle. I have plenty of bedroom space, so you can stay here."

"Thank you! That is very generous of you, Sophia."

"Anything to make 'my girl' happy," she said with a soft laugh.

"You might as well spend the night and get started back in the morning."

Paolo looked at Isabelle and her eyes were saying yes. "I guess I could do that. Thank you!"

After dinner Isabelle and Paolo unloaded the boxes from Paolo's truck. Sophia had a storage room for Isabelle's belongings. She could go through the boxes later. After they finished that, they went for a walk in Sophia's beautiful flower garden. Dino, the gardener sure had everything looking immaculate. He had already gone home for the day. They walked for awhile then went to the gazebo and sat down. It overlooked a small fish pond. Isabelle could see large gold fish swimming around. "Isn't this breathtaking?"

"It certainly is," answered Paolo.

"What a wonderful place to sit and relax. It is a good place to forget any worries one might have."

"You are so right. Do you have any worries Isabelle?"

"I guess my biggest worry would be my best friend, Fallon, who died about a year ago."

"What happened?"

She proceeded to tell him the whole story of how she survived the car crash and her best friend didn't. She told him about the hard time she had dealing with it. She also told him about Tracy and Dustin. Paolo was very sympathetic as she told the story.

"I am so sorry you had to go through this and sorry for the loss of your best friend."

"Thank you, but I know that God had a purpose in it. I

just don't know what it is yet. I know we are not supposed to question God, but it's hard not to when a tragedy like that happens. Still I know He is in control and His will was done. I cling to the fact that I will see her again one day."

"I admire your strong faith in God, Isabelle."

"It's all I have ever known. I was raised in a good Christian home and I feel very blessed. My grandparents were Christians also."

"That's wonderful. My family is Catholic and has been for generations. That is all I have ever known."

"I guess we had better go back inside. We have been sitting here for two hours. The time passes so quickly when you're enjoying yourself. Thank you for being here for me, Paolo."

"It's my pleasure. There is nowhere else I would rather be."

They stood up and he took her into his arms. He kissed her ever so gently, yet very passionately, leaving them both breathless. He laughed, "Yes, it is time to go in."

They walked to the house holding hands. It seemed so natural to both of them. Paolo was already in love with her and decided to tell her. "Isabelle, there is something I need to tell you." She turned and faced him. "I love you, girl. I have loved you from the first moment I saw you."

She smiled at him and replied, "I know, Paolo. I have fallen in love with you, too."

He was all smiles, "You have made me the happiest guy in the world. I have waited so long to hear those words."

"Now that you've heard them, do you feel better?" she smiled.

"Absolutely! My heart feels so light and fluttery. One day I will ask you to marry me. I know you are not ready and I understand. I will be patient, Isabelle."

"Thank you for understanding, Paolo."

Paolo left the next morning and headed back to Rome. Isabelle dreaded to see him go but she knew it had to be this way. Absence makes the heart grow fonder...so they say. She wondered how this separation would affect their relationship. Only time would tell.

She and Sophia left the house around nine o'clock and headed to the office. Isabelle would be in training for a few days before the actual taping. She was very anxious to get started. The name of the cosmetic line was **'Sophia's Choice'.** She had everything from foundation to lipstick. The cosmetics were manufactured on site. She was always coming up with a new idea for a product in a rainbow of colors.

Sophia introduced her to Eduardo, the makeup artist. He was a short, stocky man of about forty, who wore black horn rimmed glasses with thick lenses. He had been with Sophia from the beginning and was a very talented makeup artist. After showing her around the factory where the products were manufactured, she told Isabelle that Eduardo would do her makeup. Then she would meet the photographer/videographer.

Eduardo took his time with Isabelle. When he was finished he told her to go look in the big mirror. She was stunned at what she saw. Her face was flawless. Her eyes sparkled like they had never done before. Her pouty lips were perfectly framed with a liner and he had brushed the lip color within the line. He did a perfect job! She was very impressed with his work. To look at him, one would not believe he would be capable of the miracle he had just performed on her.

Sophia showed up just as he had finished. "You look amazing, Isabelle! I told you he was a miracle worker. Not that you needed it."

"He is fantastic!" exclaimed Isabelle.

"Now let's get you to the photographer." They walked a short distance to where he was. He turned around and stared at Isabelle. She could tell he liked what he saw. "Isabelle, I'd like to introduce you to my photographer, Fabio Moretti." Sophia turned to him and said, "Fabio, this is your next subject, Isabelle Colter, from the United States. She comes from the beautiful western state of Montana."

Fabio took Isabelle's hand and kissed it. She could feel her face heating up. As they looked into each other's eyes, she suddenly felt a connection. He was undoubtedly the most handsome man she had ever seen in her life. His dark chiseled face with his thick black hair hanging slightly in his eyes was the most romantic thing she had ever seen. He should be in the movies, not taking pictures, she thought. Just then he brushed the hair from his eyes showing his strong muscled arm. He was wearing a T-shirt which showed his perfectly shaped body. She was sure he worked out every day at the gym. You didn't get a muscled body without it. He had broad shoulders and slim hips. He was perfect! Finally, reality set in and she said, "So nice to meet you, Fabio."

"Nice to meet you as well," he replied with a smile. "I am looking forward to working with you."

"Then let's get started," suggested Sophia. "May I have a moment with you, Isabelle?" She started walking away.

"Sure," replied Isabelle as she followed her.

"Isabelle, I must warn you about Fabio. I saw the way you two looked at each other. It happens all the time. Fabio is a great guy, but he is also a player. He is twenty eight years old and has never been married. He has dated dozens of women and so far, none of them have been able to catch him. They all fall head over heels in love with him.

He dates them until the newness wears off and then he's off looking for a new face. I felt I should warn you."

"I appreciate your frankness, Sophia, and I will keep it in mind. Anyway, I am in love with Paolo."

"Then you shouldn't have a problem, right?"

"Right."

They walked back over to Fabio who had a mysterious look on his face. He knew they were talking about him. He figured Sophia was warning the young Isabelle about his philandering ways. It wasn't the first time she had done that. He smiled to himself as he thought of how Sophia tried to protect the young girls like she was an old hen with baby chicks. Well, at least she cared about the girls. He had to admire her for that.

"Fabio, I am going to turn Isabelle over to you and let you start filming her with some of my products. I think two will be enough to let her practice on today. Let's do a foundation and eyeshadow."

"Here's the script for the foundation, Isabelle. It's short so I'm sure it won't take you long to learn it."

"I'll do my best."

"Practice on these today and see if you can do it without the script tomorrow."

She walked away and left the two of them to get on with the filming. Isabelle read the script the first couple of times, then decided to try it without the script. She did amazingly well.

"I think you're a born natural," said Fabio.

Isabelle grinned at him and said thanks. They filmed it over and over until it seemed to be perfect. Then they started on the eyeshadow. It was the same routine, over and over. Finally, when Fabio felt it was right, they called it a day. Isabelle was beginning to feel tired. "Wanna go for a cup of coffee or tea?" he asked her.

"I think I will pass on this today. I need to find Sophia and see when she is going home. I don't want to miss my ride," she said smiling. "See you tomorrow."

She went to find Sophia, who was sitting at her desk in her office. She was on the phone and Isabelle assumed it was a client by the way she was talking. When she got off the phone she asked Isabelle if she was finished for today. Isabelle told her she was, so Sophia said they would call it a day and go home.

The next day seemed to go easier. Fabio was impressed at how much better Isabelle was today. She must have studied the script last night. He didn't think she could be any better if he filmed her a second time, so he paged Sophia and asked her to come and view the tapings.

"These are wonderful!" exclaimed Sophia. "You did a great job, Isabelle. I knew you could do it."

"Thanks, Sophia."

Isabelle was rather proud of the videos. It was hard for her to imagine that was actually her in the videos.

Day after day she learned new scripts and Fabio filmed her. They did two new products each day. She would take the script home and learn it in one night. Hardly ever did she make a mistake so that it had to be filmed a second time. She was loving her new job!

The first time she saw her video on TV she was ecstatic. She couldn't believe that was actually her. Her life sure had changed. The next week Sophia told her that sales for the foundation and eyeshadow had sky-rocketed. She gave Isabelle a check for $5,000.

"I can't believe this!" she exclaimed as she looked at the amount of the check.

"This is just the beginning, my dear."

Isabelle was bubbling over with excitement. "Now I have money to pay rent."

"NO! NO! NO! That is your money. I offered you a home with no strings attached. I am a rich woman and I can afford to supply a home for you. You are going to bring in lots more money for the company."

"That is very generous of you, Sophia. Thank you for everything you have done and are doing for me."

"It's my pleasure. You don't realize how much it means to me having you live in my home. You have brought joy where there was much sadness. I can never repay you for that."

"I am glad to hear that. I love living in your beautiful home and you are such a sweet, generous lady. I am so glad our paths crossed. I feel like God had this in His plans for me and I humbly thank Him."

Company sales kept going up and up. Sophia was paying Isabelle $5,000 a week. She took her to the bank and encouraged her to open a checking and saving account. Isabelle was so thankful for her job and her boss, who was so helpful to her.

Paolo was very proud of her. He came to Milan a couple times a month. Isabelle was always happy to see him. They spent every waking moment together. He was there for her nineteenth birthday. Sophia had a large cake made at the bakery nearby. The three of them celebrated her birthday. She thought about her family back home and wished they could be here. Paolo had to leave early the next morning.

That same day at work, Fabio wished her a Happy Birthday. "May I take you out for lunch?"

Hating to be rude, she accepted. They went to a restaurant nearby and ate. They decided to not talk about work. He wanted to know more about her. After answering his questions, she decided it was her turn. She found out he was an only child born to his father and mother. Thinking they would never have a child of their own, they adopted a boy and girl. Several years later, Fabio was born. His aging parents lived about twenty miles from the city.

"I bet they spoiled you."

"I guess they did, to some extent. They were very strict on me as a child. I was not allowed to do things that other boys did. I know now it was for my own good. As a child, it is hard to accept."

"I know what you mean. My Dad had a hard time dealing with me going to modeling school in New York. I had never been away from home and to leave at eighteen did not set well with him. Then when I got the job offer in Rome, he really had a hard time dealing with that. I guess he is used to by now." She laughed as she continued. "Mom was easier to deal with. I think she understood how much I wanted this and to my Dad, I was just still his little girl."

"I'm sure it's different with girls. Boys can take care of themselves better than girls."

"That's what everyone thinks," she added.

"Isabelle, are you seeing anyone?" he asked bluntly.

"I have a boyfriend in Rome. Paolo and I have been seeing each other since I came there to work."

"Does he come to visit?"

"Twice a month."

"That's not very often. You need to go out and have a good time. You're too young to sit at home and dwindle your life away."

Isabelle laughed. "I don't mind. I don't have a lot of time for dating anyway."

"I would love to take you out to dinner and a movie one night. How about it?"

"That would be nice. Thank you, Fabio."

"How about Friday night?"

"I think that could be arranged. What time?"

"I will pick you up at seven."

"Sounds good. For now, we had better get back to work. Sophia might fire both of us."

"Fat chance of her firing you. It might be different with me."

"I couldn't see that happening. As a camera man, you are the best and she knows it. I think your job is secure as long as you want it."

Friday night came and Isabelle was more excited than Sophia. She could tell her boss wasn't happy about her going out with Fabio. "What about Paolo?" asked Sophia.

"Paolo has nothing to worry about. Fabio and I are just friends."

"I hope you won't live to regret it."

"Don't worry Sophia. I can handle it." (Famous last words)

Chapter 28

By the end of the second year, Isabelle was making $1,000,000 per year. Sophia had kept her promise; she had turned Isabelle into a supermodel. Her face was plastered on the cover of lots of magazines as well as TV. She had made it big time. Her parents were so proud of her and Jennifer bought magazines, just to have her daughter's picture.

Paolo was still coming to visit twice a month. She loved him but she didn't know if it was fair to 'string' him along. He was old enough to get married, but she wasn't. She was approaching twenty. Her career meant more to her than getting married any time soon.

She still had lunch or sometimes dinner with Fabio. They had become good friends. She never asked him about his personal life but she often wondered 'WHO' he was dating and how many girls there were in his life. He was very attentive to her when they were out and never seemed to notice any beautiful girl that might walk by. He seemed to only have eyes for her. One night as they were having dinner, he paused from eating and said, "Isabelle, there is something I must tell you. I have tried to hide it but I can no longer do so. I have fallen in love with you."

Isabelle almost choked on the food in her mouth. "WHAT?" she asked in disbelief. "I thought we were just good friends."

"We started out that way, but you have become more than a friend to me. I didn't mean for it to happen, but it has. I could hold it in no longer. Now you know...and I feel relieved."

"I don't know what to say, Fabio. Sophia warned me that this could happen. I told her I had everything under control. As you know I will soon be twenty. I have my career ahead of me and I cannot think about marriage any time soon. If you are looking to get married, then you had better find someone else."

"I don't want anyone else, and I am willing to wait for you."

"Oh, Fabio, I am in a mess now. Paolo told me the same thing. He is waiting until I am ready for marriage and he wants to marry me."

"One thing for sure...you can't marry both of us. You will have to choose."

"I need to set both of you free and let you get on with your lives. It may be several years before I am ready for marriage."

"I love you enough to wait."

"What about all your other girls?"

"What girls? There are NO other girls. Since I fell in love with you, I haven't gone out with another girl. I don't intend to. I'm a patient man, I will wait."

Isabelle could see the love he had for her as she looked into his dark brown eyes. She was in a fix. She would have to make a decision soon. It wasn't fair to either guy, or to herself. She would pray about it and ask God for an answer.

The weekend was approaching and she received a call from Paolo. "Hi Isabelle, something has come up and I won't be able to visit you this weekend. I'm sorry. I will talk to you soon."

There was no 'I Love You' or anything else. Isabelle thought he sounded strange and wondered why. Then it hit her...I bet he has met another girl. Could this be the answer to her prayer? The more she thought about it, the more she was convinced it was. She felt a little sad, but on the other hand she was relieved. Paolo may have answered her prayer in her having to make a choice. She would wait and see. He called her a week later and gave her some stunning news. "Isabelle, I am so sorry to have to tell you this, but I have met someone else and we are engaged."

"WHAT?"

"Christina is my new protégé and we hit it off immediately."

"What, like we did?" she asked sarcastically.

"Don't be sarcastic, Isabelle. It isn't becoming to you."

"I'm sorry, Paolo. I guess I was just shocked and disappointed."

"I hope you will meet someone, if you haven't already. I know you aren't ready to get married, but I am. I will never forget you, Isabelle and you will always have a special place in my heart."

"Thanks for everything you have done for me, Paolo. I appreciate it and I will never forget you either. I wish you the best with Christina. I sincerely hope you have a long and happy life together."

"Thank you, Isabelle. Goodbye."

As she hung up the phone the tears started to fall.

She wasn't sure if it was tears of pity for herself or tears of relief. Paolo had taken care of the problem she had been praying about. She was sure God worked through him.

She went downstairs to find Sophia reading in the den. She looked up as Isabelle entered and saw her wiping the tears. "What's wrong, my child?"

"Paolo just broke up with me. He is engaged to another girl."

"I can't believe that!" exclaimed Sophia. "That sure was fast."

"He is going to marry his latest protégé. Her name is Christina."

"It is very hard to have a long distance relationship."

"I know. He wants to get married and I am not ready, so he found someone who is."

"Oh well, it's not the end of the world. I guess Fabio will be happy to hear the news."

"I will tell him tomorrow at work. He has already confessed his love for me and said he would wait until I was ready to get married. I guess we'll see."

"How do you feel about him?" asked a concerned Sophia.

"I think I am falling in love with him. I don't want to get too serious yet. It seems like the timing is wrong for both guys. If I were older, things would be different. I have my career to think about now and I don't want to get married at twenty."

"Speaking of twenty...I want to throw a big party for your twentieth birthday."

"You don't have to do that. You have done too much for me already. I should be looking for a house to buy."

"I won't hear of that. Save your money. I want you to live here."

"Whatever you say, Sophia. You're the boss!"

The next day at work Isabelle approached Fabio with a sweet smile. "Good morning, Fabio. How are you this morning?"

"I'm doing well. How are you?"

"That's what I want to talk to you about. May I have a few minutes before we start work?"

"Sure, what's on your mind?"

"I had a call last night from Paolo. He broke up with me."

"He did what? Has he lost his mind?"

Isabelle laughed, "I don't think so. He has met another girl and wants to marry her. I guess he got tired of waiting on me. I couldn't rush into marriage just to hold on to him."

"If he had really loved you, he would be willing to wait. You are most definitely worth the wait."

"Thanks, Fabio. You know how to make me feel better. I think the distance made a difference also. He probably got tired of the long drive."

"It could be. Oh well, his loss is my gain. At least I hope so!"

Isabelle smiled sweetly at him and replied, "We never know what the future holds; we only know WHO holds the future."

"You are exactly correct."

"Thank you for listening Fabio."

"You're very welcome, my love."

Later that night, Isabelle went to find Sophia, who was in the den reading a book. "Sophia, I hate to interrupt, but may I speak with you for a minute?"

Sophia could see she looked troubled, "Of course you may, my dear, what's on your mind?"

"As you know, I was raised in church. I have really missed going since I have been in Rome. I need to find a good church. I know I have let God down and I am not happy with myself. Do you know of a good church nearby?"

"The closest one I know is the 'Milan Bible Church'. I have heard good things about it."

"Maybe I will check it out this Sunday. Would you like to go with me?"

"Not now," replied Sophia. "Maybe some time."

"Okay. Thanks for telling me about the church. It might just be what I am looking for."

When Sunday morning came, Isabelle was up early getting ready for church. She felt her spirit lifted and she had a song in her heart. She knew this was definitely what she should be doing. She arrived at the church just before the eleven o'clock service was about to begin. The pastor came to greet her as soon as she was seated. He was very friendly and welcomed her with a big smile. He asked where she was from and he seemed amazed when she told him she was from the United States. He wanted to know what state and she told him Montana. He told her he hoped she would enjoy her visit at their church and would come back again. She thanked him.

The singing was good and the sermon was even better. She felt like it was meant for her. It was like he knew exactly what she needed to hear. She had been told by preachers that God enlightens them about certain needs of people. Not knowing who it is for, the preacher has to preach what God tells them to do. She noticed that he never had his sermon written out. He read scripture from the Bible and then preached his message. She took in every word, even though he was 'stepping on her toes'. She knew what she needed to do, so when the altar call was given; she went up and rededicated her life to the Lord. She felt like a burden had been lifted from her shoulders. She felt light and as free as the air. God had given her another chance. Not that she had done anything bad; she just wasn't where God wanted her to be. After church many of the members shook hands with her and told her they would be praying for her. They invited her to come back. None of them seemed to recognize her and that was just the way she wanted it. She might be making big money, but in the sight of God she was equal to those who didn't have much. That was when she realized that she needed to be helping those who were less fortunate. She felt good. God had blessed her and she would give in return.

Week after week she attended church. She enjoyed every moment of it. It didn't take her long before she realized there were some in the church who could use help. She talked to the pastor to confirm it. She did tell him about her work and that she had the means to help those who needed it. He seemed to be surprised that she would actually do that. She asked him for a list of people and their needs. She wanted to remain anonymous. "God Bless You, Isabelle!" he said.

He gave her a list and she fulfilled every need listed. She managed to get the things to him during the week, unbeknown to the church members. He was so excited when she brought carload after carload and dropped the items off at the church. "You sure are going to make some people very happy!" he remarked.

"I think I will be happier than them. God has blessed me so much and I want to share with others."

"Thank you, Isabelle. God will bless you for your effort."

"If there is anything your church needs please let me know."

"We have been thinking about a new roof."

"Say no more. Let me know how much you need and I will pay for it."

"Thank you so much, Isabelle. God saw our need and sent you here to help us."

Chapter 29

Sophia had been busy for the past week planning a twentieth birthday for Isabelle. She wanted everything to be perfect. The last party she had planned was for Adriana's sixteenth birthday and that seemed so long ago. She never dreamed that she would ever be planning another party, but here she was with a new young friend. Isabelle had become like a daughter to her. She knew that eventually Isabelle would get married and move away, but for now she was enjoying her company. Her heart broke for Isabelle when Paolo broke up with her. Although she had warned Isabelle about Fabio, she was glad that she had him for a friend. He would help her get through the breakup with Paolo. Sophia wondered if there was more than friendship between them. Isabelle had never said and she never asked her. She didn't believe in prying. She would let Isabelle come to her in her own time.

The invitations had gone out two days ago. The party was in three weeks. There was so much to do. She ordered a huge birthday cake which was to be decorated with **'Gone With The Wind'** decorations. She wanted this birthday to be perfect for Isabelle. She was sparing no expense. The party would be held outside near the flower garden. She had ordered three large tents in case of rain. She called a caterer with her menu. She had a friend who was a decorator and she agreed to take care of everything. Fabio had agreed to take the pictures and to video the party. He hadn't mentioned it to Isabelle. He wanted to surprise her.

Isabelle knew about the party, but knew none of the details. Sophia wanted to keep it that way and surprise her. She didn't even know who Sophia had invited and how long the guest list was. She was in awe of how Sophia had taken her under her wing and wanted to do so much for her. She knew she was truly blessed.

She and Fabio seemed to be getting closer. He was not trying to rush her into anything. He understood her feelings about her career. She was soaring to the top and he was extremely proud of her. They worked a few days a week. She modeled and he filmed. Sophia wanted Isabelle to model all the cosmetics in her *'Sophia's Choice'* line. No model had ever been as popular as Isabelle had become. She was so proud of her and of course, the money was rolling in. This was the happiest Sophia had been since before Adriana died. She had gotten to where she could talk about it easier and the memory of her daughter's death was not as painful. She was thankful for that. She thanked God for sending Isabelle to her.

The day of the birthday party arrived with the sun shining brightly and not an ominous cloud in the sky. The birds were merrily singing like they knew something special was about to take place. Nikki prepared a special breakfast for Sophia and Isabelle. They both ate heartily and didn't worry about calories this time.

The party was scheduled for two o'clock. The tents were set up the day before. The tables and chairs were in place. The cake and the food arrived around one o'clock. The decorations had been hung that morning. Everything was falling into place. Isabelle was excited when she saw all that was happening. *'Vanilla Sky'* band arrived at one-fifteen and began to set up their equipment. Isabelle had never heard of them so she was anxious to hear them. They started playing ten minutes before two. She liked the sound of most of their music although it was very different from what she was used to. She grew up on country music. This band seemed to be pop/rock. It would take some getting used to. She realized she was a country girl and most people didn't like her kind of music. She realized she needed to broaden her horizon.

The band started singing at exactly two o'clock. After a couple songs they quit and joined the crowd at the food tent. Isabelle was very surprised at the amount of people who showed up. She only knew a few of them and they were from the Sophia's Cosmetic Company, which included Fabio. She was happy to see him. "I'm glad you could come," she said. "You look great today!" He was dressed in dark gray pants and a silver silk shirt. His black wavy hair was covering his ears slightly and a piece of hair lay on his forehead. Isabelle had never seen him look more handsome. Looking at him took her breath away. He was undoubtedly the most handsome man in the world and he could be hers if she wanted him. She did want him. She hoped he would be willing to wait for her. Paolo had told her that he would wait and he never, so how did she know Fabio would be true to his word?

"Thank you. You look very beautiful today!" She was wearing a sundress with small violets on a white background. It was a perfect fit. She was wearing purple sandals which matched.

"Thanks and thank you for coming!"

"I wouldn't have missed it. I will be doing the videoing and taking pictures."

"Sophia would. She wants to hang on to these memories. This is her first party since she gave her daughter a sixteenth birthday party."

"I'm glad to see her coming to life again and it's all because of you!"

"Now Fabio...I don't want to take credit for it."

"It's true. I have seen a drastic change in her since you arrived."

"I think we have been good for each other. I know she certainly made my life easier by allowing me to move in with her."

"I'm sure she is the one who feels more blessed. Come on Birthday Girl, let's go get some food." He took her hand and guided her to the food tent.

They joined the long line and waited. There was so much food and so many things to choose from. When they reached the table they filled their plates and went to another tent and sat down. After everyone finished eating, it was time to cut the cake. Sophia came and got Isabelle. Fabio followed them. Isabelle was surprised when she saw the cake. "You have outdone yourself, Sophia! This cake is beautiful and you knew exactly what I like. Thank you very much!"

"My pleasure! The delight I see in your eyes is worth everything I put into this party. I have loved every minute of it!"

"I appreciate it and YOU very much, Sophia!"

"Come on, let's make a birthday wish and cut the cake."

Isabelle thought for a minute and then she blew out the candles. She knew what she wished for but would never say a word to anyone about it.

Cake and Ice Cream were served. Everyone was having such a good time. The band was playing and singing.

Next was the opening of the birthday gifts. The table was piled high. Isabelle was surprised at how generous everyone had been. The gifts consisted of many different things, DVD's, CD's, Books, lingerie, perfume and assorted jewelry. Isabelle was grateful and excited with every gift she opened. Just when she thought she had opened the last gift, Sophia told her that she saved her gift for last. She took out her cell phone and dialed a number. "Bring it on," said Sophia. That was the end of her conversation. Isabelle heard a motor start and looked toward the driveway entrance just as a beautiful red, Ferrrari California Convertible came cruising down the driveway. Her heart skipped a beat. The guy pulled up as close as he could and got out of the car. "HAPPY BIRTHDAY, ISABELLE!!!" exclaimed Sophia extending her hand toward the car.

Isabelle's hand flew over her mouth in total shock. "FOR ME?" she asked in a very excited voice. "YOU BOUGHT THIS CAR FOR ME?" another shocking question from Isabelle. "I think I'm dreaming. This can't be for real. Sophia you have been more than generous to me. Why would you want to buy me this expensive car?"

"You have become very dear to me, Isabelle. You are like a daughter and I guess I just wanted to spoil you a little more."

"You shouldn't have been this generous though!"

"Don't dampen my spirit by rejecting my gift to you."

"I would never do that, Sophia. I very much appreciate everything you do for me. I guess it just hasn't sunk in yet. You were overly generous and I thank you from the bottom of my heart."

"You are most welcome, my precious friend. You have

no idea how much you have changed my life. I have the courage to go on now and it's all because of you."

"I am so humbled that I could help you, Sophia but I feel I can never repay you for all you have done for me."

"I am not asking for anything in return. I just love having your friendship and companionship. It has changed my life more than you will ever know and that is worth more than all the money in the world."

Isabelle wiped the tears from her eyes. "God must have sent me here to help you, Sophia. There is no other explanation." Isabelle hugged her and kissed her on the cheek.

"Perhaps you are right."

It had been the best twentieth birthday a girl could ever have. Isabelle felt so humble and blessed. After the party was over and everyone left, Isabelle and Fabio went for a stroll in Sophia's flower garden. It was so beautiful with every color of rose bush you could think of. There were all kinds of other flowers but the rose was Isabelle's favorite. It was hard for her to choose a favorite color. She could narrow it down to two, the sunshine yellow and the scarlet red. Sophia had made a center piece for the main table mixing the red and yellow roses. It was so beautiful!

They stopped and sat down in the gazebo. Fabio put his arms around her and kissed her passionately. "You know I'm in love with you, Isabelle!"

She smiled and replied, "I know you are and I am grateful for your love. In my heart I know I love you too, but I am not ready for marriage."

"I know that and I am not rushing you. I just want you to know how I feel. Don't ever forget it. I will be here for you as long as you want me."

"Thank you. That's good to know."

"I would like to take you out in the country to meet my parents. Would you be willing to go?"

"Yes, I would like that."

"How about next Saturday?"

"I think that would be fine."

"Great. I will call my Mom and let her know that we are coming."

"Can we take my new car?"

"Sure, if that's what you want."

"That will give you a chance to drive it."

"I would love that."

Chapter 30

The next Saturday came and they left Milan at ten in the morning. It was an hour's ride to Fabio's parent's home. When they arrived Isabelle saw a man outside on the front porch. "That's my Dad," said Fabio.

They came to a stop and got out of the car. The man walked over to them. He hugged his son and turned to Isabelle. "Dad, I would like for you to meet Isabelle Colter." He turned to Isabelle and introduced his Dad as Dante Moretti.

"So nice to meet you, Isabelle. We've heard quite a lot about you."

"It's very nice to meet you, Sir."

"Oh, please call me Dante," he said smiling as he took her hand and kissed it. She looked into his eyes and was shocked at how much Fabio looked like his dad. It was like she was seeing Fabio in the future. Well, she sure liked what she saw. Mr. Moretti was a handsome man and looked more like an older brother to Fabio. His hair was silver streaked which made him look even more handsome and distinguished. "Come on in the house. I know your Mom is anxious to meet Isabelle."

They followed him into the house where a woman was leaning over the stove cooking. She was wearing an apron over her dress and looked so completely at home in this surrounding. "Hi Mom," said Fabio as he hugged and kissed her. "I would like for you to meet Isabelle Colter. Isabelle, this is my mom, Leora Moretti."

"It's so nice to meet you, Isabelle. Welcome to our humble home."

"I'm glad to meet you, Mrs. Moretti."

"Please call me Leora. I feel like my husband's mother, God rest her soul, when someone calls me Mrs. Moretti."

Isabelle laughed, "Okay, Leora."

"Come sit and talk to me while I finish lunch."

"Is there anything I can do to help you?"

"Oh no, you just sit."

"As you wish."

"Tell me, where in the United States did you come from? Fabio only said that was where you are from."

"I moved here from Montana. It is a beautiful state in the western part of the United States. My parents own a ranch in Laurel. I grew up in the country and enjoyed all the things that city people never know about. I love to ride horses. I guess that was my most favorite pastime."

"I would like to see the United States but I'm sure I will never get there."

"Never say never."

She smiled at Isabelle and continued to cook lunch.

"Do you have other children besides Fabio?"

"He was our only child, born to us late in life. We thought we would never have a child of our own so Dante and I adopted two children before Fabio was born. Elmo is forty and Eleonora is thirty-five. They are brother and sister and were in an orphanage. We couldn't separate them, so we adopted both of them. We have never had any regrets as they have made us proud."

"That's wonderful! I know they are very thankful to have you for their parents."

"I think they are."

"Do they live nearby?"

"About an hour away. They come to see us once a month."

"That's nice. Family is very important. I really miss mine. It's been two years since I last saw them. I plan to go home soon. I have asked Fabio to go with me. He hasn't given me an answer yet. I know it's expensive, so I told him I would buy his plane ticket."

"That's very generous of you. It would be a trip of a lifetime for him since he has never been to the United States."

"I would love to show him my home place and have him meet my family."

"May I ask you a question?"

"Sure. What is it?"

"Are you serious about Fabio?"

"Yes, Ma'am I am. I know he loves me and I love him. He has been very patient in waiting until I am ready for marriage. He knows I wanted to get my career off the ground. I am doing quite well now. Maybe in a couple years or so..."

"Fabio must love you because he has dated a lot of girls and never seemed to find one he wanted to settle down with. I like you...I am happy he found you."

"Thank you, so am I. The first moment I saw him I thought he was the most handsome man I have ever seen in my life and I still feel the same way."

Leora laughed, "That is exactly the same way I felt

when I first saw Dante. Fabio looks so much like his Dad did when we met."

"I can see why you fell for him!"

Lunch was ready and Leora asked Isabelle to go tell the men. They were sitting on the front porch talking. They looked up as Isabelle opened the door. "Lunch is ready," she said with a smile. "Are you hungry?" she looked at Fabio.

"I'm starving!" he exclaimed. "I never ate breakfast."

The men followed Isabelle into the dining room and they were all seated. The table was covered with delicious looking food. Suddenly, Isabelle felt extremely hungry. Conversation flowed as they ate. Isabelle felt so at ease with Fabio's parents. She loved them already. They were so kind and down to earth. They were her kind of people. She may be earning big money now, but she was still a country girl at heart and always would be. She was most comfortable with people like this. She could tell they weren't rich, but she was sure they had enough to get by. They lived in a modest home, nothing fancy but very comfortable and she could tell this was a home filled with love. It reminded her of the atmosphere at her home in Montana.

After lunch she offered to help Leora with the dishes but was told to spend the time with Fabio. He took her for a walk on the farm. They had a few cows, a couple of horses, some pigs, goats, chickens, ducks and geese. Isabelle was beginning to feel more at home. She loved farm life. That is where she was the happiest. They walked over to a rather large pond where several ducks were swimming. They were so beautiful. They sat down on the bench beside the pond. A large maple tree shaded the bench. They sat there for an hour talking and occasionally commenting on the ducks.

"We should bring a picnic lunch here sometime," suggested Fabio. "Do you like picnics?"

"I love picnics! We used to go on picnics back on the ranch. That was one of my favorite things to do."

"Then that should make you feel right at home."

"It will help."

"Are you free next Saturday?"

"As far as I know I am."

"Let's plan a picnic for that day. I will tell Mom we are coming out here, but she won't have to cook for us."

"Sounds like a splendid idea. I would like that very much."

"Then it's a date!"

She smiled and agreed with him. She felt so happy and at ease when she was in the company of Fabio. Every now and then she thought of the day that Sophia warned her about him. She had seen no sign that he was like that. He was very attentive to her and when they were out, he only had eyes for her. She loved that quality in a man.

Chapter 31

The years went by and she and Fabio were still dating. They had grown closer than ever. She was about to turn twenty-five. He was seriously thinking of proposing to her on her birthday. He thought she might finally say yes to his proposal. He had already bought a beautiful two carat diamond and was ready to pop the question. Sophia was planning another big birthday party for her and he thought this would be the perfect time to propose. He hoped she would think so too!

Business was booming! Isabelle was earning $2,000,000 a year now. She was a famous super model. Although she was famous and made a lot of money, she never let it go to her head. She was still the same sweet Isabelle he had met several years ago. He was so proud of her and could hardly wait to make her his wife.

The morning of her birthday he arrived on the front doorstep at ten o'clock. Sophia knew he was coming. He had told her his plan. Isabelle was wearing blue jeans and a t-shirt. She hadn't gotten dressed for her party yet. She was surprised when Fabio showed up. "I wasn't expecting you this early," she said as she let him in the door.

"I was in the neighborhood," he winked at Sophia as she walked out of the room.

"Really?" she asked. One could tell that she knew something was amiss. "Now truthfully, what are you doing here this early?"

"I have something I need to ask you."

"Okay..."

He kneeled down on one knee in front of her and pulled a box out of his jacket pocket. He opened the box and looked at her with love in his eyes, "Isabelle, will you marry me?"

A tear trickled down her face as she smiled at him. "Yes, Fabio, I will marry you!"

He placed the ring on her finger and let out a yelp. Sophia came rushing back into the room. "She must have said yes!"

"She did! She has made me the happiest man alive!"

"Congratulations to both of you!" exclaimed a very happy Sophia. "Now we can plan the wedding, Isabelle."

"Of course we can, Sophia. I will be honored to have your help."

"I am very happy for you, but I certainly will miss you when you move out of my house."

"Maybe we can find a house nearby, so we can see you often. Of course I will see you at work, but that's different from being at home."

"Do you think your family will come over for the wedding?" asked Fabio.

"I would say yes. I don't think they will want to miss it."

"How soon can you get this wedding planned?"

"It takes about a year."

"Couldn't we do it in six months?"

"Are you in a hurry?"

"Yes, I am. Remember I have been patient and waited for you for several years," he teased.

"I know you have and it will be worth the wait. I promise."

"I think we can do it in six months," added Sophia. "I know people and can pull some strings."

"That sounds wonderful. Six months it is. Does that make you feel better Fabio?"

"It sure does."

"I need to call my Mom and tell her our news. I know my twenty-fifth birthday party is today, so I have to focus on that. I do want to tell my family first."

"I'll be going and get ready for your party. I will be back soon."

Isabelle smiled and gave him a kiss before he left. She could hardly wait for his return. She missed him very much when they were apart.

Isabelle gave her Mom a quick call. Jennifer wished her a happy birthday. She thought that was why Isabelle was calling. "Mom, I have some other news for you!"

"What is it, dear?"

"Fabio just asked me to marry him?"

"He did? What did you say?"

"I said 'YES'. The wedding is in six months. Can you make arrangements for you, Dad and Rachel Rose to come over here for our wedding?"

"You'd better believe I will. We wouldn't miss your wedding for anything!"

"I will let you know as soon as we set the exact date."

"That sounds wonderful. Also, have fun today on your twenty-fifth birthday. I can hardly believe you have reached that milestone."

"I know, Mom. Sophia is having a party for me. I told her to keep it smaller this time."

"Your Dad and I really appreciate her for being so good to you. I can't wait to meet her."

"She is a wonderful lady! I don't know what I would have done without her."

"You're going to make me cry," said Sophia in the background.

"I will talk to you later, Mom. I love you and miss you!"

"The same goes for me, my dear Isabelle. We all love you very much!"

"Bye Mom!"

"Bye Darling."

Isabelle wiped the tears from her eyes. She was so happy, yet she felt sadness. Her family was so far away. She wished they could be here to help her celebrate her twenty-fifth birthday. She would never forget this birthday. Fabio had picked the perfect day to propose to her. She was happier than she had ever been in her entire life. He was perfect for her.

She went to change into the outfit she would be wearing for her party. Somehow she wasn't into this party like she was her twentieth one. Could it be because Fabio had just proposed to her and her mind was on planning their wedding? She couldn't let Sophia know because she had worked very hard at planning this party. Isabelle knew that Sophia enjoyed it as much as she did.

As she dressed in the lavender sundress with yellow roses in the background, her mind was wandering. She slipped on lavender sandals to match. She was thinking about her wedding day and having her family here with her as she married the love of her life. Then her mind drifted back to Tracy Kelley. She had thought he was the love of her life. She must admit, she hadn't thought about him for quite some time. She was living in another world now. Everything from her past seemed so far away. She hadn't seen her parents for seven years. She called them several times a week and that helped. She had grown up so much since that girl of eighteen left her home in Montana. She could hardly believe she was twenty-five now. She was almost as excited about seeing her family as she was about the wedding. Having them here would make everything perfect.

She went downstairs where Sophia was putting the final touches on everything. She was more like a child than a grown woman in her early fifties.

Fabio arrived shortly. He was wearing a smile from ear to ear. As he approached Isabelle his eyes widened, "You look absolutely beautiful, my love! You have made me the happiest man in the world!"

"Thank you, Fabio. You have made me the happiest girl in the world. I must say you look as handsome as ever!"

He leaned over and kissed her briefly as Sophia walked in the door. "Don't let me interrupt," she teased."We had better go outside. Guests are starting to arrive. The birthday girl needs to be out there to greet them."

So they went outside and welcomed each guest and thanked them for coming. It was another great party with **'Vanilla Sky'** as the entertainment again. The food was plenteous and very delicious. The large cake was done in white icing with red and yellow roses and 'Happy "25th" Birthday' Isabelle' on it. After they finished eating, Isabelle opened her gifts. She received lots of pretty and useful things. Sophia gave her a beautiful diamond necklace and earring set. Fabio gave her the bracelet to match. He had been conspiring with Sophia. It was a wonderful day, but Isabelle was glad when it was over and just the three of them were alone.

"Let's go for a walk," she suggested to Fabio.

"Sure," he replied. "Are you okay Isabelle?"

"I need to unwind. I wouldn't want to hurt Sophia by seeming ungrateful, but I don't want any more parties, except our wedding reception. I have everything I want and if I don't, I have the money to purchase it. I hate to see all these people spending their money on me."

"I understand how you feel."

"I do love the book your parents sent me. The first edition of **'GONE WITH THE WIND'** will always be special to me. How did they find it?"

"They didn't. I found it for them. I had to do some searching before I located it."

"My thanks to you, as well as them."

"Anything for you, my love!"

Chapter 32

The next several months were very busy for Isabelle. Between work and planning her wedding, she had very little free time. Sophia had insisted that she pay for the wedding, which Isabelle graciously accepted. She knew there was no use arguing about it. It meant a lot to Sophia to do this for her. So they did all the wedding planning together with a little input from Fabio every now and then.

Isabelle had her wedding gown ordered from New York. It was a beautiful white organza flounce Lazaro bridal ball gown, with a sweetheart neckline. It had a sheer Alencon lace bodice, dropped waist, with a voluminous layered organza skirt and a chapel train. She ordered the veil to match. She would wear the diamond necklace and earring set that Sophia had gotten her for her birthday, along with the matching diamond bracelet from Fabio.

The invitations were ordered. The photographer, caterer, musicians were booked. The cake and flowers were ordered two months in advance to be delivered on that special day. Everything seemed to be falling into place.

Rachel Rose was going to be Isabelle's Maid of Honor.

She was now nineteen years old and had grown into a very beautiful young lady, looking so much like her Aunt Miranda and Grandmother Rachel. She would be wearing a rose colored floor length organza dress, detailed with sequins and beads on the bodice below the sweetheart neckline. Isabelle knew she would be beautiful. She had carefully chosen this dress for Rachel Rose, who would be her only attendant. Since none of her brothers would be coming, she decided to have a small wedding party, just her Maid of Honor and Fabio's Best Man. She told Sophia to keep the guest list small. The wedding would take place in Sophia's beautiful garden. It would be the perfect place for a wedding.

Gabe would walk his daughter down the aisle. They were to arrive in Milan, a week ahead of time so that any changes to their clothing could be made in time for the wedding. Fabio would rent a tuxedo for Gabe when he rented his own.

Fabio's dad would be his Best Man. Isabelle was glad he chose his dad. They had a very close father/son relationship and Isabelle was happy about that. That told her a lot about both of them. She really liked Fabio's brother and sister. Although Elmo and Eleonora were adopted, they were as much a part of the family as Fabio. His parents showed no favoritism. That said a lot for them.

Elmo was married to Gaby. They had a son, Alanzo and a daughter, Fontana, who were both teenagers. Eleonora was married to Georgio. They had two sons, Gino and Lanzo, who were also teenagers. They were all planning to come to the wedding. Isabelle was happy, but it made her sad that the rest of her family couldn't come. Of course, it was her uncles and aunt. Rachel Rose was her only sister. She was very happy that her immediate family would be there on her special day.

Everything for the wedding was falling into place. Isabelle's dress fit perfectly without any alterations. It was hanging in the closet waiting for the big day to arrive.

Gabe, Jennifer and Rachel Rose arrived the following week. It was a very happy reunion. Isabelle met them at the airport and brought them to Sophia's house. They were very impressed with the house and with Sophia. They thanked her for being so kind to Isabelle and opening her home and heart to their daughter. "It is my pleasure," she assured them. "Isabelle is like a daughter to me."

"I'm so sorry about your daughter," said Jennifer.

"Yes, it was a very hard thing to go through. Having Isabelle here has helped me get over it tremendously. She has helped my heart to heal."

"That's good. I know how hard it is to lose a child also."

"Yes, Isabelle told me. I am very sorry for your loss."

"Even though it happened so long ago, the wound opens from time to time."

"I can relate to that," said Sophia. "Anyway, welcome to my home. I am so glad you could come over for Isabelle's wedding. I know it means everything to her. Just look how excited she is talking to her sister."

"I know. Rachel Rose has really missed her."

"She is a beautiful girl! You have two beautiful daughters...both beautiful, but so completely different."

"They are, for sure."

Isabelle took them upstairs and showed them to their rooms. "After you unpack, come back downstairs."

By the time they finished unpacking and came downstairs, Fabio had arrived. "Mom, Dad, Rachel Rose, I would like for you to meet my fiancé, Fabio Moretti."

Fabio shook hands with Gabe and told him it was nice to meet him. Gabe expressed his greeting also. Fabio kissed

Jennifer's hand and expressed his happiness in meeting her. Then he took Rachel Rose's hand and kissed it. Her big green eyes were wide with admiration as she stared at him. She was speechless. "Oh, the beautiful Rachel Rose. I have heard so much about you. Welcome to Milan!"

"Thank you," she stammered. Isabelle had never seen her like this. She just kept staring at Fabio.

"Rachel Rose, are you okay?" asked Isabelle.

"Yes, but he is so beautiful," she whispered.

"Indeed he is. I thought he was the most handsome man I had ever seen when I first met him and I probably acted just like you are acting," she said smiling.

"I'm sorry, Isabelle. I didn't mean to act this way. It's just that I have never seen such a good looking man in my life. Does he have any friends that look like him?"

"You'll have to ask him."

"I can't do that!" she exclaimed.

About that time Nikki announced that dinner was ready. They entered the dining room and were seated. The food was delicious, as usual. Everyone except Rachel Rose ate like they were starving. That always pleased Sophia to see her guests enjoy a meal at her house. Isabelle noticed that her sister was eating very little.

"Aren't you hungry Rachel Rose?" asked Isabelle.

"Not really," she answered moving the food around on her plate with her fork.

"Mom, does she eat like this at home?" asked Isabelle.

"She has been eating skimpy lately."

"Doesn't that concern you, Mom?"

"It does. I figure it's a phase she is going through. Most young girls are afraid of getting fat."

"I never worried about that and I don't think Rachel

Rose is in danger of being overweight. Have you taken her to the doctor lately?"

"No, I haven't. She says she feels okay."

"She is too skinny," replied Isabelle.

"I am not! Don't worry about me, sister dear!"

"You look a little pale to me," said Isabelle with concern.

"I wasn't lucky like you. I don't have a dark complexion."

"I'm just concerned about you little sister! That's all."

"I'm okay."

"I won't mention it again!"

"Thank you. I don't want to talk about it anymore."

After they finished eating, Sophia suggested that Isabelle show them the flower garden. So she invited her family to follow her. They garden was in full bloom with a variety of flowers in an array of colors. It was breathtakingly beautiful.

"This is so beautiful! What a wonderful place for your wedding," said her Mom.

"I know. I just hope it won't rain that day. Tents will be set up just in case."

"That's a great idea," replied her Mom.

Isabelle changed the subject. "Any news from back home, Mom?"

"Matter of fact there is. Tracy got married two weeks ago."

Isabelle felt her face heat up. "Oh really? Who did he marry?"

"Some girl he met in college. Her name is Sara. They had a big church wedding."

"Really? Have you seen his new wife?"

"Yes and she is a very lovely girl."

"Oh well, I am happy for him. Tracy is one of the nicest guys I have ever met!"

"But you let him get away," teased her Mom.

"I know," she sighed. "Our lifestyles were different and that drove us apart. I truly hope he will be happy. Do you know what career he is pursuing?"

"Oh yes...I thought you knew. I guess I never thought to mention it to you. Tracy is a minister."

"A MINISTER? You're kidding, right?"

"I'm afraid not. He graduated from Warner University in Florida. He recently became Pastor of a First Church of God near his home."

"I am so happy for him. I guess I am just surprised, but I shouldn't be. Tracy is a wonderful Christian guy."

"He surely is."

"When you see him again, tell him I said congratulations on his marriage."

"I sure will. He has asked about you from time to time."

The wedding was one week away. Isabelle was so glad her family had arrived early and safely. It felt so good to have them here. She had missed them terribly. She was the happiest she had ever been. She was about to marry a wonderful man and her family was here to support her.

Chapter 33

Isabelle had just gotten into bed when the phone rang. She reached over to her nightstand and picked it up. "Hello," she said.

"Isabelle," there was a pause. "Isabelle, this is Paolo."

"PAOLO? Why are you calling?"

"I really need to talk to you. Can you spare me a few minutes?"

"Sure Paolo. What's the matter?"

"Christina broke off our engagement tonight."

"I'm sorry, Paolo. I guess you know how I felt when you dumped me," she said a little sarcastic.

"I am so sorry that I broke things off with you. I still love you, Isabelle. In fact, I never stopped loving you. Will you give me another chance? Please, Isabelle!"

"You sure had a funny way of showing your love for me. I'm sorry Paolo; I can't give you another chance."

"I know I was a fool and I'm sorry!"

"It's too late now. I am about to marry the love of my life. In fact, our wedding is only one week away."

"Are you sure this is what you want?" he asked almost in tears.

"I am certain."

"Remember all the good times we had and the love we shared?"

"Of course I do, but apparently it meant more to me than to you."

"I deserved that. Again I am so sorry!"

"You'll find another girl soon. I'm sure you won't be alone very long. One thing I learned in life is you don't go back. If someone hurts you, there is no going back. You need to pick up the pieces and move on. That is exactly what I have done. Fabio and I have a wonderful relationship and I am really looking forward to becoming his wife."

"Congratulations! I wish you the best."

"Thanks, Paolo. I honestly hope you will find love again."

"Thanks, Isabelle and goodbye."

"Goodbye Paolo."

Isabelle lay there in the darkness pondering over the conversation of the phone call she just had. She was very surprised to hear from Paolo again. He had hurt her very badly when he broke it off with her. Part of her felt sorry for him and the other part said he got what he deserved. She knew she shouldn't feel that way. God would not be pleased with her. You have to forgive, even if you never forget. She was about to begin her life journey with Fabio and she couldn't let Paolo or any other man upset her or come between them. She intended to make him the best wife ever. She loved his family and would be very happy being a part of it. His parents had treated her like a daughter from the first day that they met. She had grown to love them very much.

Fabio came over the next day after work. Isabelle noticed how Rachel Rose could hardly take her eyes off him. This made her feel uncomfortable and she knew that Fabio could see what her sister was doing.

"Rachel Rose, may I speak with you for a moment?"

"Sure, what's up?"

"Follow me," said Isabelle who got up and left the room with her sister following her.

"My dear sister, I am going to come to the point. It is plain to see that you cannot take your eyes off my fiancé. I find this upsetting to say the least."

"I'm sorry Isabelle. I don't mean anything by it. He is just so good looking and I find it easy to rest my eyes upon him."

"You are very obvious about it though. I know you are making him feel uncomfortable. Please try to stop staring so much."

"I'll try. I promise."

"Thank you!"

They walked back into the other room where the rest of the family was. Fabio looked at Isabelle with a questioning look. Did he really not know? She couldn't believe he could be that blind.

The rest of the day went well. Rachel Rose stayed true to her promise. She went into Sophia's library and found a book to read. That entertained her for the rest of the day.

The week flew by and the day of the wedding dawned with a bright sun early that morning. Birds could be heard singing their melodious songs in the trees. It was like they knew something special was about to take place. Spring was a beautiful time for a wedding. Everything was fresh and new. The tents had been set up the day before. Chairs were in place and the aroma of the flowers permeated the air. Sophia had the gardener cut flowers from her garden for the wedding. Basket after basket decorated the area where the ceremony would take place. You couldn't tell the garden had been touched. The flowers were so thick and beautiful.

Isabelle and Rachel Rose went upstairs to get dressed for the wedding. Rachel Rose looked beautiful in the rose colored dress Isabelle had chosen for her. After she was completely ready, she helped her sister with the wedding gown. They stood in front of the full length mirror when they finished. "Don't we look fancy?" asked Rachel Rose laughing.

"Indeed we do. This is the only time I plan to wear a wedding dress," said Isabelle smiling.

"I don't know if I will ever get married. It seems like too much work."

"When you meet the right guy you will change your mind."

"Perhaps."

"You're still young and have plenty of time. Don't ever rush into anything. Take your time and make sure he is the 'one' for you."

"Oh, don't worry big sister. I have no intention of getting married anytime soon."

"That's good to know."

They stayed in the room until Jennifer came up to get them. "Oh my goodness, how beautiful you both look!"

"Thanks, Mom," they said in unison.

"It's time to go down. Fabio is already standing with the minister. The family is already seated as well as the guests. It's show time girls!"

Rachel Rose went down the stairs first with Isabelle following. Gabe was waiting at the bottom of the steps. He whistled as he watched his daughters descend the stairs.

"You both look absolutely beautiful!" exclaimed an excited Gabe.

"Thanks Dad!" they answered in unison.

The music started and Rachel Rose walked slowly on the white carpet until she came to where Fabio, his father and the minister were standing. Now it was time for the bride... On the arm of her proud father, Isabelle walked slowly toward her bridegroom. She never took her eyes off him. His eyes were glued to hers. It was almost like they were the only two people on earth. His heart was overflowing with love for this beautiful girl he was about to marry. The smile on his face said it all. It seemed to take forever for her to get to him. Her father released her arm as she stepped forward and took her place beside her bridegroom.

The ceremony was the most beautiful and sacred one that she had ever witnessed. She and Fabio had written their own vows. With tears in their eyes, they earnestly recited their vows to each other. She could hear sobbing in the crowd. She hoped it was tears of joy as hers was. She had never been as happy as she was at this very minute. She was marrying her best friend. God had surely blessed her. She gave Him thanks for sending her this wonderful man.

The ceremony was over when the minister pronounced them husband and wife and told Fabio to kiss his bride. He gave her a long passionate kiss, which made the guests laugh. Isabelle felt her face turning red as she gently pulled away from him. The minister announced, "I now present to you, Mr. & Mrs. Fabio Moretti."

Isabelle whispered 'I love you' before they turned and headed back to the house. Bird seed was flying through the air as they walked. They could feel it hitting their heads. Isabelle even felt it going down the bodice of her dress. She smiled as she walked past them. Meanwhile, the photographer was taking dozens of pictures. He was snapping one right after another. Isabelle wanted to make sure there was plenty to choose from.

They walked back to the front for lots more pictures of the two of them and also ones with both families. Of course Sophia had to have her picture taken with the bride and groom. She felt as if Isabelle was her daughter.

Afterward everyone gathered under the tent for the reception. Fabio, Isabelle and their families, along with Sophia, formed a line so that the guests could congratulate them. Then it was time to eat and enjoy. The band *'Vanilla Sky'* had been hired for this joyous occasion. Today they had changed their style of music. They were performing some love songs, per Isabelle's request. Her favorite was *'The Rose'*.

The reception lasted for two hours. Guests left a few at a time. It had been a glorious day for Isabelle and Fabio. Having their family and friends with them on this joyous occasion meant everything to both of them. "What a way to start our new life together," Isabelle said to Fabio.

"I agree with you. It couldn't have been any better than this."

"Look at Rachel Rose. I think she has found someone interesting to talk to."

"It seems that way," replied Fabio.

"I'm glad. Maybe she won't be staring at you so much," she teased.

"Oh, she's just a kid. You don't have anything to worry about."

"I know...I was just teasing you."

Finally, all the guests were gone. The family gathered in Sophia's den and enjoyed catching up. Isabelle and Fabio decided to wait until her family left before leaving for their honeymoon in Paris.

Jennifer, Gabe and Rachel Rose stayed three more

days. They did some sightseeing while they were in Milan. Isabelle was sad when the time came for them to leave. She and Fabio drove them to the airport. Fabio watched as the family said their tearful goodbyes. "Don't worry...I will bring her to see you soon. Maybe next May or June we can come to Montana. I would love to see your ranch, Gabe."

"You would be welcome anytime. Take good care of our daughter," he said as he hugged his new son-in-law.

Isabelle wiped the tears from her eyes as she watched them board the plane. She watched until they were out of site. The she spoke to Fabio. "I'm sorry for crying. I should be the happiest girl in the world. I am, but it was hard to watch my family leave, knowing they are so far away."

"I understand, Darling. We will go to see them soon, I promise! On another note, we are leaving for Paris in the morning."

"I know and I am very excited! I have to go home and pack."

"So do I. Bring your suitcases over and we'll stay at my place tonight," he said.

"That sounds wonderful. We will finally be alone."

"Sophia had said you could stay here but I told her we wanted to be alone."

"Was she upset?"

"No, I don't think so. I think she understood."

Chapter 34

Their plane left early the next morning. Isabelle was very excited since she had never been to Paris. She had heard a lot about it, but never dreamed she would go there. She wondered if Francine was still there. She would give her a call once they got settled and see what she was up to these days.

After several hours in the air, they landed at the Roissy-Charles de Gaulle Airport, which is the second busiest airport in Europe, with some 200,000 passengers moving through daily. It is located about fifteen miles northeast of central Paris and offers quick and reliable ground transportation in to Paris.

They took the Limousine that Sophia had reserved for this joyous occasion. It was a pleasant ride to the *'Hotel Ritz Paris'* where they would be spending the next two weeks. After their luggage was taken to the honeymoon suite, they went downstairs to the restaurant to eat an early dinner.

Sophia had rented the limousine for the entire two weeks they would be in Paris. She had been so generous with them. She just kept giving and giving. Isabelle knew it was because she was trying to capture 'what might have been' if her daughter was still alive. She was very grateful for Sophia and how she had taken her 'under her wing' and given her the opportunity to become a supermodel. She felt very blessed.

The next morning the limo picked them up and took them to see the 19th century *'Eiffel Tower'* which is the tallest building in Paris (1,050'). It was built in 1889 and means the *'Iron Lady'*. It was named after the engineer, Gustave Eiffel, whose company designed and built the tower. It is the most visited, paid monument in the world. Millions of people ascend it every year. It was truly a sight to behold.

They went to visit the 12th Century Cathedral *'Notre Dame de Paris'*, which means *'Our Lady of Paris'*. Construction started in 1163 and continued into the 1240's. It suffered desecration during the radical phase of the *'French Revolution'* in the 1790's. Extensive restoration returned the cathedral to an 'original' gothic state.

The next day they went to visit the *'Napoleonic (Arc de Triomphe)'* which was constructed in 1806 and is 164' high. It was designed by Jean Chalgrin. Beneath the Arc is the *'Tomb of the Unknown Soldier'* from World War I. He was interred here on Armistice Day in 1920. It has the first eternal flames lit in Western and Eastern Europe since the Vestal Virgins' fire was extinguished in the fourth century. It burns in memory of the dead, who were never identified (now in both world wars). According to sources, the flame has only been extinguished once, by a drunken Mexican football supporter on the night that France beat Brazil here in Paris, most likely referring to the 1998 FIFA World cup Final.

Next on their things to see was the *'Musée d'Orsay Museum'*. It was housed in a former railway station built between 1898 and 1900. The museum holds mainly French art dating from 1848 to 1915, including paintings, sculptures, furniture, and photography. It is probably best known for its extensive collection of masterpieces by such painters as Monet, Manet, Degas, Renoir, Cézanne, Seurat, Sisley, Gauguin and Van Gogh. Isabelle was so excited to see all these paintings by such famous artists.

These are just a few of the places they toured in their two week stay in Paris. The time went by too swiftly and soon it was time to go back to their new home that was waiting for them. Isabelle was excited that they would have their own home now. It was only a few miles from Sophia, so it wasn't like they were going to be a long distance from her. She had been so good to them and they were committed to helping her in any way they could.

When they arrived home, Sophia was waiting for them. She had ordered fresh flowers and the aroma permeated the entire house. The dining room table was laden with all kinds of delicious looking food. What a homecoming! After a cheerful greeting, Sophia started to leave. "Oh no you don't!" exclaimed Isabelle. "You are going to stay and eat with us!"

"I don't want to intrude," said Sophia.

"You won't be intruding," added Fabio. "We will be happy to have you dine with us, especially since you furnished all the food." He was smiling.

She stayed and had dinner with them and left shortly afterward. Isabelle and Fabio were tired from their trip so decided to retire early, but not until after they called their parents to let them know they made it home safely.

Two days later, it was back to work for both of them. Fabio had not recovered as quickly as Isabelle. They never thought much about it until he kept feeling tired day after day. "Maybe you should go to the doctor, Fabio."

"I don't need a doctor. I'll be okay in a few days. Besides, all I need is you, Isabelle."

"As sweet as that is, I am going to look out for your health also."

"To keep you from worrying, I will go if I don't feel better soon."

He did begin feeling better several days later. Isabelle was relieved. She was so happy being married to Fabio. She knew he was going to make a wonderful husband. They continued to work for Sophia. Isabelle was still high on the list of top paid super models. She was conservative with her money as far as material things go. They had everything they needed and more. She still felt the need to help those less fortunate. God had blessed her with a great job and she knew she had to use some of the money to help others. She received such a blessing when she saw how happy she made others. She was very involved in church work and helped with missions. She was not just a fan of Jesus, but a follower. She was heeding the call to help others, just as Jesus would do. She couldn't perform miracles, but many people considered it a miracle when she did nice things for them. She didn't want any glory or praise for what she did. God blessed her and that was all she needed.

An idea came to her and she wanted to discuss it with Fabio. After dinner one night she brought up the subject. "Fabio, I have been thinking. God has blessed us both more than we deserve. I have a very strong feeling that I should be doing more. I am thinking about buying some land and building a homeless shelter. I want to have plenty of beds and also a soup kitchen. These people need food and a place to sleep." She looked at him and waited for his reply.

"Are you sure you would have time to do all this? After all, you are very busy with your modeling."

"Yes, this is something I have to do. God has impressed me with this idea and I can't forget about it. I must heed God's calling."

"Wow, Isabelle."

"What's the matter?" she asked puzzled.

"I am just very surprised that you would want to do something like this. Helping at church is different. This would be much harder."

"God didn't call me to do the easy work only. I feel guilty having all this money while many people are homeless. I have to make a difference in their lives."

"Whatever, you say. I will stand by you in your decision."

"Thank you, Fabio. You are a wonderful husband."

She began looking for land by contacting a real estate company. They found the perfect place for her and recommended a contractor also who came to talk to her. After much planning, the homeless shelter was started. She was very excited! She had a deep feeling of contentment in her heart. She knew she was doing the right thing. She had asked for God's guidance in her life and now she knew exactly what He wanted her to do. She thought back to the plans she had before entering modeling school. She had planned to go to an Indian Reservation to teach and help the misfortunate. She remembered how she had felt that she was letting God down by not pursuing that field. As she thought back she realized if she hadn't chosen to become a model, she wouldn't have the money to be building this homeless shelter. She definitely felt that God had this planned for her all along. Her heart was so tender and she mourned for those who had nothing. Becoming famous had never gone to her head. She was the same sweet Isabelle she had always been, with the same compassion for others. Money changes some people and she knew God was not pleased with that. She was so glad she had been brought up in church and taught the right way to live. She never forgot to give God the praise every day for what He had given her.

Chapter 35

One year later the homeless shelter was up and running. Isabelle had hired a staff to run it for her. Gina was the head chef and dietician. Isabelle always checked in every afternoon when she finished working. Lots of times she stayed and helped serve the meals. She got such a blessing out of seeing the love these people showed from day to day. They never ceased to let her know how much they appreciated what she was doing for them. This pleased her but in return she thanked God that He had blessed her with the resources which allowed her to do it.

Fabio came by some days to help out. He was not feeling up to par these days. He seemed to stay tired all the time. One evening while he was there helping, he slumped to the floor. One of the servers screamed. Isabelle came running to find him in the floor with his arms and legs jerking. His eyes were rolled back in his head. "Call 911," she screamed to anyone who was nearby. Gina pulled her phone out of her pocket and dialed the number. Five minutes later the ambulance arrived. The EMT immediately told Isabelle that Fabio was having a seizure. They loaded him on the stretcher and headed to the nearest hospital. Isabelle followed behind in her car.

Fabio was taken to the ER where they performed some tests on him. They verified it was a seizure. After he roused up, they asked him if he had ever had a seizure before and he told them no. They sent him home with Isabelle.

One week later, he had another seizure. This time it was while he was videoing Isabelle. She immediately called 911. They decided to do a brain scan. Isabelle was not prepared for what they had to tell her. "He has a brain tumor," said the doctor.

Isabelle felt faint and had to sit down. "Are you sure of this?" she asked.

"Yes, I am sure. We will have to keep him here this time and do an MRI to see what type of tumor we are dealing with."

"When will you do the MRI?"

"First thing in the morning."

Isabelle wouldn't leave Fabio. They put him in a room with a recliner that made a bed. She was going to be beside him all night.

Early the next morning they wheeled Fabio down to the x-ray department. An hour later they brought him back to his room. Isabelle was there waiting. He looked so helpless lying there in bed. She walked over and put her arms around him. "I'm here for you Fabio. I won't leave you."

He looked up at her with tears in her eyes and said, "Thank you."

Tears welled up in her eyes as she said, "I love you Fabio, now and forever."

"I love you, too."

Isabelle continued to stay with Fabio, only leaving long enough to get a bite to eat in the hospital cafeteria. Two days later the doctor walked in early in the morning. "I have the results from the MRI," he said with a solemn face. "I'm afraid it's not good news. The tumor is cancer."

"How bad is it Doc?' asked Fabio."How long do I have?"

"The cancer is advanced. I would say one year at the most."

Fabio turned pale. "I guess I had better get my affairs in order soon."

"That would be a good idea," replied the doctor.

Fabio turned to Isabelle and said, "I knew from the start that you were 'too good to be true' and now it looks like it will all be over soon."

Isabelle couldn't hold back the tears. "Don't say that Fabio! As long as you are alive, there is always hope. God is in control and we must pray for His will to be done."

"I wish my faith was as strong as yours."

"It could be. All you have to do is surrender your heart and life to Jesus and ask Him to forgive you of your sins. I know with your Catholic upbringing it may be a little hard to understand, but I am willing to help you."

"Please do."

So for the next half hour she explained the plan of salvation to him. She told him how God sent His Only Begotten Son, Jesus, to die on the cross for our sins. She quoted John 3:16 to him.

"It sounds so simple," he said with tears in his eyes.

"It is simple. You can't pay your way to Heaven or go by doing good works. You have to accept Jesus as your personal Savior. Invite Him to live and reign in your heart forever."

"I want to do that."

Isabelle knelt down by his bed and prayed with him. When she finished and stood up she saw he was crying and had his arms lifted toward Heaven. His eyes were closed. She stood there quietly for a few minutes and then he opened his eyes. "I did it. I asked Jesus to forgive me of my sins. I asked Him to come and dwell in my heart for the remainder of the time I have left. When I get out of here I am going to church with you, Isabelle."

"That sounds great! I am so proud of you and I thank God for giving you the understanding to make things right between you and Him." She wiped the tears from her eyes. No matter how much time he had left, she felt so at ease knowing he had made things right between him and the Lord.

She called her parents again that night. They had been earnestly praying for Fabio. When they heard the news of the cancer, they mourned with Isabelle. "I have some good news to tell you."

"Good news?" asked her Mom.

"Yes, Fabio got saved today."

"Oh my, that is wonderful news! Tell him we are praying for him."

"I will, Mom. Please pray for God's will to be done."

"We will. Please keep us updated. My heart is with you, Isabelle."

"I know, Mom. Thanks and I love you all."

Fabio came home from the hospital a week later. Isabelle hired a nurse to care for him during the day while she was working. Sophia had hired a new photographer for her. His name was Lothario Benetti. Isabelle wasn't sure she liked him. He was a big flirt and thought he was God's gift to women. His name suited him well since it meant 'seducer of women'. She wasn't interested in his games. She did her work and left. He knew about Fabio and asked her out to eat. He thought she needed someone to talk to and someone to cheer her up. "Please don't ask anymore. I am not interested in your games. Find a single woman to hit on. I am happily married."

"But not for long I hear."

"Lothario, I am disappointed in you. How could you talk about my husband in such a manner? I don't know how long God will choose to leave Fabio with me. It's all in His hands. I want you to know that I will cherish every day we have together for the rest of my life."

"I'm sorry, Isabelle. I didn't mean to offend you."

"Apology accepted. Just don't bother me anymore. I would like for our relationship to be strictly professional."

"As you wish, my dear."

"No 'my dears', either."

"Are you going to be hard to get along with?"

"Not if you keep your thoughts to yourself!"

"I guess I know when to shut up," he replied.

Isabelle never answered him. She went to the makeup department and got ready for the photo and video shoots. Her heart was not into her job anymore. She and Fabio had always been such a good team, even from the beginning. Oh how she missed him. Tears welled up in her eyes and she wondered how she would ever get through the photo shoots without her mascara running. She just wanted to get finished and get out of there. Fabio was waiting for her at home. He was the love of her life.

Morning after morning she went to work with a heavy heart. She could tell that Fabio was getting worse. His vision was beginning to fail but he was so brave and never complained. This hurt her even more. He was dying in front of her eyes and there was nothing she could do about it. Soon God would be calling him Home. Hospice was called in five months after his cancer diagnosis. She was hardly working any now. Sophia told her to take time off and spend her days with Fabio. So that's what she did. Sophia hired another young model to take her place. In her heart, Isabelle knew her modeling days were over. It didn't bother her since she knew it would only last a few years. She's had her time and she was ready to give it up. Right now all she could focus on was Fabio. She loved that man so much and he had been everything she had wanted in a husband. They had talked about having children and even tried, but she was glad it never happened since he wouldn't be here to help her raise them. God knew what was in their future.

It broke her heart to watch him go through one chemo treatment after another. She watched as he grew weaker and that was hard to deal with. If she hadn't had the Lord to comfort her, she didn't know how she would have made it through all those difficult times. Near the end, he slipped into a coma. He had already requested that he die at home. Isabelle obeyed his wish. He lay there for eight days before he slipped away. She hardly left his side. Even though he was in the coma, she somehow sensed that he knew she was there with him and heard her when she talked to him.

Ten months and three days after his cancer diagnosis, Fabio went home to be with the Lord. He had suffered a lot during the last several months but when the time came, there was a sweet peace in the air. Isabelle could feel it. She didn't cry for him right then as he was out of his suffering for good. She did cry for herself and the all the lonely days she knew would be ahead of her. Their marriage was brief but so full of love. She was so thankful for the time they had together and she would never forget him. Not as long as she lived...

Her Mom and Dad flew over for the funeral. Rachel Rose stayed with a friend. Isabelle was so glad her parents were able to come. She didn't realize how much she needed them until she saw them again. She had missed them so much. They tried to console her and reminded her that God's will had been done and that Fabio was no longer suffering. They were so happy that he had become a Christian before he died. That made it much easier to give him up.

The funeral was a blur. So many people came to her house bringing food and offering their condolences. So much food...and she had no appetite. Somehow she made it through the next few days. She was glad she had so many friends but sometimes she longed for all of them to go away, except for her family.

A week later the friends were gone and it was just her family, except for an occasional visit from Sophia who made a suggestion to her on a particular day. "Isabelle, why don't you go back home with your parents? I think it would be good for you to get away for awhile."

"But I have so many things to take care of here."

"Let me do what needs to be done. I can represent you."

"I know you can, Sophia. I really appreciate you!"

"Maybe Sophia is right," suggested Gabe. "It would do you good to be back home and in your own room for awhile. Maybe a month or so..."

"I'll think about it, Dad."

"Rachel Rose would be thrilled," said her Mom.

"It would be good to see her again also. Maybe I will go back with you. Did you get round trip tickets?"

"No, we didn't because we weren't sure how long we would be staying," answered her Dad.

"Good, then we can get tickets on the same plane."

"Sure can."

"Let me take care of this for you, Mr. & Mrs. Colter," suggested Sophia.

"That would be wonderful," spoke up Jennifer.

"I want to buy your tickets also."

"You don't have to do that, Sophia. That is too much," said Gabe.

"I want to do it for all of you!"

"That is so sweet and thoughtful of you," added Jennifer.

"Isabelle is like a daughter to me, you know."

"I'm glad you have enjoyed our daughter. She is a wonderful girl," said Gabe.

"She surely is!" exclaimed Sophia.

A week later, Sophia reluctantly watched as the three of them boarded the plane heading for the United States. She would miss Isabelle but knew this break was just what she needed.

Isabelle had given instructions to Gina at the homeless shelter and she knew things would be fine in her absence. She was blessed to have Gina and the staff who was so capable of carrying on without her. She thanked God for them.

After several stopovers, they landed in Billings, Montana the next evening. It felt good to Isabelle knowing she was almost home again. It seemed like she had been gone forever.

Rachel Rose flew out of the door as they pulled into the driveway. After many hugs and tears they finally went into the house. "I still can't believe you are actually here, Isabelle," said her sister.

"I know. It doesn't seem real to me either."

"I am really looking forward to spending time with you."

"Me too," answered Isabelle.

"I have two weeks of vacation coming up and I am going to take it while you are here," said Rachel Rose excitedly.

"That would be great. We have a lot of catching up to do."

"Did Mom tell you that Tracy Kelley's wife has breast cancer?"

"NO! I am so sorry to hear that!"

"I know me too. She has been taking chemo and radiation. Right now she is in remission."

"That's good to hear. Cancer is such a terrible disease and almost always a killer unless you catch it early. Is she at home?"

"Yes."

"I would like to visit with them. I would love to meet Tracy's wife."

"I think that could be arranged. I will call him for you."

"Not for ME...for us!"

"Okay Isabelle...for us."

The next day was Saturday so she called Tracy's house. He happened to be there and answered the phone.

"This is Rachel Rose Colter. How are you Tracy?"

"What a nice surprise. I'm doing well, considering..."

"I was very sorry to hear about your wife and I have been praying for her."

"Thank you!"

"I have a surprise for you. Hold on a minute."

"Hello Tracy," said Isabelle. "Do you remember me?"

"It's not Isabelle, is it?"

"One and the same."

"How in the world are you, Isabelle?"

"I have been better. I just lost my husband to brain cancer."

Silence...and then he responded, "I am so sorry, my friend. I know what cancer is about."

"I know you do. I am so sorry to hear about your wife."

"Thank you, Isabelle and I am so sorry about your husband! How long did he live after his diagnosis?"

"Ten months and three days."

"Wow that was fast."

"It was and I surely wasn't ready to let him go."

"I don't think you ever are. My wife was diagnosed two years ago. She's in remission right now after many chemo and radiation treatments."

"Do you think she would be upset if Rachel Rose and I came over for a visit? I would love to meet her and of course see you again."

"I think it would be fine. In fact, it would probably be good for her. She sits here day after day. Unless someone comes to see her, she never sees anyone. She refuses to go anywhere except to the doctor."

"How about us coming over sometime on Monday? What time would be best?"

"Probably around eleven in the morning. Sara always goes to bed after lunch."

"We'll see you Monday morning or will you be at work?"

"I do a lot of studying and reading my Bible, but I will take time off to see you," he laughed. "I do most of my reading while Sara is sleeping."

"Great. We'll see you then."

Chapter 36

Sunday was a pleasant day. Isabelle went to church with her family and it took her back in time. Sometimes she wished she was a little girl again. Time stands still for no one. After church they took a picnic basket out to the tree beside the brook where her Grandfather Grayson, had proposed to her Grandmother Rachel. This story had been told many times as she was growing up. It was such a romantic story...much like a fairytale.

This was her third night sleeping in her own bed on the ranch. It felt weird being back in her old room, but also felt good being with her family once more.

Monday morning came with the sun streaming in her window. She could hear a Mockingbird singing loudly in a nearby tree. She loved the sound of his music. She looked at her clock and saw it was after eight. She jumped out of bed and got into the shower. Only after she was completely ready did she go downstairs and fix herself a cup of coffee and some toast.

The kitchen was vacant. She knew her Dad got out early and she supposed her Mom was getting ready for work. She had to be in her office at nine o'clock. She was only working four days a week now. They had enough doctors to cover, so she decided to cut her workload. In her heart she wished she could take the whole month off and spend all her time with Isabelle before she returned to Milan, Italy.

Rachel Rose came downstairs and joined Isabelle. "Are you feeling okay?" asked Isabelle.

"I'm okay," said her sister.

"You look pale this morning."

"Oh, it's because I am excited to have you home. I never slept well last night. I guess I was just too excited!"

Isabelle laughed, "It sure is good to be home!"

"You can say that again. I didn't know if I would ever see you again."

"Now, Rachel Rose...you know better than that."

"Anyway, I am glad you are here. I want us to make every minute count!"

"We will do that. I promise."

The girls left the house at ten-thirty and headed over to Tracy's house. They stopped at the local florist and bought some flowers for Sara. Isabelle was feeling a little nervous. It had been years since she had seen Tracy. In fact, she was only eighteen the last time they were together. Time makes a change. They arrived at his house a few minutes before ten-thirty. As they pulled into the driveway, the front door opened and a handsome man walked out. Isabelle noticed how much he had matured in the past several years. He came to meet them as they exited the car. "Hello Isabelle. Hello Rachel Rose. How are you both?" He hugged both of them. Isabelle noticed how nice he smelled and smiled to herself.

"We're doing well," answered Isabelle. "It's really good to see you again Tracy."

"The same to you. I had no idea I that I would ever see you again."

"That goes to show that time changes things."

"It surely does," he added. "Well, come on in. Sara is waiting."

"How is she this morning?" asked Isabelle.

"About the same. I am hoping your visit will perk her up some. Thank you for bringing the pretty flowers to her."

Isabelle smiled and replied, "You're welcome." They followed him into the house. Sara was sitting on the sofa. She looked up and smiled as they entered.

"Sara, I would like for you to meet two longtime friends of mine, Isabelle and Rachel Rose Colter."

"Lovely to meet you both," she said in a soft voice.

"It's very nice to meet you also, Sara. I have heard many good things about you from my Mom," added Isabelle as she handed the flowers to Sara.

Sara smiled and said, "Thank you. They are very beautiful. Please sit down,"

They sat down near her and had a pleasant conversation until she began to get tired. "I'm sorry," she explained in a weak voice. "I tire easily."

"We understand," replied Isabelle. "We will be going and let you rest."

"Please come back to see me."

"We will," they promised.

Tracy followed them outside. "I'm sorry you had to cut your visit short. It is so good to see you again," he said looking at Isabelle. She could see the sorrow in his eyes. It made her want to take him in her arms and hold him. Right now he looked like a little boy who had lost everything he owned. Her heart went out to him. "Please come back, Isabelle. I need someone to talk to. I know that you understand since you just lost your husband. I am so sorry for your loss, Isabelle."

"Thank you and we will be back as soon as possible. I will be here for a month."

"That's good. I'm glad you're home even if it's only for a brief time."

"It sure is good to be back with my family."

"We are so happy to have her," added Rachel Rose.

"Goodbye Tracy. Take care of Sara and yourself," said Isabelle as she gave him a hug. She held him tightly for a few seconds. When she let him go, she saw tears in his eyes. She felt her own eyes tearing up. She wished there was something she could do to help ease the pain, but she had been there and knew there was nothing anyone could say or do. You had to deal with your own grief.

The month went by too fast. Isabelle dreaded leaving her family. She and Rachel Rose had such a special time together. They had gone horseback riding, shopping, visited friends including Tracy and Sara, gone on picnics, gone to the movies, as well as spending time with their parents. Each day was packed full.

The morning she left, the house was full of tears. Something seemed to be pulling at her not to go back to Rome, but she knew she had to. She had her house, the homeless shelter and of course, Sophia.

Gabe drove her to the airport. Her Mom and sister said goodbye to her at home. They didn't want to see her get on that plane and leave. It was too painful. She had a smooth trip back and arrived in Rome late the next evening. She was exhausted. Not only physically, but mentally as well.

She slept in the next morning. It would take her awhile to get adjusted to the time change again. After she finally got up and ate a bite, she showered and got ready to go see

Sophia. It was a happy reunion. "I missed you so much, Isabelle!"

"I know. I missed you too! I sure enjoyed spending time with my family though."

"I knew that would be good for you. Are you ready to go back to work?"

"I thought I had been replaced."

"Never! You can work as long as you want to."

Isabelle walked over and hugged Sophia again. "Thank you, Sophia. You are the best."

Sophia smiled and thanked her for feeling that way. "I don't have to tell you again, because you already know you are like a daughter to me."

"I don't know how I would have made it here if it hadn't been for you Sophia. I thank God every day for you."

"I think I should be thanking Him for you because you were a life savor for me."

"I guess I came along at the right time, didn't I?" asked Isabelle smiling.

"Yes, you sure did."

"How would it be if I work three days a week for awhile?"

"Anything you wish, Isabelle. I am just happy that you are willing to go back to work. We have enough work for both of you models."

Isabelle went back to work four days later. Lothario seemed very happy to see her. He was all smiles when she walked in the room. "Welcome back, Isabelle. I am sorry for the loss of your husband."

"Thank you, Lothario, on both accounts. How is the new girl working out?"

"She's great, but she's not you!"

"She is young and very beautiful though."

"Even so, her personality is not like yours. You are very pleasant to be around."

"Thank you. Now let's get to work."

They worked for several hours without taking a break. Finally, at one o'clock he put down his camera and asked, "May I take you to lunch today?"

"I don't think so."

"Why not?"

"I don't feel like it...that is why. I just lost my husband, or have you forgotten?"

"No, I haven't forgotten. I thought you could use some cheering up."

"Not today, Lothario." She turned and walked out of the room. She headed to her car and went straight home. She ate a bite and headed over to the homeless shelter. She felt more at peace here than anywhere in Milan. This was something she and Fabio had built together. His spirit would always be here with her. In her mind she could picture him working in the kitchen serving food to the homeless people. Tears welled up in her eyes as she continued to hold on to this thought.

After everyone had been fed and retired for the night, she went back home. She was exhausted, but in a good way. Her heart was so full of love for these people. They had fed over one hundred people tonight. She showered and slipped into bed. She drifted off to sleep with Fabio on her mind. She dreamed they were back home on the ranch and there had been an accident. He had fallen off a cliff. She looked down and saw his lifeless body lying there. She started to descend the cliff, lost her grip and started falling. She immediately woke up and sat up in the bed. Her heart was pounding. It took her a few seconds to realize it was only a dream and that Fabio had died from cancer some time ago. This brought the pain of losing him back. It felt so real like it had just happened. "Please Dear God; give me the strength to endure these trying times of having to adjust to Fabio being gone. It is so hard...I loved him so much! Please God, put your loving arm of protection around me and let me sleep in peace and not dream these horrible dreams. Forgive me where I have failed you. Thank you, God! In Jesus' name I pray. Amen."

She lay back down and drifted back off to sleep. When she woke the next morning, she realized she'd had some peaceful hours of sleep, with no more nightmares. She thanked God for giving her peace of mind.

She continued to model three days a week and spent most of the other days working at the shelter. Although she missed her family dearly, she felt this was where she belonged, at least for now. She called her family every weekend and sometimes during the week. She received a call from her Mom just before bedtime on Wednesday night. It was two months after her visit on the ranch.

"Is something wrong, Mom?"

"Not in our house. We are all fine. I just wanted to let you know that Sara Kelley passed away this morning."

"Oh, I am so sorry. How is Tracy?"

"Not doing well at all. He is very heartbroken."

"Please tell him that I am so sorry and give him my love."

"I will do that, Isabelle. I think he already knows how you feel."

"What do you mean, Mom?"

"Don't deny it. I know you and Tracy still have feelings for each other."

"Why on earth would you say a thing like that?"

"Call it a mother's intuition."

"Mom, will you order some special flowers for Sara?

Make them red and yellow roses and have them put in a big basket. I will send you the money for them. Let me know how much."

"That's very nice of you, Isabelle. I will do just that."

"Thank you, Mom!"

She crawled into bed thinking about what Tracy was going through. She knew exactly the pain that came with losing the one you loved. Losing Fabio was still fresh in her mind. She wondered how long it took for the pain to ease or did it ever go away? She hadn't had any more nightmares about Fabio and she gave God the credit for that. Fabio was on her mind almost every waking minute though. She tried not to dwell on it and think about other things, but somehow it slipped back into her mind.

She would wait until after Sara's funeral was over, then she was going to call Tracy. She felt it might help him to have someone to talk to. Someone who actually understood what he was going through.

Chapter 37

Tracy was surprised when he received a phone call from Isabelle a week later. He was sitting in the recliner reading his Bible when the phone rang. He reached over and picked up the phone. "What a nice surprise!" he exclaimed after hearing Isabelle's voice.

"I want you to know that I am very sorry about Sara! I thought I would call and see how you are doing."

"Not too well. It is very lonely with Sara gone."

"Boy, do I ever know that feeling! That's why I'm calling. I thought it might help to have someone to talk to that has been through the same thing."

"Thank you so much for calling Isabelle. It always helps to talk and especially to a dear friend."

They talked for over an hour. It seemed like only a few minutes. Conversation flowed, mostly about Sara and Fabio. They both felt so much better after sharing their thoughts. "I will call you again sometime, if that's okay Tracy."

"Sure, I would like that."

Isabelle felt better after her talk with Tracy. He had

always been very special to her and she knew she could talk to him about anything.

Back in Montana, Tracy's heart was lifted after talking to Isabelle. She had always been special to him but time and separation had taken a toll on their relationship. Then he met Sara in college and married her after graduation. She had made a wonderful minister's wife and they had been very happy together. When cancer struck her, he felt that his world had collapsed around him. Then he realized that God had a purpose in this happening to Sara. Although he thought he was as close to God as he could get, he realized he wasn't. He knew that God allowed this to happen to draw him closer to Him. He would deal with it and with the help of his good friends; he would learn to live again.

Months passed and Isabelle and Tracy talked about once a month. He called it his 'pep talk' from Isabelle. He always felt stronger in the Lord after talking with her. He truly believed that God had sent her into his life at the perfect time. He called her his Angel. She had helped to save his life.

On a Saturday morning about a year after Fabio's death, Isabelle called home. Rachel Rose answered the phone.

"Rachel? Is that you?" asked a concerned Isabelle.

"Yes, it's me," she answered softly.

"Are you okay?"

"I think so."

"What do you mean?"

"I stay so tired all the time."

"Have you been to the doctor?"

"No, but Mom checked my blood and it is low. She is taking me next week."

"Good. Let me know when you find out something."

"I will."

Isabelle questioned her Mom about Rachel Rose. She could hear the concern as she talked about her youngest daughter. "I am taking her in to the doctor next week. I will let you know when we know something."

The next few days Isabelle constantly thought about her sister. She prayed that nothing serious was wrong with her. A week later the dreaded call came... Rachel Rose had been diagnosed with Leukemia. Isabelle's heart fell to her feet when she heard the terrible word cancer again. All the memories of Fabio came rushing back into her mind.

"How bad is it Mom?" Isabelle asked in tears.

"Dr. Barrington said she is in stage II and needs a bone marrow transplant as soon as possible. Your Dad and I are going to be tested next week. Just pray that one of us is a match."

"I am coming home, Mom. I want to be tested first. If I'm a match, I want to be her donor."

"Are you certain about this Isabelle?"

"I've never been more certain, Mom. I will catch the next flight out. Tell Ray Ray I love her."

"I sure will. I will be praying for a safe flight for you. Let us know when you need to be picked up at the airport."

'I will, Mom. See you soon."

Next she called Sophia and relayed the bad news to her. She told her she had to make a trip back home to Montana because she was going to be tested to be a bone marrow donor for Rachel Rose. "I am so sorry about your sister! That is a brave thing you are doing for her." Sophia exclaimed. "Is there anything I can do to help?"

"Yes, since I am leaving as soon as I can book a flight, I need for you to check on the homeless shelter every day or two. I know Gina is capable of running things, but it might help if she knows she has a back up."

"I can certainly do that. In fact, I might volunteer to help serve on the days I have free."

"Sophia, that would be so wonderful! I know Gina would be grateful and I think you would get a blessing from helping. I know I always do."

"Isabelle...go and take care of your sister. I will see that things keep running here. Don't worry about your job or the shelter. They will be here when you return."

"Thank you so much, Sophia. You are a true friend!"

She hung up and called the airport. She was able to make reservations for day after tomorrow. That would give her time to get things packed and everything in order for her departure. She had no idea how long she would be gone, so she packed a large bag and a smaller carryon bag.

Sophia volunteered to drive her to the airport so she could leave her car at home. Early the morning of her departure, Sophia picked her up and drove her to the airport. They said their tearful goodbyes and Sophia drove away.

Isabelle had a smooth flight for most part. She had a couple of short layovers and then she was headed for Montana. She was so excited but wished it was under different circumstances. She could hardly wait to see her family again. Gabe, Jennifer and Rachel Rose were all at the airport waiting. They were all smiling and welcomed her with open arms.

"Welcome home!" exclaimed her Dad.

"It's good to be home." She turned to her sister and asked, "How are you feeling?"

"I'm very weak. Other than that, I feel okay."

'Mom, do you have a date set for my testing?"

"As a matter of fact, we do. It's day after tomorrow."

"Great. Let's get this thing on the road," she said as she

smiled at her sister. "I think I will be a match, so you and Dad won't have to go through the testing."

"That sure is selfless of you, Isabelle."

"I don't think of it that way. I am doing what any good sister would do."

The twenty minute drive home was pleasant, even though the circumstances weren't. Isabelle was so excited just thinking about being home. It took her back in time when her life was simple. She missed that. She got settled into her old room which was beside Rachel Rose's room. That was nice. She would be nearby in case her sister needed her.

Two days later she was up early. This was the day for the bone marrow testing. She had been praying that she would be a match. It would be better if her Mom and Dad didn't have to go through the testing.

She was admitted to the hospital as soon as she arrived. They took her to the operating room for testing thirty minutes later. She was sedated and the procedure began. They used a needle and syringe to extract the bone marrow from her hip. Multiple bone punctures were required to extract the requisite amount of bone marrow. One to two quarts were harvested and would be frozen and stored at -80 to -196 degrees until the day the transplant occurred. Isabelle would feel slight discomfort when she woke up. She would spend one night in the hospital as a precaution.

Rachel Rose would begin chemo tomorrow. She would take several treatments. Two days following her last chemo treatment, a battery of tests would be performed on her to ensure she was she was physically capable of undergoing the transplant. Bone Marrow is a spongy tissue inside the breast bone, skull, hips, ribs, and spine. It contains stem cells that produce the body's blood cells. The white blood cells fight infection and the red blood cells carry the oxygen and removes waste products from the organs and tissues; platelets which enable the blood to clot.

The procedure was over and Isabelle was brought back to her room. She was still drowsy when her parents came into the room. When she woke up she was feeling some pain and discomfort in the hip area. Dr. Barrington told her parents that she did great. They would keep her overnight for observation.

On the day she went home Rachel Rose started chemo. After several days of treatments and a two day rest period, the doctor began her testing. Everything seemed to be going well. Her age was in her favor.

Isabelle was the perfect match to become the bone marrow donor for Rachel Rose. They were all excited.

Rachel Rose was given the treatment in her room since this was not a surgical procedure. It was given intravenously. She was checked very often for fever, chills, nausea, vomiting, and diarrhea. She had some of these symptoms. This could continue for several weeks after the procedure. Now it was wait and see. The first two to four weeks would be the most critical time. She would be in the hospital for four to eight weeks. Days and weeks of waiting would begin. One day she might feel good and then the next day be very sick. Her family was by her side praying. Jordan and Miranda had come to be with them. Jennifer was so thankful to have her brother and sister here at this difficult time. Since Jordan lived in Billings, it was easy for him to join them. Miranda, on the other hand, lived in Medicine Bow, Wyoming. She drove over five hours to be with her family. She planned to stay a few days. She had asked Sallie and Bobby to move into her house and care for the children while she was gone. Since Bobby was retired, it was no problem. He said he would be glad to help Eli on the ranch. So it all worked out well for Miranda.

Tracy Kelley came over to be with the family and had prayer with them before the transplant was started on Rachel Rose. He assured the family that she was in God's hands and that everything would be okay. Isabelle was happy to see Tracy again and thanked him for coming to be with them. "You guys are like family to me. I had to come," he said.

"It means so much to all of us having you here," replied Isabelle with a smile.

Tracy reached out and took her hand. "We will always be friends, Isabelle."

"Yes, we will. We have a long history, don't we?"

"We surely do. You know we are both blessed to be here. We could have been killed in that accident long ago that took your best friend, Fallon."

"I know and I thank God every day for giving me another chance."

"So do I Isabelle. So do I."

Tracy visited Rachel Rose once a week while she was in the hospital. Sometimes Isabelle happened to be there when he arrived. They had some great conversations.

Week after week went by. Isabelle had no plans to return to Italy until she knew Rachel Rose was going to be okay. Finally, after week seven, Rachel Rose was discharged from the hospital. She was so glad to be home in her own bed. Even though she was still having some symptoms, she was feeling better.

She went back to see Dr. Barrington in two weeks. He was amazed at how well she was doing. He told her to come back in two more weeks and he would check her blood. By the time she went back she could tell she was gaining strength. The blood test was good. The transplant seemed to be working so far. She was so thankful to have such a loving sister who stepped up when she needed her the most. She was so happy they were a close family. She thanked God every day for her family. She knew she was really blessed to be in this family.

She went once a month for blood work. So far, everything was looking great. Dr. Barrington was very pleased at the success of the transplant. When she completed her six month checkup, he told her she could come back in two months. He also told her if she needed him, just call.

Isabelle stayed for six months and reluctantly headed back home to Milan. She had gotten so used to being here on the ranch that she dreaded leaving. She had seen Tracy every week. They took some walks together and would reminisce old times. She could feel the two of them becoming closer. It was almost like she had never gone away. She found herself wishing she didn't have to go back to Italy. Tracy must be feeling the same way because on their last night together he told her he wished she didn't have to leave. She knew she would be leaving with a heavy heart...not only for her family, but Tracy as well.

She had kept in touch with Sophia, who was doing a marvelous job at helping with the homeless shelter and keeping an eye on her house. She had told Isabelle to take as long as she needed.

Chapter 38

Sophia was at the airport to pick up Isabelle. It was a happy reunion. "I have missed you so much!" exclaimed Sophia as she hugged her tightly.

"I know. I have missed you too! I had no idea I would be gone this long. It was so hard to leave though. I cherish the time I had to spend with my family and watching my sister getting better every day."

"I was praying for Rachel Rose and your family."

"Thank you, Sophia. You can't have too many prayers."

"I know. Isabelle, I want you to take the rest of the week off and get rested. You can start back to work on Monday."

"Thank you, Sophia. You are the kindest, most thoughtful boss a girl could ever have!"

Sophia laughed, "Thank you but you are more than an employee. You are like a daughter to me and don't ever forget that."

"I won't, Sophia. You have treated me like a daughter from the beginning. I will forever be grateful."

After Isabelle got everything back in order from her

trip, she decided to go to the homeless shelter. Gina and the crew were very happy to see her and gave her a big welcome. That made her feel good, knowing that they liked her as a friend and not just as a boss. She helped serve the people their dinner. It felt good to be doing this again. In the back of her mind, were Rachel Rose and the rest of the family. She wondered if they missed her. Of course they did, she told herself. Then her mind turned to Tracy. She knew she would miss him very much. On their last night together he had left with tears in his eyes. He had kissed her goodbye. All the feelings she had for him had rushed back in. All it took was that one kiss. She knew he felt it too. Neither of them said anything. It was such a sacred moment and words were not necessary. "What am I going to do?" she asked herself aloud.

"Did you say something?" asked Gina.

"I'm sorry. I was thinking out loud." She smiled at Gina.

She helped at the shelter the rest of the week. Sophia had told her to rest but that left too much time on her hands to think. She just couldn't stop thinking about Tracy. It didn't matter if she was working or at home, he was always on her mind.

A week later she approached Sophia. "I have been thinking...I feel that I have been gone from home too long. My family needs me and I have also reconnected with an old friend. In my heart I know what I have to do. I have to go back home to Montana."

Sophia wasn't surprised. "I guess I knew this day would come and I have been dreading it. I have seen a change in you since you returned this time. Although I will miss you greatly, you have to do what is best for you."

"Thank you for being so understanding!"

"That's how you are when you are close to someone."

"I appreciate everything you have done for me. You have been like a mother to me. I have been very blessed. I do have something to ask you. Would you be interested in buying the shelter from me? I feel that I need to sell it since I will be so far away."

"Yes, I am interested. I have enjoyed what time I worked there and it has enriched my life. Not only will I be helping those in need but I will feel your presence when I'm there. We'll discuss a price and get the paperwork done."

"Thank you so much! I know the people will be in good hands."

"Thanks for your confidence in me."

Sophia contacted her attorney and started the paperwork. Isabelle was so thankful things were working out for her. She wasn't going to tell her family or Tracy until all the legal issues were resolved. She wanted to be free of obligation when she told them. Meanwhile, she worked at the modeling agency three days a week. Lothario was very happy to have her back. "I have missed you, my dear," he stated the first day she went back to work.

"It's good to be missed. How's the new girl, Cara doing?"

"Oh, she is great! In fact, she and I have been seeing each other outside of work."

"Good for you." She was thinking he would leave her alone now.

"How about having dinner with me tonight?"

"WHAT? You just told me you are seeing Cara."

"I am, but that doesn't mean I can't see you or anyone else for that matter."

"It sure does to me. I don't play second fiddle to anyone!"

"Come on Isabelle. Don't you want to have some fun?"

"Not your kind, I'm afraid."

"Have you met someone new?" he asked.

"As a matter of fact I have. He is not new, but he is an old friend from back home. We spent a lot of time together when I was there."

"How can a long distance relationship like that work? You need to go out, have a few beers and loosen up."

"First of all, I don't drink! I never have and never will."

"You don't know what you're missing!"

"I won't find out either. I have heard of those who wake up with hangovers and I want no part of that."

"What are you a Miss Goody Two Shoes?"

"Call me what you want. I am a Christian and I want to be a follower of Jesus."

"Jesus? I don't believe in him."

"I feel sorry for you. One day you WILL believe and it may be too late. There will be many good moral people on that Judgment Day who will be turned away because Jesus will say, 'Depart, I never knew you'. There are many FANS of Jesus, but not many FOLLOWERS. One must have a deep, intimate relationship with Jesus to be a Follower."

"It all sounds like garbage to me!" he exclaimed with a smirk.

"Oh no, it's very real. I will be praying for you, Lothario."

"Save your prayers for yourself. Let's get to work."

Isabelle never answered him. He spent the next two hours videoing and photographing her. They had very little conversation. She was praying silently. She knew she needed to get out of there as soon as possible. She was trusting God to work everything out for her and she knew He would in His time.

Later that evening she called Sophia and told her about

the events of the day. Sophia was sympathetic with her and apologized for Lothario.

"You don't have to apologize for him. He and I are just too different. I don't enjoy working with him and I think that will make my decision to leave even easier."

"I'm sorry. I will contact my attorney and try to put a rush on things."

"Thank you, Sophia. I just want to go home. I hope this won't be too difficult for you, but I don't want to work with Lothario anymore. I am ready to give it all up."

"Just as you wish, my dear. I just want you to be happy. I will be sorry to lose you but I do understand."

"Will you come to visit me in Montana?"

"You bet I will."

"Good. I will be looking forward to it."

Two weeks passed and Isabelle had spent most of the time at the shelter. At night she began to pack a few things. She knew that she could only take her personal things. Her house had been on the real estate market for almost two weeks. She would be selling it furnished. Several couples had come to look at it and one couple was very interested in buying it. She would find out as soon as they heard from their loan application.

A couple of weeks later she heard from Jon and Marcy Lazarino. They were ecstatic! Their loan had been approved and they were buying the house. Isabelle couldn't have been happier. Thank you God, she prayed silently.

She couldn't stand it any longer so she called her parents that night. "Mom, I have some good news for you."

"What is it?"

"I sold my house today."

"YOU WHAT?"

"I sold my house. I am moving back to Montana. Mom,

I am coming home." There was a silence and Isabelle could hear weeping. "Mom, are you okay?"

In a broken voice Jennifer replied, "I am more than okay. I guess I am in shock. I never dreamed you would ever move home again. You have made me the happiest I have been in a long time."

"I'm glad Mom. Can I stay with you and Dad until I find a house?"

"I won't hear of you buying a house. I want you to move into the ranch house with us. Rachel Rose will be so happy to have you here too. She needs her sister. I can't wait to tell her and your Dad! How soon will you be here?"

"I have to close on the house and also on the shelter. Sophia is buying the shelter."

"That is wonderful. I'm sure she will do a great job running it."

"I know she will. She has enjoyed what time she worked there with me."

"Well, get all your paperwork done and hurry home. What about your job?"

"Oh, I quit that a few weeks ago. My photographer and I had too many differences. I have already transferred my funds to the Yellowstone Bank in Laurel and the Western Security Bank in Billings."

"That's good. I'm glad you have that taken care of."

"I'm trying to tie up loose ends as quickly as possible, Mom. I just want to come home!"

"You're not any more anxious than we are!"

She called Tracy and told him the news. He was very excited and said he had been praying for God to make it possible for her to come home. She laughed when he told her that and promised to call him as soon as she arrived home.

Chapter 39

The long awaited day finally arrived. Isabelle had bought a one-way ticket to Billings, Montana. She had never been more excited in her life. Even when she found out she was going to Rome, she wasn't as happy as she was now. Knowing that she was going home had really lifted her spirit. She had grown up a lot since she had left home at age eighteen. Looking back she realized how young and naïve she was then. She had learned so much from living in Italy for these several years. Now she was ready to leave it all behind and go home. The only thing that bothered her about leaving was Sophia. She would miss her terribly. Sophia had promised to visit them at the ranch and she knew that would happen one day. Isabelle signed over her new car to Sophia. She didn't want to sell it. It was something she wanted Sophia to have of hers to remember her by. She hadn't forgotten the new car Sophia had bought her for her twentieth birthday. It felt good doing something for the friend who had treated her like a daughter. She would never forget Sophia and all she had done for her.

Sophia insisted she drive Isabelle to the airport. She

stayed until time for Isabelle to board the plane. It was a tearful goodbye with promises to stay in touch. Sophia watched Isabelle board the plane and then walked away with tears in her eyes. This was almost as heart wrenching as the day her daughter died. When she got into her car, she let the tears flow. She sat there for ten minutes before she was able to drive away. Her heart felt so empty. Isabelle had been such a big part of her life for the last several years. She vowed right then to never let another girl become such a big part of her life. It was just too painful when they left.

Isabelle felt sad at leaving Sophia but the need to go home overruled those feelings. The flight was smooth. She met a nice young man who was seated next to her. He was in the United States Army and had been stationed in Rome, Italy. His overseas tour was over and he was heading home to his family in Wisconsin. He was married and had a three year old son who was just a baby when he left. He was so excited to be going home. Isabelle could hear the love in his voice as he talked about his wife and son. She hoped his wife had been faithful while he was away. She had heard so many stories...

She arrived at the Billings airport the next evening. For the most part, they had a smooth flight. At one point there was turbulence which upset some of the passengers. Isabelle closed her eyes and prayed. She was at peace with God and knew He was in control. She was ready to meet Him, should He call for her now. The turbulence only lasted a few minutes and the rest of the flight was smooth. She thanked God for watching over them.

Her Mom and Dad were waiting at the airport when she arrived in Billings. Gabe helped her with her luggage. Just as they were heading to the car, Isabelle saw a familiar face and let out a gasp, "TRACY! I didn't know you would be here!"

Tracy was smiling as he walked toward her. "I wanted to surprise you," he said as he gave her a big hug.

"You did just that," she replied. "Did you know he was coming, Mom?"

"I must confess...I did know. He didn't want me to tell you."

"I am very happy to see ALL of you!" Isabelle exclaimed. "It is sooo good to be back in the USA!"

"We're all glad to have you back, Isabelle," added her Dad. "I hope you won't go running off anymore."

"I plan to stay right here in Montana!"

Tracy looked at her with loving eyes and said, "That sure sounds good to me. Would you like to ride with me, Isabelle?"

"Only if you'll stay for dinner."

Tracy looked at Jennifer who responded, "Sure Tracy, you are very welcome to stay for dinner. Rachel Rose should have it ready by the time we get there."

"Then it's settled," said Isabelle as she headed toward Tracy's vehicle. He opened the door for her and got her settled in. They followed Gabe and Jennifer home.

A wonderful aroma filled the air as they stepped inside the door. "Oh, this smells wonderful!" exclaimed Isabelle as she headed to the kitchen. Her sister was busy with the final touches. She turned around and saw Isabelle. A huge smile crossed her face as she enveloped Isabelle in her arms. "I am so glad to have you back home Isabelle! I have missed you more than you know. I hope you never leave again!"

"I have no plans of leaving, little sister. I am home to stay."

"Are you staying here with us?"

"Dad insists that I do."

"Great! It will be like old times!"

"It will except we are much older now."

"That doesn't matter. We are still sisters and if we want to act silly, we can."

Isabelle laughed, "Sounds like fun. I sure do need to unwind. By the way, are you dating anyone?"

"I have been dating for a long time. You still think of me as a child, don't you?"

"I guess I do. You are six years younger than me."

"Yes, I am dating a very nice guy. His name is Anthony Fontaine. Everyone calls him Tony. We have been dating for over six months."

"Do you think he is the one?"

"Could be. We get along so well and seem to have so much in common. We love the outdoors."

"What kind of work does he do?"

"He works for the Montana Game & Inland Fisheries."

"That sounds exciting."

"It is. You should hear some of the stories he tells. They are true stories of things he has experienced in his job."

"I hope things work out for you if he is the one. Is he a Christian?"

"Oh, yes...he is a very devoted Christian! He goes to church when he isn't working and even sings in the choir. He has a wonderful voice!"

"That's great. Guys like that are few and far between. You had better hang on to him."

"I plan to Isabelle!"

"I will be anxious to meet him."

"I have invited him to dinner tomorrow night."

"Great. I will give him the 'once over' like you did Fabio," said Isabelle laughing.

"Please don't do that. You know I apologized for my actions."

"I know and I was only teasing you. I promise I will be on my best behavior."

"Good!" Rachel Rose was smiling.

Rachel Rose put the finishing touches on the meal and they all sat down to eat. Gabe asked Tracy to say the blessing. He prayed a beautiful prayer thanking God for the safe return of Isabelle. Rachel Rose had prepared a wonderful meal and they thoroughly enjoyed it as well as the lively conversation. Everyone seemed to be so happy to have Isabelle back home with them. It was like a new beginning...

Isabelle and Tracy went to the living room at Rachel Rose's insistence. She knew they had a lot of catching up to do, so she volunteered to clean up the kitchen alone. She would accept Isabelle's help tomorrow night when Tony was there.

"Have a seat, Tracy. I am so glad you are here."

"Me too! I was very happy when your Mom invited me. It's been so long since I've seen you. I have missed you more than you will ever know."

"I've missed you too, Tracy. I am so glad to finally be home and look forward to spending time with you."

"That sounds wonderful to me!"

"As you know, my family goes to Laurel Baptist Church. I think I need to go with them Sunday as this will be my first time since returning home. I hope you understand."

"Of course I do, Isabelle. Maybe you can visit our church some too."

"I would love to do that, Tracy. I am anxious to hear you preach."

"I make it simple so that even children can understand."

"That's the way it should be. I am so proud of you Tracy!"

"Thank you!" he exclaimed shyly.

They talked for three hours. The time flew by. "I had better go and let you get some sleep. I know you are tired from your trip."

"I guess I am. I've had so much fun I haven't thought much about being tired."

"I'll call you," he said as he got up to leave.

"Great," she replied. "Can you come to dinner tomorrow night? Rachel Rose is having her boyfriend, Tony, for supper. I would like for you to meet him."

"Sure, I will come. It's not as if I already have plans," he said laughing. "I'll see you tomorrow night. What time?"

"Be here by six. Dinner may be a little later, but we can continue catching up."

"I'll be here, Lord willing." He hugged her and left. Isabelle watched him drive away. Somehow even though she was happy, her heart felt sad watching him drive away.

Isabelle felt like a school girl again. She lay in bed that night thinking about Tracy and what they used to have between them. So many years had gone by and she wondered if they could ever feel that way again. The love they shared was very special and Isabelle never thought they would ever separate. It was hard leaving him when she went to New York but she had no idea the pain he suffered when she left him. Then her mind drifted to another scene. She thought about that horrible night when her friend, Fallon Hollister had been killed. It all came rushing back to her. She hadn't thought much about it recently, but somehow being with Tracy tonight had brought back many memories. She and Fallon had been best friends and never thought they would ever be apart. She was taken young, not even eighteen yet. Isabelle found herself wondering what Fallon was doing in Heaven. She knew that she was having a wonderful time and as much as she missed her, she wouldn't want her to come back to this sinful earth. Fallon was the lucky one that fateful night!

She finally drifted off to sleep. She slept until seven o'clock the next morning. She woke up feeling rested. She thanked God for the good night He gave her. She was also thankful that she never had any bad dreams. She got up and looked out the window. The sun was shining brightly and there was a slight wind blowing in the trees. It was indeed a beautiful day. In the distance she could see the horses grazing in the field. She had missed the ranch and all it encompassed. She was anxious to go riding. Her mare, Velvet, was getting old. She was happy that her Dad hadn't sold her. He knew how much this mare meant to her as she was growing up. She might take Velvet for a short ride, but would choose another one for her long ride.

She went downstairs to find Rachel Rose in the kitchen. "Good morning, little sister."

"Good morning. I hope you slept well."

"Actually, I did. I had a lot on my mind before I went to sleep, but once I drifted off, I don't remember waking at all until seven this morning."

"That's good. We sure are glad to have you home."

"It is sooo good to be here. By the way, I invited Tracy to dinner again tonight. I thought it would be nice if he and Tony met. Hope you don't mind."

"Why should I mind? You'll be helping me cook."

"Really? I don't remember volunteering."

Rachel Rose laughed. "You didn't. I volunteered you."

"I don't mind. I was only teasing. I will be glad to help you. Just tell me what you want me to do."

"I will be home from work around five, so you can have the potatoes peeled. I am going to start a beef roast in the Crockpot and it will be done by the time I get home. We will have time to fix some other vegetables and bread later. Oh...you can make a couple coconut pies today. They are Tony's favorite."

"It's been so long since I've made a pie, but I will give it a try. I'm sure they won't be as good as yours."

"Thanks for helping me out!"

Rachel Rose left the kitchen and went to get ready for work. She was a lieutenant with the Billings Police Department. She had always been intrigued with law enforcement. From the time she was small she said she was going to be a cop. She came back to the kitchen fully dressed in her uniform. The uniform fit her perfectly slim figure. Her long blonde hair was flowing down her back. "WOW!" exclaimed Isabelle. "You look beautiful. I bet you have to fight the guys off!"

"Not really," she answered as she took a scrunchy, tied back her golden mane and stuffed it up under her police hat. "They don't allow us to wear our hair down. I guess that's why most girls have short hair. I haven't been able to bring myself there yet."

"Please don't! You have such beautiful hair...just like Grandma Rachel and Aunt Miranda."

"Thank you! I have no plans to cut it. Besides, Tony loves my long hair."

"That's a man thing. They all like long hair. Actually, I do to. I never wanted to look like a man," Isabelle laughed.

"I don't think that would happen even if you shaved your head."

"I know I am changing the subject but I am so happy to see you looking so well. You look very healthy now."

"Thanks to you! I feel great now. I will never be able to thank you enough for saving my life."

"That's what sisters do. I know you would have done the same for me."

"Without a doubt. I would not have thought twice."

"So now you know why I did it."

"I will forever be grateful. But for now, I have to go to work. See you this afternoon. Love you, Isabelle," she said as she gave her a hug.

"Love you, too."

After Rachel Rose left for work, Isabelle got dressed to go horseback riding. She would make the pies later. Her Dad was at the stable when she entered. "Good Morning, Dad!" she exclaimed as he slowly turned around.

"Good morning Sweetheart. What's on your mind?"

"I want to go riding. It's been so long."

'Fine. I will saddle up a horse for you."

"No, Dad. I want to ride Velvet."

"But she is so old, Isabelle."

"I know. I won't ride her far. I just want to spend some time with her."

"As you wish, Dear. She is your mare."

Isabelle put the saddle on Velvet and walked her out of the stable. She mounted her and slowly they went out the path down by the creek. It felt so good to be on her mare once more back here on the ranch. Right at this moment she never wanted to leave this place again. This took her back in time to when she was a child. She wished those days had never ended.

She stopped Velvet under the big maple tree and

dismounted. She tied her to a tree limb where Velvet immediately started to eat the lush green grass. She walked over to the creek and sat down on the bank. She picked up a rock and threw it in the creek. This brought back childhood memories. She sat there for at least a half hour daydreaming. The snort of her mare brought her back to reality. She looked around and saw her Dad riding up. Velvet had alerted her.

"I was just checking to make sure you are alright," said her Dad.

"Sure, I'm fine. I guess I just lost track of time." She got up and walked toward Velvet. She mounted her mare and headed for the house. After showering, she headed for the kitchen and took out her Mom's recipe box. She searched until she came to 'Coconut Pie'. She took out the recipe and began to gather the ingredients she would need. Two hours later, she had two pies cooling on the counter. They turned out great. She was rather proud of herself considering the fact that this was the first time she had ever made cooked pie filling with meringue on the top. She hoped they would be as good as they looked.

She was so excited about the pies that she decided to try her Aunt Miranda's yeast roll recipe. She found it and began to read. It didn't sound too difficult. She figured if she started it at three o'clock, they should be ready by six. This was her first time to try rolls. She had no idea how to make them, so she called her sister. After Rachel Rose explained the procedure, Isabelle told her sister that she thought she could make the rolls.

Chapter 40

Tony and Tracy arrived just before six that evening. Rachel Rose, Isabelle and Jennifer, were in the kitchen finalizing everything.

Gabe went to the door and invited the guys in. He took them into the den so the girls could finish the dinner. "It's good to see you guys. Have you two met?"

"Yes, we introduced ourselves outside. It's good to see you again Gabe," replied Tracy. "Thanks for having us for dinner."

"Yes, thanks. I am really looking forward to it."

"So am I," added Tracy.

"I'm sure the girls are happy to have you here and you're both welcome in our home any time," said Gabe.

"Thanks," they said in unison.

Rachel Rose came to the entrance of the den and announced that dinner was ready. They guys followed her to the kitchen. "Tony, I would like for you to meet my sister, Isabelle. She has just moved back home from Italy."

Tony extended his hand to her and replied with a

smile, "So nice to meet you Isabelle. I don't think I have ever met a supermodel in person. I'm honored!"

"Thanks, Tony. It's very nice to meet you. I've been hearing some good things about you from my sister."

Tony looked at Rachel Rose, smiled and replied, "That's nice to know. I am very fond of your sister. Actually, I am in love with her." He turned to Rachel Rose, "It's true. I think you already knew it."

"No, I didn't. You haven't told me," she teased.

"Sorry, I should have told you first. I do have something I want to speak to you about after dinner."

"Okay." She gave him a puzzled look.

They all sat down at the dinner table. After Gabe said the blessing, they started passing the food around. The table was full of delicious looking food and the three guys helped themselves and no one was bashful about eating. Both Tony and Tracy commented on how wonderful the food was. Isabelle and Rachel Rose looked at each other and smiled. Jennifer smiled at both her daughters. She had taught them well.

After they finished eating Jennifer told her daughters to go spend time with their guests and she would do the cleanup. This didn't happen too often, so they took advantage of the offer.

Tony and Rachel Rose went out on the porch and sat in the swing. It was such a beautiful night. The sky was full of stars and the moon was giving off her light. What a perfect night to sit on the porch with the one who held your heart. Tony couldn't wait any longer. "Rachel Rose, I have something to ask you and I can't wait any longer. Will you marry me?"

"What?" she asked in amazement. "We've only been dating for six months."

"Time doesn't matter. It's what I feel in my heart and I am hoping you feel the same way."

"I do love you, Tony, but this is so sudden."

"What if we get engaged now and wait a year to get married? I know it takes you girls about a year to plan your wedding."

"You're right, it does." She paused for a moment and replied, "Yes, Tony, I will marry you one year from now." She reached over and kissed him briefly on the lips.

He grabbed her and gave her a long kiss. "You've made me the happiest man in the world! I can't wait for you to be my wife!" He pulled a box out of his pocket and opened it. Taking the beautiful diamond from the box, he placed it on her finger.

She gasped as she saw the beautiful ring and exclaimed, "Oh Tony, it's beautiful! You are such a wonderful man and I look forward to becoming your wife. How about having the wedding next June? That is my favorite month for weddings."

"Anytime you wish, my dear. I'm just so happy that you said yes." He smiled at her and hugged her tightly. "Now I need to go ask your Dad's permission to marry you. I will be back shortly. Wait here for me."

He was gone fifteen minutes. He came back with the biggest grin on his face. "He said YES!"

"I knew he would. He really likes you a lot Tony. Now we need to go back in the house and tell my Mom and sister."

They started toward the door and Jennifer met them with a smile on her face. "I just heard the good news. CONGRATULATIONS to both of you!"

"Thanks, Mom," said Rachel Rose. "Does Isabelle know?"

"I thought I would let you tell her."

"ISABELLE!" yelled Rachel Rose as she walked in the door. "I HAVE SOMETHING TO TELL YOU!!!"

"What is it?" asked Isabelle as she hurried to see what her sister wanted to tell her.

"Tony just proposed to me!"

"CONGRATULATIONS!" exclaimed Isabelle as she hugged her sister. "When is the big day?"

"It will be sometime next June."

"That is a good month. At least that will give you plenty of time to plan your wedding. I am so happy for you." She turned to hug Tony and said, "You are getting a wonderful girl. Be good to her. If you're not, you will have to answer to me."

"I will treat her like a baby. I give you my word. I love that girl so much!"

Rachel Rose and Tony went back out on the porch. They sat in the swing and talked for two hours. Rachel Rose was so happy and full of ideas. Tony let her talk and agreed with all her ideas. He was getting the girl he wanted and he didn't care what kind of wedding she planned. He just wanted to marry her.

Meanwhile, Isabelle went to the living room where Tracy was waiting for her. "Sorry I took so long but Rachel Rose has some exciting news. Tony proposed to her tonight."

"He did? That is awesome. I'm sure she said yes."

"Of course she did. My sister is no fool."

"When is the wedding?"

"Next June. That will give her plenty of time to plan it."

Tracy looked at her with a serious look on his face and asked, "Do you think you will ever remarry?"

"I don't know. How about you?"

"I would like to...that is, if the girl I love will have me."

Isabelle wondered if he was in love with a girl that perhaps didn't even know it yet. She bravely asked. "Who is she?"

Tears welled up in Tracy's eyes as he lovingly replied, "It's you, Isabelle. I have loved you for a long time. In fact, I don't think I ever really stopped loving you."

"Wow! I don't know what to say!"

"Just tell me that I have a chance with you."

"Well, Tracy, it's like this...There is no other man in my life and I don't expect there will ever be. There is a bond between us that has lasted for all these years. As far as I am concerned, there is only one more step for us."

"Oh Isabelle...I am so happy to hear you say that. I didn't know if going away and becoming famous had changed you so much that you would never have time for me again. I am so thankful that you are the same Isabelle that I knew and loved all those years ago. You are truly a blessing from God!"

"Oh Tracy, you're going to make me cry."

Out of the blue he asked, "Isabelle, will you marry me?"

"WHAT???"

"Will you marry me? I love you with all my heart and the only happiness I will ever have is if you agree to marry me."

"Deep down I know I love you Tracy and yes I will marry you. We can't say anything to the family tonight, because this is Rachel Rose's night. I don't want to take that away from her."

"I fully understand. We will wait awhile before telling anyone. Don't make me wait too long."

"I won't. I promise. I just had a thought...what if we have a double wedding with Rachel Rose and Tony?"

"That would be fine with me. That way the family who lives so far away would only have to come one time. I know your Uncle Rob, lives on Prince Edward Island."

"You are right. If we let all of them know this far ahead of time, maybe they can make plans to attend the double wedding. I have to talk to Rachel Rose first before we plan anything. I will wait a couple weeks and gently approach the subject with her. I think this is a wonderful idea. I just hope she and Tony agree."

A couple of weeks went by and both girls were extremely happy only Isabelle had to keep quiet about her plans. One day they were in the kitchen and Rachel Rose caught Isabelle smiling to herself. "What are you thinking, dear sister? You have the biggest grin on your face and yet you are not saying a word. I can tell you are deep in thought."

"You caught me. I may as well tell you. Tracy has asked me to marry him."

"He what??? Isn't this sudden? You just got back home."

"Maybe so, but if you remember...Tracy and I go back a long way. He was my boyfriend when we were in high school. I loved him then. All that we felt for each other has rekindled these past few weeks."

"Are you going to marry him?" asked Rachel Rose looking shocked.

"Yes, I am going to marry him."

"When?"

"That's what I want to discuss with you. Now this is only an idea and you can say no if you want to."

"What is it?" she asked seeming to be a little agitated.

"What do you think about us having a double wedding?"

"You're kidding, right?"

"No, I'm not kidding. I think it would be perfect. If you don't want it, just say so and we will make other plans."

Rachel Rose paused a moment and Isabelle could tell she was in deep thought. "You know, that might be a good thing to do. I will have to ask Tony first and see if he has any objections."

"Great!" exclaimed Isabelle. "Let me know as soon as you find out something."

"Oh I will. I think I will call Tony now." She called and talked to him for half an hour. When she got off the phone she found Isabelle in the den. She was smiling as she approached her sister. "I talked to Tony and he said it is fine with him. In fact, he thinks it's a great idea."

"Really? I can't wait to tell Tracy. Have you decided what day in June?"

"June 28th."

"June 28th it is. I am going to call Tracy." She proceeded to call him and relayed the good news. He was as excited as Isabelle.

"May I come over tomorrow night? There is something I have to do."

"Sure Tracy. You know you are welcome anytime. Come over for dinner."

"Thanks, I will see you then."

The next evening Tracy arrived around six o'clock. He was all smiles. "You sure look happy!" exclaimed Rachel Rose.

"I am very happy."

"Could this have anything to do with my sister?"

"It has everything to do with your sister."

Isabelle was smiling. She never thought she could

ever find happiness again with a man as wonderful as Tracy. When she left Montana years ago, she actually never thought she would ever leave Italy and come back home. Of course she didn't know that her husband, Fabio, would get cancer and die. Her world was shattered at that point. If it hadn't been for God and her wonderful friends, she would never have been able to make it through that difficult time. She knew this was God's plan for her now. If Rachel Rose had not gotten sick with cancer, she may never have moved back home. She wouldn't be marrying Tracy either. She was so happy that everything had worked out for her. She was so thankful to God for sparing the life of her beautiful sister, Rachel Rose.

After dinner Tracy asked Isabelle to go outside. She followed him out on the porch and sat down beside him in the swing. He put his arms around her and kissed her gently. "You know I love you with all my heart, Isabelle and I always have. Now I would officially like to ask you again. Will you marry me?" He had pulled a box from his pocket which held a beautiful diamond engagement ring. The diamond wasn't nearly as large as the one Fabio had given her, but that didn't matter. It was just a material thing anyway. When she saw the love in his eyes as he placed the ring on her finger, it could have been a twine string and she would have been just as happy. She knew she was marrying the BEST man in the world!

Isabelle looked up at him with tears in her eyes as she answered, "Yes, Tracy, I will marry you."

They kissed again to make it official and he said, "You have made me the happiest man in the world."

"That works both ways. I have never been happier in my life."

"I'm glad to hear that. Let's go tell the family, as if they don't already know," he said teasing her.

Her parents and sister were very happy about **'Isabelle's Choice.'** She had gone around the world and back to find her soul mate waiting for her. The grass is not always greener on the other side of the fence. Sometimes true love is in front of us and we can't see it.

After Tracy left, Isabelle took Rachel Rose aside and told her, "Thank you for allowing Tracy and me to intrude on your wedding with Tony."

"You are NOT intruding at all. In fact, I think it will be fun getting married together."

I have something to tell you and you can't say no. I want to pay for the entire wedding, which includes your dress and all of your attendant's clothes."

"WOW!" exclaimed Rachel Rose. "That is a huge expense!"

"I don't care. It's not like I don't have the money to pay for it. I don't want you to feel bad or obligated to me. I am doing this out of my love for you!"

"I don't know what to say..."

"Just say YES!"

"YES! I would be honored to accept your generosity."

"Good. We need to start doing some planning soon."

"Indeed we do. You know, I always thought you would be my Maid of Honor. Now I will have to find someone else."

"I'm sure you won't have a problem with that."

"I have a good friend at work. I may ask Julie to be my Maid of Honor."

"That's good. I think we should have Kati and Haley to be our Bridesmaids. I am going to ask Aunt Miranda to be my Matron of Honor.

"That's a splendid idea!"

"Maybe we could have Taylor and Savannah as junior Bridesmaids."

"That's another great idea. I know they would love to have a part in our weddings."

"Let's make this the biggest and fanciest wedding ever held in Montana. Of course we will want to have it here on the ranch, right Rachel Rose?"

"Of course, where else would we have it?" she asked laughing.

"There's nowhere else. Mom and Dad will be happy. Mom loves planning events so we will include her in our planning."

"Sure, that's fine with me."

"Now, I have someone special that I need to call. I just have to share the good news with Sophia and invite her to come to our wedding. She should be up by now."

Isabelle had a smile on her face as she dialed Sophia's number and waited for her to answer. "Sophia, it's Isabelle. I hope I didn't wake you."

"ISABELLE!!! I am so happy to hear from you! How are you doing? I miss you very much!"

"I miss you too, but things are going great for me. Remember I told you about Tracy Kelley, whom I was dating when I left for New York?"

"Sure I remember."

"Well," Isabelle paused for a few seconds. "Tracy has asked me to marry him and we are having a double wedding with my sister, Rachel Rose, and her fiancé, Tony Fontaine."

"What exciting news!" exclaimed Sophia. "I am so happy for you!"

"Thank you, Sophia. I want you to come to our wedding if you can. That's why I am telling you early, so you can make plans. The wedding is next June 28th."

"Oh, that is a good way off, so I will definitely arrange

my schedule and make plans to come. It will be so good to see you and your family again."

"GREAT! All you have to do is let me know when you will be arriving and we will meet you at the airport in Billings. Come a few days before the wedding if you can and that will allow us to spend some time together. I want you to stay here on the ranch."

"Thank you! That sounds like a great idea. I am going to mark my calendar as soon as we get off the phone."

Isabelle called her Aunt Miranda next. She was so excited to hear the news of her two nieces getting married. "I think a double wedding will be lovely."

"Aunt Miranda, I would love for you to be my Matron of Honor."

"Sure. I would be happy to unless you want one of your younger friends to do it."

"I've lost touch since I've been gone so long. Besides, there is no one I would rather have than my beautiful Aunt Miranda."

"Oh thank you, Isabelle. You are so sweet! Yes, I accept. I will be honored to be part of your wedding."

"Do you think Taylor and Savannah would like to be junior Bridesmaids?"

"I'm sure they would love it," replied Miranda joyfully.

"We are going to ask Kati and Haley to be our Bridesmaids."

"What about a ring bearer?"

"Tracy has a small nephew who will be perfect for that job."

"It sounds like you are getting things together. I am very happy and excited for both of you girls!"

"Thanks," replied Isabelle. "I'll talk to you later."

Meanwhile, Rachel Rose had called Haley and Kati,

who said they would be very happy to be in the wedding. They offered their congratulations to both the girls.

Things were falling into place. They had their part of the wedding party established. It would be up to the guys to do their part in selecting their best man and groomsmen.

"I think we had better call it a night dear little sister. I am tired and I know you need to rest and not overdo yourself. As Scarlett O'Hara said, 'Tomorrow's another day'."

"Goodnight, Isabelle."

"Goodnight, Rachel Rose," answered Isabelle as they hugged and each went to their own bedroom.

"Mom," said Isabelle to Jennifer the next evening. "Is *'Et & Em Catering'* still in business?"

"Yes, they sure are."

"Great! Would you call them and see if they would be interested in catering our wedding?"

"Sure, I will call them tomorrow. It is no longer just Emily and Ethel; they had to hire help. Luckily for them, their niece Debbie was available, so she joined them about five years ago."

"That's great. It's nice when families can work together."

"Whatever happened to their older sister, Sallie?"

"She is still living in Medicine Bow, Wyoming. She and Bobby are still together."

"That's great. Does she still help Aunt Miranda?"

"Not since the children have grown up. She loves living in Medicine Bow and feels that Miranda, Eli and the children are 'her' family."

"That's great!"

"I hope she and Bobby will be able to come to the wedding."

"I'm sure they will if they are well at that time. It will also give Sallie a chance to see her sisters and niece."

Chapter 41

The months flew by and the girls were very busy planning their weddings. Everything was falling into place. *"Et & Em Catering'* had been hired. In addition to the food, they were also making two wedding cakes. A photographer and a local band had been booked. Flowers had been ordered and were on hold to be delivered the morning of the wedding. The wedding gowns hung in an upstairs closet, along with the attendant's dresses. Fittings and alterations had been done and everything seemed to be perfect. They were just waiting for the 'day' to get here.

Sophia arrived a week before the wedding. Isabelle was excited and knew that Sophia would be a lot of help. She always had so many good ideas. It was so good to see her friend again.

Rob, Kati and Grayson III arrived a few days before the wedding as did Miranda, Eli, Savannah, Taylor and Tommy. All the children were growing up. There were no little ones in the family anymore.

Jordan, Haley and their daughter arrived the morning of the wedding. They lived in Billings, so it was a short drive for them. Blake flew in from Hollywood the day before. He was accompanied by a beautiful model named April. In fact, he introduced her as his fiancée. She was wearing a huge diamond engagement ring as well as a huge smile.

"So our playboy has finally been captured!" exclaimed Jennifer smiling.

"Yeah, I couldn't resist April." Blake smiled at his fiancée.

"I told him he was old enough to be thinking about marriage. After all, if we want to have children, we can't wait forever."

"You are exactly right," said Jennifer. "So, when's the big day?"

"Actually, we haven't set a date yet," replied Blake.

"Well, don't put if off too long. This beautiful girl might get tired of waiting on you."

"Oh no, I can't risk that! I'm sure we will be married within the next couple of years."

The rehearsal dinner was for the family and wedding attendants. Jennifer ordered BBQ and the fixings. Miranda made several cakes. She had always enjoyed cooking and baking. She was the great cook of the family, after their mother, Rachel passed away. It was a great family time. Everyone was relaxed and enjoyed themselves.

Just before bedtime, the phone rang. Jennifer answered it. "It's for you, Isabelle," she said.

Isabelle picked up the phone and said hello. "Hello Beautiful," said a voice which seemed somewhat familiar.

"Hello," replied Isabelle. "Who is this?"

"Don't tell me you have forgotten me already!" he exclaimed with a slight laugh.

"I'm sorry...but I don't know who you are."

"It's Paolo."

"PAOLO? What are calling me for?"

"I heard you were getting married again and I called to say congratulations and wish you the best."

"That's very nice of you, Paolo, but who told you I was getting married?"

"Sophia, of course. Who else?" he snickered as he told her.

"Did she call you?"

"No, I called her. It just came up in the conversation."

"I bet it did!" she exclaimed.

"Isabelle, I must confess...I did call her asking about you. I was surprised when she said you had moved back to Montana. I thought you would stay in Milan."

"My family is here and this is where I belong. After Fabio died, there was nothing to hold me there. My sister, Rachel Rose, had cancer and I gave her my bone marrow."

"That was a remarkable thing for you to do."

"No, it wasn't. I did what any good sister would do."

"How is your sister?"

"She's fine and cancer free. In fact we are having a double wedding tomorrow."

"Well, I wish you both the best. Who are you marrying?"

"Tracy Kelley. He was the boy I dated in high school. I left him to be a model."

"You mean to say that he waited for you all this time?" he asked.

"No, he got married and his wife died with cancer also."

"So let me get this straight...your husband dies...his wife dies...and you came running back into his arms. Is this correct?"

By now Isabelle was feeling a little irritated. "I have to go Paolo. Thank you for calling. Oh, and by the way...have a good life!" Isabelle hung up the phone.

Isabelle walked back into the den. Jennifer could tell her daughter was irritated. "Are you okay, Isabelle?"

"Yeah, I'll be okay. Paolo just called. He found out that I was getting married and wanted to say congratulations. That's all there was to it."

Jennifer could tell that Isabelle didn't want to talk about it, so she didn't pursue the subject. Isabelle surely didn't need to be upset the night before her wedding.

Isabelle got up the next morning being her usual self as if the phone conversation had never happened. She decided not to mention it to Sophia. This was her wedding day and she didn't want to have another man invading her mind. She was so much in love with Tracy and she thanked God every day that He had brought them back together.

She ate a light breakfast and went outdoors where all the action was taking place. It was like a circus out there with all the hustle and bustle. Everyone seemed to know their job and did it. Isabelle had spared no expense to have the wedding that she and her sister wanted. She wanted everything to be perfect.

A few hours later, she and Rachel Rose were putting on their wedding gowns. They giggled and laughed until they were in tears. This was the happiest day of their lives. Both of them were marrying their soul mate. Their makeup, hair and nails were done before they dressed. They both looked beautiful. Their attendants were dressed and helping them in any way they could. They were wearing pale pink floor-length dresses adorned with tiny rosebuds just a shade darker. Their bouquets were pink rosebuds.

The bridal bouquets were white roses mixed with a few pink rosebuds. The flowers were all beautiful.

Then it was time for Gabe to walk his two daughters down the steps on the white carpet and out to the colorful flower garden. The attendants were all there waiting for them. Tracy was on the right and Tony was on the left. Neither guy took his eyes off his beautiful bride as she approached him. A big smile graced their faces. Gabe led Isabelle to Tracy, then Rachel Rose to Tony. After giving them away, he seated himself beside his beautiful wife, Jennifer.

The ceremony began with Isabelle and Tracy. When the minister came to the part where he asked if anyone objected to this marriage, a dark, handsome man stood up and exclaimed, "I object! Isabelle should be marrying me. We were meant to be together!" Then he made his way out to the aisle and headed toward Isabelle. The minister looked horrified, as did all the wedding party. They could hear whispers from the crowd. The ushers started toward the man and Isabelle spoke up, "It's okay guys...I will speak to him."

"Do you know this guy?" asked a frustrated Tracy.

"I'm afraid I do. I was engaged to him in Rome. That is until he broke it off."

"Why is he here now?" asked Tracy. "He let you go and now you are mine!"

Isabelle met Paolo in the aisle and took him over away from the crowd. "Paolo," she said. "How could you do this to me?"

"Because I love you!"

"If you had loved me, you wouldn't have set me free. You broke my heart, Paolo. It took some time to get over you."

"I know I made a big mistake. Please forgive me and let's start over!"

"No, Paolo...it's too late for us. I have given my heart to Tracy and I plan to marry him in a few minutes. If you want to stay for the wedding, that's fine. If you cause any more trouble, I will have you escorted out of here."

"Okay, Okay...I won't cause any more trouble. I would really like to stay."

"Make sure you keep silent or you know what will happen."

"I promise," he said and Isabelle could hear the sadness in his voice. She walked back to her future husband and reassured him with a smile, "Everything is fine!"

She looked at the minister and said, "Please continue with the ceremony."

The minister was still frustrated but somehow managed to get through the ceremony. He pronounced them husband and wife...then Tracy kissed his bride. They stepped aside and stood while Rachel Rose and Tony were married. Everything went smoothly for them. Soon both couples walked back up the aisle as birdseed was flying through the air. Smiles graced all four faces.

Gabe and Jennifer were excited. They had just gained two sons in one day. They couldn't have been happier. Ever since little Isac's death, Gabe had always longed for a son... now he had two. He was very happy with the choice his daughters had made.

Then it was on to the reception. Emily and Ethel had outdone themselves with the food. The wedding cakes were beautiful and delicious too. These ladies were very talented. Everyone seemed to enjoy the food and lingered awhile after they had eaten. Finally, everyone left except for the family and the caterers. Sallie and Bobby had made it for the wedding and were helping Emily, Ethel, and Debbie with the cleanup.

The family gathered in front of the flower garden for the wedding photos. It was so good to have all the family together for this joyous occasion. After all the wedding pictures were taken, the photographer took portraits of every Parker/Sterling family there. These portraits would hang in the family home here on the Parker Ranch. They would grace the walls in the den along with Rachel Hargrove Parker Sterling, Mitch Parker, Grayson Sterling and little Isac Colter. Their legacy would carry on for many generations to come...

About the Author

Sally Campbell Repass is the youngest of three children born to Warren & Ethel Aker Campbell, in Marion, Virginia. She is a Christian wife, mother, grandmother and great-grandmother.

She has been married to her loving husband, Paul, for 10 years. They are going through a very difficult time now, as he battles Stage IV Colon cancer. Their faith in God, the love of their family and dear friends, has helped ease the pain.

Recently her 34 year old son, Trent Fisher, was diagnosed with Cutaneous Follicular Lymphoma. He took 20 radiation treatments for the cancer. Sally feels that her faith is really being tested as both her husband and son battle cancer. She is a strong person and has placed Paul and Trent in God's hands. She knows that God is in control and prays for His will to be done. She also knows that God never makes a mistake. She is at peace with this.

Sally and Paul sang together at church and at home until

his illness. They enjoyed singing and she has written several songs of faith. She has always loved to write and in 2008 she wrote her memoirs, 'MY LIFE...MY CHILDREN'. This was written for her children. The same year she wrote a short story called, 'MEMORIES OF DAD'.

She has written other short stories such as, 'BOOTS...THE LUCKY CAT'...
'LOOK OUT BOYS, ZEUS IS COMING HOME'...
'A WALK INTO THE PAST'...
'LIFE ON THE FARM'... (as told by her husband)

Sally wrote and published a Children's Fairytale Book, 'PRINCESS KARI & THE GOLDEN HAIRED BOY' in early 2010. This book was inspired by her granddaughters, Katie and Campbell.

Later that year, she published her first Inspirational Romance Book, 'FOR THE LOVE OF RACHEL'.

In 2011 she followed with a sequel, 'RACHEL'S DAUGHTER'. Not being able to let go of the family she had created, she decided to write a third book. In 2012, 'FROM THE RANCH...TO THE ISLAND' was born.

Her fourth book in the series was also published in 2012. 'BACK HOME TO MONTANA' is the continuing saga of the Parker/Sterling families.

It is followed by Book #5 in the series. 'MEDICINE BOW...A NEW BEGINNING' brings about a turn of events.

Book #6, 'ISABELLE'S CHOICE' is the final one in this series. As this book ends, so will the saga of this family she has grown to love. She has spanned 4 generations of the Parker/Sterling families and hopes you have enjoyed the journey as much as she has.

Just because she has finished this series doesn't mean she has quit writing. In fact, she is working on 'SARA'S QUEST' at the present time. She wishes for God's Blessings to be upon you and thanks you for your love and support!

Website: www.fortheloveofrachel.com

Email: virginiawriter2010@gmail.com
       screpass2008@yahoo.com